Chinese Tonic Herbs

by Ron Teeguarden

Japan Publications, Inc.

This health care system is not meant to replace medical diagnosis or treatment. If symptoms are severe or persistent, you should always consult your physician.

Published by JAPAN PUBLICATIONS, INC., Tokyo and New York

Distributors:
UNITED STATES: *Kodansha International/USA, Ltd., through Harper & Row, Publishers, Inc., 599 Lexington Avenue, Suite 2300, New York, N. Y. 10022.* SOUTH AMERICA: *Harper & Row, Publishers, Inc., International Department.* CANADA: *Fitzhenry & Whiteside Ltd., 195 Allstate Parkway, Markham, Ontario, L3R 4T8.* MEXICO AND CENTRAL AMERICA: *HARLA S. A. de C. V., Apartado 30–546, Mexico 4, D. F.* BRITISH ISLES: *Premier Book Marketing Ltd., 1 Gower Street, London WC1E 6HA.* EUROPEAN CONTINENT: *European Book Service PBD, Strijkviertel 63, 3454 PK De Meern, The Netherlands.* AUSTRALIA AND NEW ZEALAND: *Bookwise International, 54 Crittenden Road, Findon, South Australia 5007.* THE FAR EAST AND JAPAN: *Japan Publications Trading Co., Ltd., 1-2-1, Sarugaku-cho, Chiyoda-ku, Tokyo 101.*

First edition: January 1985
Fourth printing: December 1988

LCCC No. 84–080650
ISBN 0–87040–551–9

Printed in U.S.A.

 *Preface*

Throughout the history of mankind, people have sought to tap the seemingly magical powers of nature to enhance the quality of life, and to heighten the experience of human life on earth. And from the very beginning, wisdom has dictated that nothing is more important than health and inner happiness. Material possessions have undoubtedly always had their attractiveness, and indeed their worth, but the wise have always known that all the material wealth on earth is useless if physical and emotional health are lost. How many sick or unhappy millionaires would gladly give up the bulk of their wealth in exchange for a healthy, vital body and a contented happy state of mind! Indeed, every culture has asked the primary question: how can we attain ultimate health and happiness?

We live in a time when the material world seems all-powerful. The material world is not innately "bad," for who does not enjoy physical beauty and, these days, the benefits of technology? But though the material world is perpetually changing, the basics of life remain unchanged. We all still seek physical and emotional well-being. It is for this reason that this book has been written. The author, an American of non-Oriental descent, has discovered that Eastern wise-men and wise-women have developed over a period of several thousand years a very wonderful means of contributing to basic health and happiness. Irrespective of changing times, of fads and changing fancies, the Chinese have tred a steady course in the study and development of what they call "radiant health."

The Chinese people, and soon after them the Japanese and Korean peoples, have learned to tap nature's marvelous resources for this purpose. With great wisdom, they have studied the ways and means of nature and have gradually learned how to use her gifts for mankind's benefit. In particular, they have learned how to use the plants, minerals and animals. The Oriental people have developed a marvelous "herbal" system, using these products of the earth and founded upon the great principles of life, that comes extraordinarily close to answering man's eternal question of how to pave the way to true health and happiness.

The Oriental people, unquestionably wise, have studied the affects of these natural products upon themselves, and over several millennia have discovered some truly remarkable products that do indeed enhance the life experience in significant ways. Some of these products have been found to prolong life. Some enhance the powers of thought and of the psyche. Others strengthen the body, and still others have been found to increase virility and fertility. Some herbal products have been found to be useful spiritually, helping to clear the inner vision, thus enhancing one's awareness of the veiled secrets of nature, and indeed even of God (or Tao, as the Chinese perceive it). And a few of nature's treasures are said to do all of these things.

The knowledge of these products has been passed on from generation to generation for a very long time and has been tested literally millions of times. The Chinese call these very special herbal products the "tonics," and together they form a unique and sophisticated system known as "Chinese tonic herbalism." This system is every bit as valid and useful in today's world as it has been historically in the East. We live in a time when natural means of attaining physical and psychic health have regained popular recognition. It is hoped that this book, *Chinese Tonic Herbs*, may be an inspiring and practical introduction to a way of health and happiness that has been proven valid in Eastern lands by many, many people for a long, long time.

The herbal products known as the tonics are special in many ways, and indeed stand out from the great majority of herbs, Chinese or otherwise. Each of these special herbs has been found to contain vital elements which enhance the life force of those who consume them. Some are considered super-nutrients, while others contain active ingredients that improve our physiological functioning and boost energy.

Yet, other factors contribute to the massive popular usage of these herbs in the East. One factor is that the tonics are *safe*. That is, they are virtually non-toxic when used properly. One can take these herbs as often as desired. But this is not to say that one should not choose their tonics intelligently. Different tonics have different effects, and knowledge of these effects serves as a basis for selection. The purpose of this book is to provide this knowledge of the tonics and their effects so that Western people can wisely select tonics for their own benefit. This book should be read carefully before trying the tonics so that mistakes are not made. If the reader has any known medical problem, it is *essential* that they consult a qualified physician first, before trying the tonics.

The tonics are not medicinal. They are not used, in this context, to treat disease. Nor are they used to prevent specific ailments. They are not drugs in this sense. They fall more appropriately into the same category as foods. The tonics provide nutrients and other biologically active agents that seem to invigorate the body and mind in a natural, gentle, balanced way. If the reader has any questions regarding the use of the Chinese tonic herbs, they should consult with an Oriental herbalist. Many acupuncturists and martial arts masters also are familiar with the tonic herbs. If no such guides are available, the reader may contact the author through the publisher of this book.

Life is balance. To do anything in an extreme way can be unsafe. The tonics were first used by Oriental sages and yogic masters for the purpose of enhancing their efforts to attain radiant health and spiritual illumination. The tonics were not, and are not, used by these masters for "healing" purposes, *per se*; but are used instead to assist, harmonize, and re-establish the natural order by encouraging natural processes and by enhancing the life force.

The tonics are taditionally used to promote a dynamic equilibrium of the psycho-physical condition and to promote maximum, indeed radiant, health. It is with awareness of this great philosophical tradition that the reader is encouraged to approach Chinese tonic herbalism. The tonics are not to be taken lightly; for as wondrous natural treasures, they demand great respect. If the reader approaches the tonics with the right attitude, incredible results may occur. Be careful, be alert. Follow instructions, be steady, and be patient. For, as an old Chinese saying goes, "Hasten slowly and you will soon arrive."

You will soon know all about Ginseng, Royal Jelly, Tang Kwei (the great woman's tonic) and many other great tonic herbs. You are embarking on an amazing journey. Over time, certain tonics will become your favorites and over more time you may master *Chinese tonic herbalism*. At that time you will truly be on the road of health and happiness.

Have a wondrous journey!

 *In Gratitude*

There are so many people who deserve recognition and thanks for contributing to this book, and/or to my physical, mental and spiritual growth. Without the support, input, encouragement, and criticism of my friends, this book would not be.

First, I must express my awed respect and gratitude to the many Oriental sages who have, through the ages, developed and passed along the profound teachings of the East. Thanks, too, to the Western teachers who shed tremendous light on my path: Alan Watts, John Blofeld, and Walter Spink.

Infinite thanks are also due to my first and foremost teacher of Chinese tonic herbalism, Taoist Master Sung Jin Park. Upon his teaching rests the foundation of this book.

I offer my deepest thanks to my beloved father, Jerry, who taught me the arts of giving and teaching. He was a great and compassionate man. I thank to my mother, Lillian, for her constantly encouraging me from my childhood to pursue the life sciences and healing arts.

My deepest love and thanks to Cynthia Teeguarden and to my children, Jeremy, Belle and Sinclair for their love and support over the years as I have pursued this path.

I wish to offer special thanks to my dear friend Iona Marsaa Teeguarden, with whom I shared growth for many years. She contributed enormously to the initial development of this book. Iona is a master therapist and teacher who continues to be an inspiration to me.

Herman and Cornellia Aihara turned my life around, opening my eyes to the real world. These wonderful, humble, altruistic people saved my life, and I will never forget them.

Michio and Aveline Kushi set my course in life. Michio is one of the great teachers of the life arts in the world today. It was Michio who encouraged me to become a teacher back in 1970. At that time I wanted to teach macrobiotics, but there were too many teachers at that moment, so I decided to teach acupressure —which eventually lead to my studies of Chinese tonic herbalism.

Thanks to all my former and present co-workers and students in the Oriental healing arts; and to the wonderful people at Japan Publications, Inc., Mr. Yoshizaki and Mr. Fujiwara, who have shown unbelievable patience with me as this book has ever-so-slowly evolved.

Thanks also to Scott Lavin and Boris Said for their generous and benevolent support and encouragement. There are many others who I would like to thank, but space does not allow.

Thank you all!

This picture has for many years been the author's favorite picture associated with Chinese herbalism. It is a rendition of Shao Lao, the Chinese "god of longevity." He carries a gourd containing the "elixir of immortality" and is accompanied by a spotted deer, a symbol of long life and harmony with nature. Shao Lao carries a magic peach, also symbolic of longevity.

Contents

 *Introduction*

The Chinese have been practicing herbalism from the dawn of their civilziation. Over the period of several thousand years, a very sophisticated form of herbalism was developed which has been used successfully innumerable times.

Among the thousands of herbs used by the Chinese are a select few which are known as the "tonics." These herbs are revered by all those who are aware of them because they enhance the life-force and increase longevity. Also called the "Superior Herbs," the tonics may be taken safely for a long duration if desired to build and maintain health.

The tonic herbs are not considered "medicinal" in the normal sense of the word. They are not specifically used to treat, nor even to prevent disease. Instead, they are used to fortify the body-mind, to strengthen the life functions, to encourage natural harmony, to enhance one's adaptability, and as a result of all this to generate what the Chinese call "radiant health."

It is common knowledge to the Orientals that disease states and symptoms of various natures may be eliminated by the use of these and other herbs. But, when using these very special herbs, it is imperative that the user realize that, according to Oriental philosophy, the change is due to the life-promoting influences of these herbs, and not due to any properties attacking specific disease agents as they are known in the West.

This is not to say that Chinese herbalism does not use such medicinal herbs. In fact, they use thousands of them. Called the "General Herbs," they are used to treat disease specifically, just as do the pharmaceutical agents used in Western medicine. Also used to treat disease are herbs known as the "Inferior Drugs" or "Poisons" which are used only to treat specific problems and cannot be used for a long period of time without resulting in unwanted side-effects. However, the subject of "medicinal" herbalism is beyond the scope of this book, wherein we will deal strictly with the "Superior Herb" class, the Chinese tonic herbs.

It seems that in the West we have been trained to see a health practitioner only after becoming ill. This attitude is being corrected in recent years, but many people do not wish to see a doctor when they feel certain that they will get a general "bill of health." Unfortunately, but undoubtedly necessarily, Western medicine has concentrated on the treatment of disease once it has become well established. Until the current revolution in medical science which is exploring the idea of "life extension," one would not see a physician in order to learn the art of developing superior health. Even now, very little emphasis is placed upon this in Western medicine. It has become apparent that each person must be responsible for their own health and well-being, unless symptoms arise that require the expertise of a doctor.

In the Orient, by necessity, a very different attitude has long been established. Though medical treatment has long since been an important part of general healthcare, emphasis has been laid on maintaining, or in fact, *promoting* health through health practices that are encorporated into one's life-style. It is upon this principle that the "tonic herbalism" has been developed and practiced in the Orient.

The greatest experts of tonic herbalism in the East have been the spiritual seekers, the sages, and yogis, who have used the Superior Herbs to benefit their life force so as to aid them in their quest for enlightenment, or as the Chinese call it, "immortality." The Chinese Taoist tradition forms the foundation of Chinese civilization. The Taoists follow the Great Principle of Yin and Yang and the laws of Nature as the guiding light on "the Way" to spiritual liberation. Though Oriental culture is ancient and many schools of thought have arisen, the Taoist principles have formed the basis of them all.

The tonic herbs have been used by all the Oriental people for a very long time. The Taoists have, however, more than any other group, used the tonic herbs and have developed their usage to a sublime level. Taoist masters have always been recognized as the ultimate "healers" by the people of the Orient. But the masters themselves invariably deny that they are "healers" and refrain from encouraging that concept. Instead, they emphasize that Tao, through Nature, is the only true "healer," and that one can only temporarily be helped by a so-called "healer." Only by learning the secrets of Nature and Life can one truly be "healed." Thus they developed the health-promoting arts such as Taoist yoga and meditation, *Tai Ch'i Chuan*, acupressure, and tonic herbalism.

Many Chinese herbalists prescribe tonic herbals to weak and sickly patients. This, of course, is a high level of medicine. But the sickly and weak are not the only ones who can use and benefit from these amazing herbs. Great men and women have used them to develop powers beyond those of normal people. The entire yogic and martial arts tradition of the East has embraced tonic herbalism. The "Kung Fu Man" of old knew these herbs well; the *samurai* found them invaluable. The emperors of China relied upon them to ensure long life, virility, and vitality. The women of the educated classes used tonic herbs to maintain youth and beauty. The common man and woman used them whenever they could find or obtain them to get the most out of their burdened lives. No, the Chinese tonic herbs are not just for the weak; they are for *anyone* who wishes to maximize life's potential.

One man, Li Ch'ing Yuen, is said to have lived to be 252 years old. His life span has been verified by modern scholars. Born in 1678 in the mountainous southwest of China, he ran away from home at the age of eleven with three travelers. These travelers were in the herbal trade. Together the boy and his three teachers traveled throughout China, Tibet, and Southeast Asia, encountering many dangerous situations, but all the while studying the herbal traditions of all the various regions.

As Li Ch'ing Yuen became older, he became a practicing herbalist, and was well known for his excellence of health and amazing vigor. But one day, when he was around fifty years old, he met a very old man who, in spite of his venerable old age, could outwalk Li Ch'ing Yuen. This impressed Master Li very much because he believed that brisk walking was both a way to health and longevity and a sign of inner health. Li Ch'ing Yuen inquired as to the old sage's secret. He was told that if every day he consumed a "soup" of an herb known as *Lycium chinensis* he would soon attain a new standard of health. Li Ch'ing Yuen, no fool, did just that and continued to consume the soup daily until he was over one hundred and thirty years old!

Naturally, he was greatly revered by all those who knew him and he had many disciples who followed him. Even at this very old age, his sight was keen and his legs were strong, and he continued to take his daily vigorous walks. One day, he was on a journey through treacherous mountains. In the mountains he met a Taoist hermit who claimed to be five hundred years old. Humbled by the great illumination of the old Taoist, Li Ch'ing Yuen begged the Taoist sage to tell him his secrets. The old Taoist, recognizing the sincerity of Li, taught him the secrets of Taoist Yoga (also known as *Nei Gung*, "the Inner Alchemy") and recommended that Li consume a daily dose of *Panax Ginseng* combined with *Radix Polygonum multiflorum*. Ginseng is well-known in the West; Polygonum multiflorum is not yet well-known here, but is highly prized in the Orient as a longevity herb, in the same class with ginseng.

It is said that Master Li also changed his diet so as to consume little meat or root vegetables and limited his consumption of grain. Instead, he lived mainly on steamed above-ground vegetables and herbs. He lived to be 252 years old, dying in 1930, reportedly after a banquet presented in his honor by a government official. He had married during his lifetime fourteen times and lived through eleven generations of his own descendants, of which he had almost two hundred during two and a half centuries of life.

Though Li Ch'ing Yuen's case is rare, in that it has been reasonably authenticated, tradition is rich in the Orient in the lore of Taoists living to ages unimaginable by us. It is well known that among the Chinese population, the Taoists far outlived all other people. Many lived to be centurians and few died prematurely. The Taoist art of longevity, known as the "Art of Radiant Health" is one of the great legacies of the East.

The author received his first in-depth instruction in the Taoist herbal arts from Master Sung Jin Park, a man of profound power. Master Park tells an illuminating story as to the efficacy of these herbs, especially when used in conjunction with Taoist yogic practices.

As a young man, Master Park became very interested in the martial arts, and like many young Koreans aspired to become a master of a martial art. Master Park soon discovered that he had great talent as a fighter and over the period of about a decade attained the level of seventh degree and eighth degree black belt in five different martial arts techniques. Such an achievement can hardly be surpassed. He became virtually invincible as a fighter and almost a superman physically.

But upon attaining this incredible level of mastery in the fighting arts, he discovered that he still felt unsatisfied at the center of his being and decided to seek out a spiritual master. Korea is the last Oriental stronghold of the true Taoist hermit. Such holymen have virtually disappeared in China and Japan. Wisemen still exist, of course, in these two great countries, but not of the hermitic type that had lived freely in the wilderness until around the time of the second World War. In the rugged and scarcely populated mountains of South Korea there still exist Taoist hermits who live in simple caves and huts and practice the ancient methods of Taoist inner alchemy. Park decided that he needed to find such a mountain holyman to truly penetrate the secrets of Tao, so he journeyed into these mountains to seek out a sage with whom he could study the teachings of Tao. Eventually, in the remote depths of these mountains, he met an old hermit who lived in a cave. His name was Moo San Do Sha. The eighty-five year old sage at first refused to accept Park as a disciple, but eventually was convinced that Park was sincere, so he invited Park into his cave and challenged him to an arm wrestling match. Park, at the peak of physical vigor and less than half the age of the old hermit, was surprised by the challenge and at first worried that he might even hurt or humiliate Moo San Do Sha. But when the contest took place, Moo San Do Sha quickly put Park's arm to the table and the shocked Park realized the vast power within the old man. Physically humbled by an eighty-five years old man, Park realized how small his power was compared to a man possessed of Tao. Park fell to his knees and again begged Moo San Do Sha to accept him as his student. Park was now ready for discipleship, and became a student of the old Taoist master.

For six years Park lived with Moo San Do Sha as his servant and student. Over this time, Park emulated the sage's conduct to the best of his ability. Moo San Do Sha was a master of the Taoist yoga, *Nei Gung*, which had been practiced in China, Korea and Japan for over two thousand years. Along with the physical exercises, meditation and breathing techniques, and other forms of spiritual cultivation, Moo San Do Sha taught Park about the Superior Herbalism.

Moo San Do Sha was a master herbalist. It was his belief that the tonics were essential to the Taoist adept. As a matter of fact, Moo San Do Sha lived *entirely* on herbs that he collected from the mountain on which he lived. Among the herbs that he and Park found and used was *wild* ginseng, one of the most powerful and profound herbs known to Man. Moo San Do Sha consumed no ordinary food, except for *one* grain of rice each day, and yet he had the strength to overcome a man half his age and in *incredible* physical condition (Park is built like a mountain). To this day Moo San Do Sha still lives in those same rustic mountains, living on herbs and air, as Taoist sages have done for at least two thousand years.

The old master's brand of herbalism had been handed down for centuries. It was traditional and simple. It did not indulge in overly complex formulations using exotic and rare substances. The herbs that he himself used were common Oriental herbs of the type found in all Chinese herb shops. The ancient formulas were designed for one purpose: to generate radiant health and to aid one in the search and achievement of "immortality." The formulations were based upon the highest levels of understanding of Chinese Taoist philosophy. These formulations, and the principles that lie behind them, were passed on to Park.

One day the old master and his disciple took a hike. They came to a valley that was bordered by two stretches of mountain. On one side the mountain took the form of a dragon and on the other side the mountain took the form of a tiger. These two animals are ancient symbols of the great cosmic forces of Yin and Yang. At the center of the valley they came to a spot where tremendous energy was being emitted from the earth. Moo San Do Sha felt that this was a very special place and thought that it would be wonderful if a shrine could be erected at the spot to attract travelers to this earth-energy spring and alert them as to its power for healing and meditation. As it turned out, the land belonged to a potatoe farmer, who would not give the two mountain men the plot of earth, but offered to sell it to them, albeit at a rather steep price. Moo San Do Sha and Park had no money, but were determined to obtain the land.

After some thought, they came upon a plan. Moo San Do Sha had heard that there was much money in America. It was determined that Park would borrow enough money to go to America, where he would teach ten people to *teach* Taoist Yoga. It was their idea that ten well-selected young Americans could sow the seed of a Taoist movement in America, and since all Americans had plenty of money (or so legend had it!), they could easily pay enough to cover Park's expenses and buy the plot of holy land from the farmer. Park did manage to borrow enough money for a one-way ticket to America. Unfortunatley, Park spoke very poor English (actually, none at first) and so had great difficulty in attracting students. He also soon found out, to his dismay that Americans are not universally wealthy. He found himself teaching small martial arts classes just to survive. Three years passed as he struggled to perform his task. One day, however, he fell prey to homesickness and a sense of hopelessness. He decided to offer his Taoist training just one more time in hopes of finding at least one student who might become a teacher of Taoist yoga in America, and who might also have enough money to pay Park enough to pay off his debts and get a ticket home to Korea. He placed a simple, archaic advertisement in a small throw-away newspaper which caught the attention of the author of this book. It was the one and only time *ever* that the author had picked up that paper. The author turned out to be the only student who responded. We took an instant liking to one another. The author had just recently opened the *Acupressure Workshop*, a holistic health center in West Los Angeles, California. Since the author was also not well endowed financially, he invited Master Park to teach classes at the Acupressure Workshop, where we could help promote his classes and simultaneously have him around all the time as our teacher. The plan worked out beautifully. We worked on his English and in a short time he was lecturing quite well in this foreign language. His powerful and wonderful character soon attracted many students. In the year that followed, Master Park revealed the secrets of ages to his enraptured students, who soaked it up like a sponge. Among his favorite subjects was tonic herbalism, and it is his teachings that form the basis of this book, both philosophically and practically.

Within the year, Park received a letter from his master Moo San Do Sha telling Park that he had taken so long that the master had decided to obtain the money himself. Moo San Do Sha had gone down to Soeul and offered a class in his Superior Herbalism, which attracted a large number of normal herb doctors, yielding enough income for the old sage to purchase the land for the shrine. He told Park that he need stay in America no longer. Park immediately made plans to return home, and invited the author and his family to come to Korea with him so that we could meet Moo San Do Sha. Within a month we were headed for Korea. Strange timing as it was, however, fighting broke out between the northern and southern governments of Korea and Americans were temporarily banned from traveling to Korea, "for our own safety." Thus Master Park returned home and the author and his family spent four wonderful months living and studying in *Japan*.

We have not seen Master Park since that time, in 1977, but his warmth, strength and wisdom live with us daily. He always emphasized the holistic natural way of healthcare. One point that he often stressed was the importance of understanding the *principles* of Taoist philosophy before blindly practicing its arts. For this reason, a major portion of this book is dedicated to the expounding of these principles, as understood by the author. There are many superior books available on these subjects, but the simple discussions are necessary to assure beneficial usage of the wonderful Chinese tonic herbs.

1 | Adaptability— The Measure of Life

1.1   The Absolute-Eternal Tao

Chinese tonic herbalism cannot be approached from the simplistic angle of "Ginseng does this and Royal Jelly does that." Though we need to know precisely how each herb acts, it is first essential that we understand Oriental philosophy and the principles of life upon which the tonic system is inseparably based.

The philosophy of the East is very subtle and even more profound. A lifetime of meditation, contemplation and experience may be necessary to become truly illuminated. The Chinese seek illumination through the merging of the body-mind with *Tao*. The Chinese word *Tao* has two major meanings. One refers to the Absolute-Eternal nature of all being and non-being. A second meaning of Tao is "the Path" or "the Way." One follows the Path, or Tao, in order to eventually recognize their unity with the Great Tao, the Absolute-Eternal. Of course, in the end both meanings of "Tao" become one.

Thus, one can be a practicing Taoist by following the principles of life set by Taoist tradition without having yet achieved perfection and illumination. But by following the Path diligently, one will eventually become attuned to the Absolute-Eternal, thus experiencing illumination, or as the Chinese call it, "Immortality." Once one has become one with the Great Tao, one still follows the Path, but now because of inner knowledge, not because of tenets set by others.

It takes a long time to know Tao. This author has no illusions that he can explain Tao to anyone. No one ever has been able to do this, not even the greatest masters of Taoism. Lao Tzu, the legendary father of the Taoist tradition began his sublime classic, the *Tao Te Ching*, with these words:

"The Tao that can be expressed in words is not the Great Eternal Tao."

But Lao Tzu, like many that have followed, including this author, felt the need to attempt an explanation that we all know cannot be given. Yet it lightens the heart, deepens the soul, and brightens the spirit to ponder the great universal concepts of which the Taoists speak. Though words cannot explain Tao, they can give us clues that may yield, if we persist, true knowledge. Lao Tzu said:

"Before Heaven and Earth were born,
There was something formless yet complete.

Silent! Empty!
Changeless! Hanging on nothingness!
Pervading all things! Unending!
We say it is the Mother of all things under heaven,
But we do not know its real name.
We call it the Way (Tao).
We say it is Great (the Great Tao).
To be Great is to go forward,
To go forward is to travel far,
To travel far is to return.
Great is the Way,
Great are Heaven and Earth,
Great is Man.
Among the four great things,
Man has his place.
Man follows Earth,
Earth follows Heaven,
Heaven follows the Way,
The Way follows itself."

And again:

"The Great Tao is unanchored—it goes left and right.
The ten thousand creatures are nourished by it and never denied,
It creates them, and makes no demand on them.
It clothes them, but has no mastery.
So it is called humble.
So it is called great.
The Tao is hidden and nameless.
Only the Tao upholds all things
And brings them to fulfillment."

Thus the Great Tao is invisible to those that cannot see behind things. It is the all-pervading force from which all things come and to which all things return. Tao has its Way, but takes no credit. In fact, the knowledge of Tao is an inner experience of immediate awareness. It is intuitive and not intellectual. When the distinction between subject and object has disappeared, when the distinction between self and non-self has vanished, one knows, or rather *is* Tao. At this point one realizes that the Tao is the great invisible, unfathomable One. Tao embraces the past, present and future; it embraces being and non-being alike. Tao is the One, without opposite, embracing all duality and multiplicity. Tao is infinite, eternal, and all-embracing. To know Tao requires a leap of consciousness, indeed!
    Does Tao have any value? Lao Tzu says:

"To know people is to be wise,

To know oneself is to be illumined.
To conquer others is to have strength,
To conquer oneself is to have true power.
To be content is to have great wealth,
To follow the Way devotedly is to fulfill all aims.
Then to die and not be lost is called "long life."

To commune with Tao is to have achieved "immortality." What is the secret to communing with Tao? Tao cannot be seen or heard. Where then can we discover its secret? Lao Tzu knew. This is his answer:

"Many words cannot fathom it
But look, it is in your heart!"

1.2 Change

Tao is manifested in Nature and Nature reflects Tao. Upon examining Nature, one soon realizes that Nature is in perpetual flux. It is everchanging. Nothing in Nature lasts forever in a constant state. Of course, some things seem to last longer than others, but change takes place none-the-less. Eventually, *everything* changes.

Everything is moving, relocating, repositioning. Even that which appears still is gradually changing. Nothing is constant, for as parameters change, constants must adapt. The speed of light is called a constant, but is now known to travel at different speeds when under the gravitational influences of any number of cosmic forces. In another universe, at another time, light will travel much differently than we think it does here and now.

The Earth moves around the Sun, and the Sun moves around the Milky Way. The Sun was born, but is changing and one day will expire. Chemical and physical principles held as "law" here on Earth may have no bearing at other locations in the universe. What one man perceives as truth may be held with equal validity to be false elsewhere. In the ephemeral world, nothing is sure; nothing is absolute.

To hold fast to something that itself must inevitably change, is foolishness. Only the Great Tao does not change. One who knows Tao, flows with the changes and avoids rigidity and attachment. Lao Tzu, like many other great teachers throughout history, recommended that we avoid extreme attachment because attachment breeds rigidity. Rigidity is contrary to the Way. Rigidity in Nature results in death, while flexibility results in renewal. This is one of Lao Tzu's most important lessons. Lao Tzu said:

"The ancient saying 'to bend is to maintain integrity' is the word of
    truth."

1.3 Cyclicity

As all-pervading as is change, there is order, there is a process by which change occurs. Central to Chinese philosophy is the recognition of this order. The principles of life, expressed by the Taoists, are derived from this recognition of natural order. One may live harmoniously in Nature's orderly process by applying these fundamental life principles.

The first of these fundamental life principles is that all processes in Nature are cyclic. Early mystics noted the many cycles of Nature and realized that all of Nature's processes had a pulse, a rhythm. Night and day followed one another without fail. But even here a shifting rhythm was observed as the seasons changed. The seasons change cyclically, as do the lunar periods. Living things experience their life cycles. The Chinese documented cyclic weather changes that helped them predict the weather and grow their crops.

The great Chinese classic, the *I Ching*, or *Book of Changes*, is a re-counting of the cyclic nature of change. In fact, it breaks a single cycle of change down to its sixty-four primary divisions—quite a detailed and sophisticated analysis.

The significance of all this has been clear to wisemen for a long time: one must not expect things to stay as they are, and predictions of following stages can be made. Heat must be followed, sooner or later, by cold—and then the cold by heat. Down-turns alternate with up-turns. Strength and weakness, wakefulness and sleepiness seem to alternate endlessly.

Modern science is very well aware of the cyclicity of things. These days, cyclicity is taken into account in virtually all scientific research. Physiologically, our hearts beat in rhythms that determine our health, brain waves pulsate, hormones are secreted cyclically; in fact, *every* function of life is now known to have its biological rhythm—that is, a natural cyclic pattern.

Becoming aware of our cycles, and of the cycles pulsing around us, is the first step to mental and physical health. The great masters have spent much time just sitting—observing the cyclic flow of things. It would do anyone benefit to take some contemplative time to just sit back and watch, with an open and clear mind. Nature will then reveal herself. Nature flows in waves. We are an integral part of Nature, so we too flow in waves. If our cycles are harmonious within ourselves and in tune with the external cycles, our life will flourish. This is the first of the life principles of Chinese philosophy.

The ancient observation that Nature's processes are cyclic has recently been "discovered" by Western science. The last two decades of research in all fields of science has now led to the same conclusions that ancient philosophers espoused.

Bertram S. Brown, M.D., when director of the National Institute of Mental Health, wrote in 1971:

> "From the moment of conception until death rhythm is as much a part
> of our structure as our bones and flesh. Most of us are dimly aware that
> we fluctuate in energy, mood, well-being, and performance each day, and

that there are longer, more subtle behavioral alterations each week, each month, season, and year.

Through studies of biological rhythms, many aspects of human variability—in symptoms of illness, in response to medical treatment, in learning, and job performance—are being illuminated. Already, some of our changes of mood and vulnerabilities to stress and illness, our peaks of strength and productivity, can be anticipated . . . . Timing promises to become an important factor in preventive health programs and medicine . . . .

No corner of medicine—from laboratory testing of new drugs and procedures to clinical and public health programs—is likely to remain untouched by the new explorations into biological rhythms."

This is not just the opinion of one man. This recognition of cyclicity is now accepted scientific law.

We all experience ups and downs in our lives. Many of our problems arise from becoming locked into one pole or another of a cycle. Growth, in the sense of human potential, is not linear. We do not set a goal and then attain that goal with constant, undisturbed steady forward progress. This is not the way of Nature. Instead, we advance and retreat, repeatedly. If the timing is right and our will is sufficient enough to flow past or through obstacles that may block our path, our advances will outgain the setbacks. This results in "growth." If the timing is poor and our will fails us, our dream will not be achieved because the setbacks will become dominant and we will become stuck or may even fall backwards. It is essential that we recognize and respect this cyclic nature of things. Otherwise we can confuse setbacks with failure and growth is terminated. To the wise, a setback is as important as our steps forward, because it is from the setbacks that we learn. Those who do not encounter setbacks cannot grow.

Of course, growth and evolution require energy. Without sufficient energy it is difficult or impossible to muster up the will or otherwise overcome obstacles which necessarily block our path. Realizing the importance of energy, generating inner strength to overcome difficulties, all wise people have sought ways to encourage their life force. Yogic practices, nutrition, meditative arts and proper living have all been widely practiced. To these essential arts the Chinese have added the tonic herbal system for the purpose of developing the vast power necessary to evolve from the finite to the infinite. With sufficient inner strength, obstacles that would mean sure failure or even death to some people are easily overcome. This is one of the great secrets of spiritual mastery, or for that matter, mastery on any plane.

The work of an evolved being, then, is not to follow rigid rules, either of society or religion, but simply to be in rhythm with life's conditions and to be in tune with Tao, that which is infinite in all things. This is not a passive process, though it may appear so when compared to one who butts their head against walls in a failing effort to succeed. The greatest danger to anyone on a path of growth is to forget that things move cyclically. It is easy for a person to become consciously

or unconsciously attached to one phase or another, and thus lose their flexibility.
Lao Tzu made the point:

> "For all creatures there is a time of advancing, a time for withdrawal,
> A time for inhaling, a time for exhaling,
> A time for growing strong, a time for decay,
> A time for creation, a time for destruction.
> Therefore the wise avoid extremes and will not be lost,
> Those who follow Tao avoid extremes,
> Because they avoid extremes they do not expire.
> They are like seeds and are constantly renewed."

1.4 Balance

What then is the secret to finding peace and happiness in a world so changing,
with extreme danger at every turn? Balance, it is taught, is the great secret. Balance yields success and happiness in a world that is continually moving in circles
from one extreme to another. Of course, we all fall off balance sometimes. This,
too, is part of growing. We must pick ourselves up, dust ourselves off, consider
the *cause* of our fall, and then step back on the track. If we lack the insight,
vitality or will for this, we must retreat for awhile and rebuild our reserves and
consolidate our will. But eventually, we learn that falling is not a necessary part
of the ultimate path. If we can learn to maintain balance, we can find Tao.

Bagwan Shree Rajneesh, one of the truly great spiritual masters of this era, has
explained this very eloquently. In responding to the question of "How can we
maintain a peaceful state of mind in a world so tumultuous?" he said:

> "Who can maintain his calm for long?
> Calmness comes, silence comes,
> But who can maintain it for long?
> By activity it comes back to life.
> By activity you can maintain it.
> If you try to maintain it by inactivity continuously, it will be impossible.
> One has to move into opposites to remain always transcendental.
> In the day you work.
> In the night you sleep.
> If you work continuously twenty-four hours, that will be death.
> If you sleep twenty-four hours, that will be death also.
> In the day work hard, and in working hard you are gaining the capacity
>   to sleep.
> In the night sleep completely, and in sleeping completely you are rejuve-
>   nating and refreshing your energies to work hard.
> Move into a rhythm.
> Lean to the right, lean to the left,

But always keep the balance.
Calm cannot be maintained by remaining inactive forever and ever.
Be a householder,
Be in the world and be out of it also, together.
Remember always that Life is a togetherness of opposites,
A deep harmony.
He who embraces this Tao guards against being overful.
Whosoever comes to know that Tao is balance, God is balance, guards
   against being overful.
Then don't move too much to one side,
For the balance will be lost.
An imbalance is the only sin for Lao Tzu.
To be balanced is to be virtuous,
To be imbalanced is to be in sin.
Because he guards against being overful,
He is always fresh and young, he's never weary, he's never tired.
Balance is vitality.
Balance is Life.
Balance gives him eternal life."

Virtually all of our mistakes reflect a lack of balance. We must be conscious to maintain balance. Yet logic and intellect are usually not the most important ingredients in this great art of maintaining balance. We must be very sensitive and very aware. We must develop our intuition to a very fine degree. Furthermore, we must be able to maintain our calm even under the most severe circumstances of change. When we are calm and centered, we easily maintain our essential balance. The person of wisdom is not afraid of the emotions or of the senses. But he is cautious not to be caught up in their extremes.

One knows not what may be hidden behind the extremes. If one must of necessity approach an extreme, the approach should be made with alertness and great care. As the great Sufi master Hazrat Inyat Khan said:

"The nature of life is illusive.
Under a gain a loss is hidden;
Under a loss a gain is hidden;
And living in this life of illusion,
It is very difficult for a man to realize what is really good for him."

A classic Taoist story further accents this most important principle of life. Once there was an old man who was very poor but was content and happy. All he had in the world were a small parcel of land, his humble cottage, an old horse and an able son. One night, the horse ran away. When the old man's neighbors heard of this, they came as a group to give their condolences and said to him; "This is indeed a great misfortune." But the old man only replied "Maybe," and smiled. The neighbors were surprised and thought him to be a bit strange as they departed.

The next night, the old man heard a great racket outside his cottage. His horse had returned, but not alone. It had returned with several other young wild horses and led them straight into the old man's corral. The next day, the neighbors returned. This time, they were very joyous and said to the old man: "Surely, good fortune shines upon you from heaven." The old man smiled as before and again replied "Maybe." His neighbors thought him ungrateful and perhaps a bit disturbed and muttered amongst themselves as they left. Soon it became time to tame the wild horses and the old man's son tried to mount one to begin the process. He was immediately thrown and broke his leg. The neighbors, upon hearing of this and being a genuinely neighborly group, once again returned as a group to the old man's house to offer their condolences. Once again, in spite of the hardship this would undoubtedly bear upon the old man, he merely smiled and said "Maybe." This time, the neighbors left in disgust, thinking the old man to be a fool, or perhaps insane. The next day, however, conscription officers poured through the village, forcing all the young men to join them. The local lord was going off to war and these young men were to be his pawns. When these soldiers came to the old man's cottage, they found the son to be unable to walk and therefore of no use as a soldier. They left him behind. Soon the neighbors came to the old man again, some weeping because their sons had been taken, perhaps never to return. They saw that the old man's son was still in his bed, his leg with a splint and bandaged. They said to the old man: "You are indeed a lucky man." The old man smiled gently and said only "Maybe." The neighbors stood quietly for some time. Gradually, they too began to smile and nod their heads. And as they slowly departed, they too could be heard saying to one another: "Maybe."

A balanced attitude and a balanced way of life help to smooth out the rocky path of life. There are times when we must work very hard: these times must be balanced with periodic withdrawal, deep rest, relaxation, and recuperation. Then there are times when all is tranquil: these times require recreation to make our time more balanced. If it is hot out, we seek the shade and drink cool liquids to cool ourselves down. If it is cold out we find a warm fire and drink hot drinks to warm up. It is our instinct to maintain balance, but sometimes our instincts are ignored and we fall into the trap of excess and imbalance. In a sense, we become addicted to an extreme position.

There is nothing in which balance does not play a factor. Even generally beneficial activities, and non-activities, can be injurious if done in excess. Breath is life, but breathing too deeply can lead to hyperventilation; shallow, insufficient breathing is a primary cause of ill-health and premature death. We must not eat or drink too much or too little. We must not sleep or work too much or too little. A little alcohol has been generally found to relax the body and mind and to prevent hypertension, but we all know what comes of those who become excessive drinkers. Salt and sugar are necessary for life, but too much can result in death. The list is endless.

Balance must be applied to every aspect of our life. When a mistake is made, the wise avoid these same excesses the next time, while the foolish repeat their error over and over. Of course, it sometimes takes a few times around to see the truth through something. Life is balance, and those who practice the art of balance succeed and are called wise.

1.5 Oneness of Man and His Environment

Human life is a part of the natural order on Earth. Though Man is a special being, capable of significantly manipulating his environment, it is a great mistake to think of himself as separate from, or superior to Nature as a whole. Man is a part of Nature and is intimately connected to his environment. Like all life on Earth, Man is dependent upon his environment for life support, and like all other beings, influences his environment. He is subject to the laws of Nature, and if these are violated, natural law determines an appropriate outcome. If he lives in harmony with his environment and abides by natural law, life flourishes.

There was a time, not many years ago, when scientists and social designers espoused a theory that Man could "conquer" Nature. This incredibly foolish belief has led to the destruction of thousands of life forms on Earth, to worldwide pollution, and to the destruction of much of our environment. Recently this selfish, egoistic attitude has become all—too transparent and our society has become aware of the need to cultivate and protect our environment if Mankind is to survive, much less flourish. There is a large effort being made by conscious individuals and groups to protect the endangered species and their environments and to clean up poisonous wastes in our soil, air and water. Some feel we are too late. Whether or not this is the case, we are certainly at the brink of disaster.

If we destroy our environment, we eventually destroy ourselves—this is biological law. If we protect and nurture our environment, it will nurture and provide for us. A truly utopian world is possible, but will only come into being when Nature as a *whole* is encouraged and protected, with balance and love as the principles guiding our actions.

The person who is conscious of their unity with all of Nature avoids polluting their environment and does not waste anything. This person gives back to Nature what he can, and in this way a balance is struck. Only in this way will Nature continue to be able to support human life.

Environmental influences were recognized by the traditional Oriental people (like all traditional cultures) to play a critical role in a person's health and well-being. All of the environmental forces were respected and recognized for their influence. Heat, cold, dampness, dryness, the wind, etc. were all studied in detail and correlated to the human condition. These forces were known to influence our condition, both physically and emotionally. The Chinese were so oriented towards naturalism, that they even categorized illness in terms of "heat," "cold," "dampness," etc. We will discuss this in more detail further on.

Unity is the very essence of Taoism: the unity of opposites, the unity in diversity. Because everything was seen to be a part of the One-Being, everything was sacred to the Taoist. As an aspect of this philosophy, the Taoists stressed the unity of the body within itself, as an integrated whole. Chuang Tzu, another great Taoist philosopher of ancient times, in discussing the human body, said:

> "In considering the human body, is it not true that its hundred bones, nine external cavities and six master organs all exist by virtue of their complete integration? May I ask which of them I shall favor the most? Should I not favor one in particular? Or is it not true that by their integration something real exists?"

Chuang Tzu is here clearly explaining that wholeness requires the proper integration of its many parts. For life to proceed, a multitude of physiological activities must proceed in harmony, as one, as it were. Of course, physiology cannot be limited to the body. The air we breathe, the food we eat, the fluids we drink, the sights and sounds we perceive, the things we touch, the ideas we receive and create, all influence us from moment to moment.

The Taoists were of the very definite opinion that the closer one lives to Nature, the closer one comes to fulfilling the purpose of life. The ancient Chinese often used the analogy of an "uncarved block" to describe simple, natural living. The great modern scholar Chang Chung-yuan has expressed it this way:

> "This world of the uncarved block is a world of free interfusion among men and men and all things. Between all multiplicities there existed no boundaries. Man could work with man and share spontaneously together. Each identified with the other and all lived together as one. Man lived an innocent and primitive life, and all conceit and selfishness were put aside. In this uncarved simplicity we see the free movement of the divine. Nature was seen in its marks of spirituality. This we cannot expect in a merely moral and intellectual world, full of distinctions and differentiations. Only in a world of absolutely free identity does the great sympathy exist: the universal force that holds together man and man and all things. To live in the world of free identity man must transform himself, get rid of his ego-conscious self."

Man is indeed a product of heaven and earth, from which he comes and to which he inevitably returns. The influence of heaven and earth are beyond question. Man wakes and sleeps with this sun's daily cycle, he eats the foods that can be procured from his environment according to the season and climate, he dresses to suit the weather, and he suffers illness for failing to adapt to climatic change.

Modern research has done much to confirm this. It is now known that actions on the surface of the sun alter the chemistry of life on Earth. Emotions change according to changes in the ion ratios in the air. Winds that blow in positively charged particles, from deserts and elsewhere, cause thousands of minor and major reactions in the human body. Winds that blow in negatively charged particles (high electron concentrations) result in an equal number of opposite effects. These and thousands of other environmental changes influence how we feel, think and act from moment to moment and day to day.

There is a great joy in realizing our total interconnectedness with Nature. Nature has bred us perfectly and can provide all that is necessary for us to live full and happy lives. Our genius, if used wisely, can perhaps enhance our experience of life, but not if we use our cleverness and skills to destroy our environment. Will mankind turn to sound ecological living or will he continue to plunder and pollute his own environment? This is probably the most important question of our era. Likewise, will he continue to pollute his own body with toxic chemicals without heed to the future consequences? Will Mankind turn to solar power, which does not pollute, or will he continue to burn hydrocarbons and use nuclear fuels, both of which yield lethal pollutants? Questions such as these must be answered soon, because the massive changes being brought about by modern Man may irrevocably alter Nature and the way of life on this planet within a mere matter of years or decades. The environment being created may not be suitable for life as we know it.

We are so intimately connected to our environment that virtually nothing goes unsensed at some level by our systems. It is utter folly to maintain an arrogant, ego-centric attitude of separateness from Nature. Man, like all life on our planet, is at-one-with all of Nature. Mankind must learn to blend progress and technology with natural principles and natural living if he is to survive and fulfill his destiny.

1.6   Adaptability

Another fundamental principle of life lies in adaptability. With everything in constant flux, every living being must constantly be adapting so as to harmonize with its environment. Man is no exception, and, as is true in all of life, most of the adjustments are automatic and subconscious.

We are constantly adjusting to a multitude of slight to large changes in the environment. It is one of the great wonders of life that a being can change in so many ways and still remain intact and maintain its integrity. Living beings are *living* only by virtue of their ability to fluidly adapt to the constant natural flux.

As human beings, we are the result of millions of years of on-going adaptation. At the present, we are capable of adjusting, whether subconsciously or consciously, to a multitude of forces constantly changing in our environment. Be it hot or cold, light or dark, windy or still, wet or dry, our bodies easily and constantly adjust—*if we are healthy*, and if these external stimuli are not so extreme as to surpass our full capacity to adapt. A healthy, adaptive person will survive and/or thrive where an unhealthy, less adaptive individual will fall and perish. Adaptability is the key to understanding evolution. Darwin said that the fittest will survive. The "fittest" in Nature are those that "fit" into their environment most perfectly and can adapt to changes in the environment so as to assure their continued success. Those that cannot adapt become extinct.

On the point of adaptability, again, both the ancient Chinese and modern scientists agree. As the great endocrinologist Hans Selye, M.D. has pointed out:

> "Adaptability is probably the most distinctive characteristic of life. In maintaining the independence and individuality of natural units, none of the great forces of inanimate matter are as successful as that alertness and adaptability to change which we designate as life—and the loss of which is death. Indeed there is perhaps a certain parallelism between the degree of aliveness and the extent of adaptability in every animal—in every man."

This quality of adaptability depends upon harmonious and energetic functioning. Adjustments must be accurate, in order that the organism adapt precisely to the changes. Over-adjustment, as well as under-adjustment will lead to disharmony and to some degree of discomfort. If for some reason a human loses the ability to adjust appropriately, sooner or later we fall prey to the forces of Nature. In a desperate attempt to regain balance, homeostasis, our bodies and psyches rely upon back-up mechanisms. If these too are insufficient, or become depleted before the adaptive response is complete, subtle signs and symptoms of illness arise, followed by overt disease and eventually death.

The Chinese tonic herbs are believed to play a significant role in the realm of adaptability. As a matter of fact, some scholars are calling the tonics the "adaptogenics." This is a very appropriate term, for it is precisely the function of the tonic herbs to enhance human adaptability so as to expand the parameters within which Man may live and play. Since our environment continually changes, we must be able to change accordingly. It is clear that if we are capable of adapting easily to changes, our life is easier. If on the other hand we suffer at every change, we become a slave to conditions, dependent upon a narrow set of circumstances for our health and happiness.

If one has developed and can maintain the high degree of adaptive capacity that one would regard as "radiant health," that person can move freely from one environment to another without fear. True freedom is the ability to flow freely from one circumstance to the next, to blend harmoniously with seeming opposites, to enjoy change. The one who can enjoy heat and cold, wind and stillness, and all the other climatic conditions without fear of illness has a great advantage in life over one who fears or shys away from certain weather conditions.

While the adaptively weak person cannot, the truly healthy person can walk in the rain and thus experience a great gift of Nature in an intimate way. On a practical level, there are many times in life when one must encounter difficult, or even dangerous circumstances that require acute adaptability. If the adaptive capacity is strong, we can succeed; but if it is not, we fail and perhaps are destroyed.

The ancient Chinese realized that true adaptability had to be cultivated and required the wisdom of balance. Ch'i Po, the mythical sage of the *Yellow Emperor's Classic of Internal Medicine*, China's earliest medical text, described three life-styles by which ancient wisemen achieved their goals:

"The ancient *Holymen* maintained their virtue and followed the Path (Tao). They lived in accord with Yin and Yang, and hence in harmony with the four seasons. They departed from the busy world of Man and retired from mundane affairs. At peace in the natural world, they were able to conserve their energy and preserve their spirit. They roamed the entire universe with infinite freedom. In this way they strengthened and increased their life, eventually achieving immortality.

"The ancient *Sages* attained harmony with Heaven and Earth and followed closely the laws of Nature. They learned the art of bending, and thus were able to adjust their desires in order to live in harmony with all men. Within their hearts they did harbor neither hatred nor anger. In this way they were able to remain in the busy world. Yet they remained indifferent to the customs. They were not concerned excessively about anything. They regarded inner happiness and peace of mind as primary, and recognized contentment as the supreme achievement. They worked with their physical bodies, but avoided over-taxing themselves. They used their minds in meditation and thought, but avoided excess here as well. By following this path, they could never been harmed physically and their power of mind could never be depleted. Thus they could reach the age of one hundred years or more.

"Then there were the men of *Supreme Virtue*. They followed Tao, obeying the laws of the universe, emulating the sun and moon, and living by the stars. They had foresight through their observations of Yin and Yang and were thus able to move in harmony with all change. They knew the art of harmony and lived as one within the four seasons and with all of Nature. In this way they achieved immortality."

With the help of the Chinese tonic herbs, we can alter our adaptive capacity and experience a new range of freedom, a freedom, the Chinese say, that is limited only by our own narrowness of mind and strength of will.

1.7 Polarity—The Great Principle of Yin and Yang

Cycles can be most easily understood by recognizing the rhythmic shifting from one pole to its opposite. Just as every process of Nature shows cyclicity, every process has a polar nature. Though oneness is the primary law of the universe, this fundamental two-dimensional view of Nature generates the concept known as "the Great Principle" to the Chinese.

The Great Principle is the law of Yin and Yang. The Great Principle of Yin and Yang provides a uniquely exquisite model of the universe, for it provides a basis for understanding the fundamental pattern of all processes. Yin-Yang is not a "mystical" concept devoid of meaning and value in the scientific age. Far from it! Actually, it is extremely logical, obvious, and practical beyond compare.

As explained previously, everything changes cyclically. Cycles occur as phenomena oscillates rhythmically between energetically active phases and resting phases. The great Chinese philosophers of old categorized all phenomena in the overtly active stage of its cycle as Yang. All phenomena in its covert, quietistic stage are considered as Yin. Many people try to explain Yang as the "male," positive force, and Yin as the "female," negative counterforce. This is a great oversimplification and is in fact quite misleading. It is far more fundamental to perceive Yin and Yang in terms of energetics.

The secret to truly understanding Yin and Yang is in the old saying attributed to Taoist master Huang-Keu:

"The Yin conserves and the Yang radiates."

Within all processes there is a time during which energy must be consumed, assimilated and stored. During this phase, energy is drawn inward and concentrated, perhaps even bound as energized matter. This phase is Yin. Once energy sufficient to the needs of the entity or process at work is accumulated and processed so as to be usable, the energy is expended and the entity or phenomena becomes outwardly, expansively energetic, perhaps even explosive or aggressive. This expansively active stage is called Yang. When the energy has been expended, the phenomena automatically seeks new sources of energy and begins the Yin, accumulative phase. Thus the cycle can repeat itself, though each cycle will bear changes that are in harmony with other cyclic processes occurring in its sphere of influence.

Examples of this process are endless. Let us take a few simple examples:

A cloud: Water evaporates from the surface of the Earth until sufficient quantities of moisture coalesce to form a cloud (Yin stage—accumulation, concentration and storage). When the cloud is concentrated to capacity, rain falls, alleviating the pressure within the cloud (Yang stage—release of energy in the form of activity).

A star: Cosmic gases accumulate and condense (Yin stage). A star is thus formed. Energy is radiated (Yang stage) until the star burns itself out.

The heart: Electrical energy flows through the nervous system into a special nerve unit (the A-V node) in the muscle of the heart. Energy builds and builds until the nerve unit reaches capacity. Until this instant, the heart is in its so-called "resting" stage. But we know that "rest" is really a phase of accumulation and concentration of the energy needed for the next phase, activity. During the "resting" stage, blood is also accumulated into the chambers of the heart. This "resting" stage is Yin. At the moment of energy saturation, the accumulated energy is discharged throughout the heart muscle causing a strong contracting action, forcing the blood out of the heart and into the lungs and other parts of the body. This Yang, "working" phase is then automatically followed by a Yin stage of energy accumulation ("rest").

The mind: As we receive information through our senses, this information is sorted and stored in the body-mind. This accumulation of information is thus Yin. When we act based upon our knowledge, experience and understanding, we are utilizing information previously received. This active stage is Yang. Of course much of the knowledge upon which we base our actions is not accumulated during our individual lifetime, but has been stored in our genetic material and has been passed on to us genetically. Instinctive knowledge is of such biological importance that Nature has built it right into our very being, and for this reason should never be ignored, though it must often be controlled.

The above examples can be expanded considerably. Upon examination, one realizes that the pattern is universal. Of course, no cycle stands alone, for every cyclic process is touched and influenced by many other cyclic processes. In these interactions, Yang causes Yin, and vice versa. To give, someone must receive; to strike, something must be stricken; to love, something must be loved.

On a physiological level, we know for example that for movement to occur in ones arm, a muscle (or actually, a set of muscles) must contract (active, Yang stage). Concurrently, a muscle (or set of muscles) which would prevent this action or would cause an opposite effect, must relax (passive, Yin stage). In a dynamic sense, the coordination of these active and passive actions of the muscles must occur in superb harmony for coordinated physical movement to occur.

Another beautiful example of Yin-Yang in human physiology lies in the nervous system. The Autonomic Nervous System is that aspect of the human nervous system that controls all of our automatic, subconscious functions. There are two components of the Autonomic Nervous System, known as the parasympathetic and sympathetic. Here is how the Autonomic Nervous System is described in a medical text recently published by the Johns Hopkins School of Medicine:

> "The physiological significance of the autonomic nervous system has been described by Pick in the following way: The parasympathetic or cranial sacral component is essentially an anabolic system, because it is directed toward the preservation, accumulation, and storage of energies in the body. In contrast, the general effect of the sympathetic nervous system is catabolic because it causes the expenditure of bodily energies and inhibits the intake and assimilation of nutrient matter. There is, therefore, a high degree of stability of bodily function under the dual control of the autonomic nervous system."

The Autonomic Nervous System exemplifies how the entire physiological process occurs. Every action and function of life takes place as opposing forces interact, first with one force predominating then the other. Every hormone, enzyme, and chemical in the body is matched by an opposing substance. If a hormone is discovered that stimulates a certain function, scientists automatically start their search for its antithesis which inhibits the action or otherwise results in an opposite response.

Another law of Yin and Yang is that opposites attract. For example, positive ions unite chemically with negative ions. In this way, a more stable, content state of being can exist. In the same way men and women attract. It is often said that men are Yang and that women are Yin. This is because men provide sexually and women receive. Also, men generally tend to be essentially aggressive when compared to women. But this is clearly an oversimplification. Men and women both have Yin and Yang aspects. In a relationship where a man is the assertive partner, he can be said to be the Yang partner and the woman the Yin. However, the opposite is often the case, and there are many women that are much more Yang than many men. Yang and Yin are relative terms when considering opposing forces. One man might be more aggressive than a woman, and he is therefore (relatively) the Yang partner and she the Yin. But she may be more aggressive than another man she knows and in this relationship she is the Yang partner. In either case, satisfaction is possible if balance is achieved.

It is a fundamental tenet of Yin and Yang that everything has its front and back sides. The wise can see both sides even while only one side is apparent. "Hot" is a term understood only in relation to "cold," "up" exists only relative to something that is "down," "behind" exists because of what is in "front." Thus the sayings: "everything that has a front has a back," and "the bigger the front the bigger the back." So often we see in humans outward strength that really hides inner fear and weakness. Occasionally we see the opposite. The saying, "the bigger they are the harder they fall" is a perfect example of Yin-Yang thinking in terms of the vulnerability of the inflated ego. For this reason, sages from all cultures have encouraged humility, and it is said that "the meek shall become great."

It is essential that we always remember that Yin and Yang are two yet one. Each contains something of the other. All things contain both. Though they appear to conflict, they in fact support one another and the two forces are mutually responsible for all change. There is no place in the universe that is free from the influence of the pairs of opposites. As the old saying goes:

"From Yang springs illumination, and from Yin darkness; yet you cannot separate them one from another."

The Great Principle of Yin and Yang can easily become incorporated into our basic logic, even if we do not use these terms *per se*. For it is the nature of existence to oscillate between opposites and in this way to maintain balance. Our awareness of this universal law can help liberate us from so many bonds artificially created by ourselves and society. Rigidity of mind and body are our own worst enemies. Flexibility with inner strength is the key to a long and happy life.

The principle of Yin and Yang is not a difficult concept to understand or to use. Its very simplicity, however, has made it subject to oversight. We can see it everywhere and in everything. We know it innately. It is so primal that it is in our souls and motivates the course of the Milky Way. It is the law of relativity and periodicity. It is expressed as rhythm, the shifting dominance of opposing forces. To recognize the unity and flow of this process is the key to wisdom.

Chu Hsi said:

> "The Yang transmutes and the Yin preserves. The Yang and the Yin
> manifest as motion and rest; moving to the utmost and resting, resting to
> the utmost and moving. Hence in the Yin is the Yang, and in the Yang is
> the Yin, inseparably interwoven, and it is thus, as a unity, that they are
> said to be one with Tao."

1.8   Life Energy—Ch'i

The Chinese felt that the entire universe is pervaded by energy. The energy on
Earth is of the precise nature to allow for life. The Earth was conceived of as the
center of cosmological forces, receiving energy equally from outer space, which
the Chinese simply termed "Heaven," and from the Earth. The importance of the
realization that Heaven and Earth each provide and receive vast amounts of life
energy is expressed in this quote from the *Yellow Emperor's Classic of Internal
Medicine*, written around the time of Confucius:

> "The principle of Yin and Yang is the basis of the entire universe. It is
> the principle of everything in creation. It brings about transformation to
> parenthood; it is the root and source of life and death. Heaven was created
> by an accumulation of Yang; the Earth was created by an accumulation
> of Yin. The ways of Yin and Yang are to the left and to the right. Water
> and fire are the symbols of Yin and Yang. Yin and Yang are the source
> of power and the beginning of everything in creation. Yang ascends to
> Heaven; Yin descends to Earth. Hence the universe (Heaven and Earth)
> represents motion and rest, controlled by the wisdom of Nature. Nature
> grants the power to beget and to grow, to harvest and to store, to finish
> and to begin anew. Everything in creation is covered by Heaven and sup-
> ported by the Earth."

The ancients were clearly aware that Man walked on the Earth and thus stood
between the two celestial forces. They recognized a difference between the forces
coming to Earth from outer space and the forces generated by the Earth. But most
importantly, they realized that they were dealing with *energy* and that life resulted
as a result of this energy. They could feel the warmth of the sun and experience
its power. They knew the relationship between vegetative growth and solar influence. They recognized the different power of the moon and observed the role
it played in human life and in Nature as a whole. And the rain, which pours
down from above was worshipped as the life-giving source of power that it is.
They observed plants growing from the Earth and knew that all life came from
the Earth.

  Their keen observation of primordial energies soon influenced the early Chinese
self-conception. They realized that, like all things, they were themselves a state of

energy, an organized microcosm reflecting the great macrocosm surrounding them. The Chinese health arts, like their cosmology, is thus vitalistic, based on energy.

The Chinese word for energy is *Ch'i*. It is Ch'i that creates life and through its careful management, the Oriental people feel that one can master life and obtain true health and longevity. This concept of energy management included the accumulation, assimilation, circulation, regulation, preservation, and utilization of Ch'i, the life energy. Ch'i has been studied in tremendous depth by Oriental scholars, yogic arts practitioners, and those specifically in the healing arts. Each of the activities and functions of the Ch'i has been observed and described in surprising detail and means have been developed by which the different aspects of energy management can be specifically influenced.

Starting thousands of years ago, Chinese spiritual seekers sat in contemplation of Nature and the Universe. The early conception of Tao and the Great Principle of Yin and Yang formed the basis of their exploration. As mentioned, they felt intimately the forces coming from the sky (Heaven) and from the Earth. They also experienced atmospheric influences. They noted that when the wind blew in from the north, it was cold and caused specific bodily reactions, while a wind blowing in from the south was warm and caused a different physical reaction. These and many other parameters were carefully observed and developed into a system of understanding Man and Nature. Each of the influences was categorized as a type of energy and each of these energies had an effect upon the same energies that composed the human body-mind. Also, sitting in meditation and practicing their yoga, the early masters discovered an energy circuitry running through and along the body, which they soon discovered had a precise pattern, including a set of points at which these energy circuits could be influenced. This new-found knowledge soon became a part of the yogic practices in a practical way. The yogis began to stimulate these spots by pressing with their fingers, rubbing, tapping, etc. as part of their regimen to develop themselves physically and spiritually. As time went by, the arts of acupressure, acupuncture and moxibustion were developed, based upon the original self-applied acupressure of the yogis.

The Ch'i has long-since been established to course through the body in the energy circuitry known as the *organ-meridian system*. Over the past several thousand years the organ-meridian system has formed the basis of virtually all of traditional Chinese medicine and the related health arts. With the coming of the scientific era, there was, of course, considerable skepticism. No such circuitry had been discovered by Western scientists and even the concept of bio-energy had been mostly overlooked by a system of research and theoretics that was dependent upon physical evidence. However, significant research, both in the East and West in the last decade has done much to validate the Chinese system which may in fact lead to changes in Western medical practice.

One interesting example was the discovery of acupuncture anaethesia and analgesia. The confirmed fact that acupoints stimulated appropriately could affect the central nervous system at specific sites encouraged considerable research into the mechanism of pain, which had remained a very mysterious phenomena until the mid-1970's. Soon after the acupuncture discovery, researchers located the receptor sites for a heretofore unknown category of neurotransmitters known as the *endorphins* and *enkephalins*. These substances were soon recognized to be *natural opiates* essential to normal human functioning. They were shown to mediate not only pain, but also emotional stress response. One type of endorphin recently isolated at Stanford University was found to be two hundred times stronger than morphine. It was found that deficiencies of these substances were responsible for many symptoms of the stress syndrome. For example, Italian researchers have demonstrated that migraines occur during periods of sudden endorphin deficiency and disappear when the endorphin level returns to normal. It has also been shown that production of these substances is integrally related to one's emotional state. An antithetical substance was also found which counteracts the euphoric, relaxing, analgesic effects of the endorphins and enkephalins: Substance P. Substance P increases stress symptoms, including pain and has an inverse relationship to endorphin and enkephalin production. It was found that acupuncture anaethesia and analgesia result due to an increased production of endorphins and enkephalins. It has since been found that other influences also increase the production and secretion of these substances, most notably acupressure, hypnosis, and long distance running. This is a brand new field of study and it will continue to yield startling results for many years to come.

Though scientists throughout the world have been attempting to understand the bio-energy phenomena, most work has not been sanctioned or supported by established scientific communities until very recently. However, the Russians began serious study of this field in the 1930's and have a forty-year head-start on the Western countries. In July, 1978, the Soviet Union's official news agency Tass published a report on the progress of the study on "bio-fields."

Alexei Zolotov, a Master of Sciences at the All-Union Geophysical Research Institute, says in the report that humans emit "bio-fields" that can perform "magic-like tricks and even cure disease." In the Tass article, Zolotov claims that a bio-field can be trained on various objects causing them to change physical characteristics. He further stated that "some people succeeded in speedily curing a running nose, boils, and bleeding in other people through training their bio-fields upon them." Dr. Zolotov said that the human organism as a whole, and each of its organs, as well as separate cells, emit bio-fields. Bio-field characteristics, he added, vary widely according to the health of the person. As an example, explains Dr. Zolotov, an ailing thyroid gland emits a bio-field in the shape of a dagger from two to three yards long. He says that a healthy person sensitive to bio-fields feels this and, "influencing by his bio-field the field of the sickly gland, can restore its normal functioning." The famed Soviet scientist stated that his research has led him to postulate that every living thing generates a bio-field, as the Western ecologist Lotke also asserted. Zolotov said that "further bio-field research will be highly influencial in advancing science, particularly medicine, and will help explain many hitherto inexplicable phenomena."

In recent years, American study has been taking a giant leap forward in the same direction, and one of the leading laboratories has been that of Dr. Thelma Moss at the University of California at Los Angeles. Relying heavily upon Kirlian photographic research, Dr. Moss' laboratory has confirmed the existence of bio-electric radiation from living substance. Among the many relevant and interesting phenomena described have been reports on the "healing" and "life-giving" properties of the human bio-electric field, as well as the trainability of the field.

Research by Dr. Moss has demonstrated that an injured leaf will show vastly improved mobilization of healing energy after being placed under the influence of the human bio-field. The human hand has been found to be an especially powerful transmitter of this energy. Research into the old concept of a "green thumb" has shown that those who are good with plants emanate an energy which is beneficial to a plant's bio-field, while those with a "brown thumb" have a detrimental effect upon the plant's bio-field—or in some cases even appear to absorb bio-electric energy from the plant, thus depleting the plant's life force. Dr. Moss' laboratory has also found that changes in the weather profoundly affect the bio-field in plants and in humans. Furthermore, it has been shown in other laboratories that the bio-fields of plants change remarkably from season to season.

Besides this generalized research in bio-electrical fields, some very interesting work has been conducted specifically into the traditional Oriental system of Ch'i and its circuitry. Dr. Robert Becker, at Upstate Medical Center in New York has done remarkable research in this area. He was one of the discoverers of the technique of applying electricity to the area of a broken bone to hasten and improve healing and has caused *regeneration* of amputated limbs in animals that normally have no such capacity. His scientific breakthroughs have been based upon the bio-field. His theory is that the bio-energy flows throughout the body, just as the Chinese described (he has demonstrated this quite eloquently as will be discussed in Chapter 3). He believes that the energy has existed in living beings since the beginning of evolution, and though it has been encorporated into other systems, it has also remained free-flowing for selective self-preservation and other reasons. Dr. Becker has concluded that the prime function of the energy is to heal and repair damaged tissue, and to maintain healthy physiological functioning at the cellular level.

Ch'i is the essential basis, physiologically, of the Chinese way of health. The tonic herbs are categorized according to the types of Ch'i that they contain and as to how they influence human Ch'i. As one becomes experienced with the Chinese tonic herbs, they will become acutely aware of their own energy and of the energies all around them. They will become quite sensitive to the energies of the foods and beverages they consume and the effects of the tonics will become obvious at an experiential level. It should not be surprising that herbs can so alter and affect our energy levels. The difference between Western and Eastern healthcare is simply that Oriental healthcare is based upon energetics while Western healthcare takes a generally grosser approach.

1.9   The Five Elemental Energies

The ancient Chinese placed cyclicity at the center of their great naturalistic philosophy. Though Yin and Yang describe the cycle in its basic polar form, the Chinese needed a more detailed description of the cyclic process. Thousands of years ago a model was developed which described the cyclic flow of change as it occurs throughout Nature. This model is called the Law of the Five Elemental Energies.

This law has been used in innumerable ways by the Chinese and a great deal of Chinese culture has been built upon it. Though it appears archaic at first glance (as does the principle of Yin and Yang), it has much to offer in terms of insightfulness of Nature's ways. Far from being archaic, it is in fact amazingly profound. Couched in old terminology, it may appear confusing to the new student of Chinese philosophy, but when explained in modern terms the Law of the Five Elemental Energies becomes quite clear.

The Law of the Five Elemental Energies describes the various stages of a basic natural cycle. There are said to be five such fundamental stages arising each in its turn as a cycle proceeds. The five stages were called by the Chinese: Water, Wood, Fire, Earth, and Metal. These terms, coined in a naturalistic age have served the Chinese well, though modern scientific thinkers often cannot get past terminology to look into meaning.

That which is known as "Water" is the elmental energy state of extreme Yin within a cyclic system. It represents the period of extreme rest and outward quietude. It is concomitantly the phase when energy is stored in its most concentrated form, awaiting an opportunity to explode outward to initiate a new stage of activity, and thus a new cycle. One great and traditional method of learning about the Five Elemental Energies is to follow the seasons of the year, which is of course a cycle. In this case, Winter is of the Water element because in Winter the energy of Nature is indrawn. Life-forms conserve their energy throughout the Winter months by being less active, preventing the loss of life-giving energy. Water energy is highly concentrated and its power is very great. On the human level, Water is attracted deep within and draws with it the blood and warmth, leaving the outer-being cool (though not cold) and still (though not frozen). It produces inner heat and strength as this, the energy of the "seed," the fundamental energy of life, concentrates and matures at the core of our system. It is indeed the very "essence," the final distillation of all accumulated energies and is thus very pure and of remarkable potential energy. It is our will to sustain ourselves, it is our self-control, it is our courage. It is the seed of all our energies, it is our emergency reserve. It is the power of the mind and provides the energy for regeneration and reproduction. It regulates the water and mineral balances in the human body. It strengthens the bones and nourishes the marrow. It provides the strength of the spine and ultimately determines our life span. If this energy can be retained it will sprout like Spring wildflowers, but if wasted will result in lack of power throughout the entire next cycle. Deficiency of Water energy results in fear, paranoia, poor resistance, a cold body, sexual weakness, lower-back and knee pain, premature senility and general bodily and mental weakness. A deficiency will also result in a shortening of the life span and in an inability to experience life at the ultimate levels. They who can retain this "essence" can live long, fruitful lives. Water is dissipated by being excessive and allowing emotions to dominate our higher Spirit, which the Chinese call *Shin*, which resides in the heart and manifests as all-embracing love. All stresses deplete the body-mind of Water energy. Detachment from that which changes and holding fast to that which is permanent (Tao) is said to be the way to nurture the Water element.

"Wood" represents the next phase of the cycle. During this phase, energy that has been concentrated and stored suddenly explodes outward, initiating a new period of activity. Wood is a powerfully expansive energy imbued with the exhilaration of reborn activity. Spring is the season corresponding to the elemental energy called "Wood" by the Chinese. The Earth shifting on its axis now receives enough warmth and cosmic energy from the sun for life to flourish, so the energy so carefully protected and stored throughout the Winter is discharged on the relatively safe gamble that a new life cycle can succeed. Anyone who has experienced a Spring and has felt "spring fever" knows the awesome power of this Yang energy state. Wood energy rises and expands and is virtually irresistible. Wood is New Yang. It is aggressive, vigorous energy which bursts forth from the depth of substance or mind in which energy has been concentrated and stored as the essence of a prior cycle, expanding, invigorating all in its field of influence, bringing forth life and creation. It is the creative urge and the procreative drive. It is the "will to become," the urge to grow and develop, to create our own existence. It is that which provokes us. We experience it as the urge to express, to manifest, to break bonds, to metamorphosize. We sense it as a reawakening. It is our will to open up, to expand. So when Wood is abundant we develop, we create and procreate. When Spring comes around, we to "spring," just as do the birds and flowers. Wood is the energy of the sprout and of all green matter. Sublimation of this powerful creative energy leads to feelings of frustration and the energy will eventually burst out as irritability, anger, jealousy, hatred and rage. When depleted there will be lethargy and depression. Free expression and satisfying creativity, in harmony with natural laws and guided by Shin, the Spirit of Universal Compassion, is the natural means of nurturing and manifesting the elemental energy known as Wood.

As time passes, the explosive Yang force of the Wood energy levels out and turns to a sustainable high level of outward activity. This phase is called the "Fire" stage. This elemental energy represents full Yang activity, the overtly energetic stage of a cycle. Energy during the Fire stage is highly mobile and is expended freely, though the work of this phase generally results in renewed sources of energy. This phase, of course, is that of Summer in our seasonal analogy. In the Summer, life flourishes (unless the heat becomes too extreme) and it is clearly the most expansive, outward time of the year. Fire is the energy of gentle growth to fullness, of warm all-embracing love and compassion and is experienced as the urge to care, to give, and to share. When Fire is unimpeded, life is joyous, loving and peaceful, and is supported by courage, strength and wisdom. Contentment, enduring vigor, a cooperative approach to life, clarity of understanding and a free-giving spirit are signs of one whose Fire element is in proper harmony with the external being (Nature) and with the internal being (the body-mind) which are in fact one. When this energy is blocked, it is expressed as heat called "false fire": tension, especially in the neck, shoulders and head, and as excitability or a tendency to over-react and to over-extend. Hysteria, insomnia hypertension, heart attacks, strokes, and nightmares are the end result. When Fire is deficient, one becomes suspicious, paranoid, loses the memory, and other organ-related emotions battle for dominance. Feeling compassion, love and joy without becoming overly excited, and giving of ourselves are the natural way to develop the Fire element.

Fire is followed by "Metal" as Summer is followed by Fall. Metal is the stage during which energy is once again beginning to be drawn inward. The abundance of the Fire stage is accumulated and energy is not so recklessly expended as it was in the Fire stage. The essential work of the cyclic process is completed in the Fire stage and the results generated by that work are ready for accumulation, processing, and storage at the Metal phase, just as the food-growing of Summer yields the harvest of Autumn. During this phase two very important processes are occurring: "harvesting" of the essential product generated during the Fire phase, and elimination of waste materials also generated by the process. If enough energy is recaptured and stored, the process will proceed to the Water stage, where the energy is stored until a new round of the cycle can proceed. If not enough energy is accumulated, the Water stage will fail to develop or will run out of energy and the whole process will discontinue, releasing what elements and energies it still possesses back to Nature. Also, excess baggage must be eliminated before the lean Water phase begins, since energy is at a premium during this period. If the stored energy is wasted supporting a bulky resting system, not enough will be left to initiate and sustain a powerful new cycle and the ensuing Wood phase may flop, or may otherwise generate a very weak new cycle prone to danger and potential failure. Metal manifests as an intuitive, meditative sifting and letting-go of that which is encumbering and useless to our inner life. It manifests as the active discarding of excess and the drawing within ourselves of that which is essential, that which is storable, that which can be concentrated and re-used. It is thus a form of harvesting. The Metal element draws life's forces toward us and draws them deep into our body-mind for storage so as to allow for passage through the dark period of rest soon to follow. Metal is the energy of release, freeing ourselves of old selves, outer attachments and emotional entanglements. If we resist this energy when it is in command and thus block its flow, we live with a constant need to "let go," to shed our old skins. This manifests eventually as occasional uncontrollable fits of grief and melancholy. The holding of strong attachments that are no longer physically present can cause intense chest and upper-back tension and pain, breathing difficulties, low resistance to colds and flus, and dull skin. Excessive letting-go can result in continuous sobbing and draining of the body's essential energy. To be able to extract the "essence" from every situation without becoming attached to the situation itself is the key to wisdom and is the way to nurture the Metal element.

In addition to these four cardinal phases, the Chinese recognized an additional elemental energy state inherent in all cycles. This fifth elemental energy sheds much light on Chinese philosophy and in many ways distinguishes Eastern thought from Western thought. This elemental energy is called "Earth." To the Chinese the Earth element represents the center and balance. It represents the balance and harmony of all the other elemental energies; it represents the pivot around which all connected processes occur. In a human being it would represent homeostasis, the balance of life that assures our continuation. Earth stands for the balancing of forces under all circumstances. Thus, the Earth element is always present and indeed dominant, for be it Summer or Winter, balance must be preserved within the context of the system or the integrity of the system would dissolve. Earth is the pivot of Yin and Yang. It is experienced as a sensation of balance, centeredness, non-striving, non-judgmental contemplation, and sympathetic understanding. It is a mature energy, the ripening soul, and proceeds any return to the Source. Earth provides the energy of memory and reflection. It nourishes the flesh and builds strong muscles. When this energy is excessive, one worries and becomes obsessed with details, losing perspective of the whole view. This in turn results in "tunnel vision," hypochondria, digestive and blood disorders, and, in women, menstrual disorders. In deficiency, the mind becomes foggy while the body becomes heavy and sluggish, often waterlogged with fatigue and resultant depression, forgetfulness. Always seeing life from a broad perspective while remaining physically and emotionally centered will nurture the Earth Element.

Thus we can see that the five elemental energies are in essence further refined aspects of Yin and Yang. Wood is the beginning of Yang, Fire is full Yang, Metal is the beginning of Yin, and Water is full Yin. Earth is the harmonizing agent, balancing Yin and Yang at all times maintaining ever-changing but continuous harmony. All of the elemental energies are always present, but their proportions change, with first one dominating then another in turn. All of the elemental energies contain both Yin and Yang aspects, as is true of everything.

An ancient scholar stated the Law of the Five Elemental Energies this way:

> "By the transformation of Yang and its union with Yin, the five elemental energies of Wood, Fire, Earth, Metal and Water arise, each with its specific nature according to its share of Yin and Yang. These five elemental energies constantly change their sphere of activity, nurturing and counteracting one another so that there is constancy in the transformation from emptiness to abundance and abundance to emptiness, like a ring without beginning or end. The interaction of these primordial forces brings harmonious change and the cycles of nature run their course. When the reality of the Unnameable (Tao) and the essence of Yin and Yang and the five elemental energies come into mysterious union, the myriad things are manifested. The interaction of these forces engenders and transforms all the myriad things.

The myriad things produce and reproduce, resulting in an unending transformation. The five elemental energies combine and recombine in innumerable ways to produce manifested existence. All things contain all five elemental energies in various proportions."

The following diagram is the classical representation of the interaction of the five elemental energies.

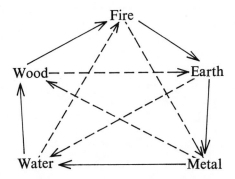

Fig. 1   The Five Elements Cycle

The generation of one phase by the next was called the "Creation Cycle" by the Chinese. Water was said to create Wood, Wood creates Fire, Fire (by logic not advisable to pursue at this time) generates Earth, Earth generates Metal, and Metal creates Water. This is represented in another diagram:

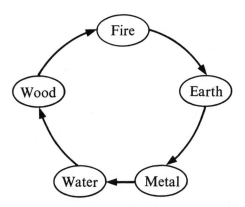

Fig. 2   The Creation Cycle

According to the Great Principle of Yin and Yang, creation must be balanced by an opposing force, which the Chinese would call "control." Each elemental energy thus counteracts an opposing elemental energy so as to limit its growth and thus prevent uncontrolled expansion of one particular state of energy. The "Control Cycle" goes as follows: Water controls Fire, Fire controls Metal, Metal controls Wood, Wood controls Earth, and Earth controls Water. The Control Cycle diagram illustrates these relationships:

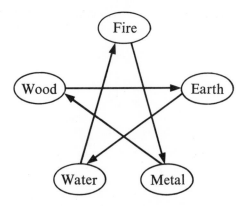

Fig. 3   The Control Cycle

The Creation and Control Cycles thus constantly interact to maintain overall balance in the system. As a model of the universal nature of cyclic change, the Chinese Law of the Five Elemental Energies has provided a vital base of understanding, unmatched by any other model. The five elemental energies play a vital role in the Chinese tonic herbal system. Each of the herbs has been found to contain one or more of the elemental energies in such free abundance as to be therapeutically valuable. The Chinese herbs are generally categorized according to the type of elemental energy which predominates in the herb and by how it influences the human energy system.

2 | The Fundamental Principles of Chinese Tonic Herbalism

2.1 The Ultimate Goal

The ultimate goal of Chinese tonic herbalism is to generate "radiant health" through the regulation of energy, so that the body may be the suitable vehicle for achieving enlightenment, or "immortality" as the Taoists called it. Not everyone uses the tonics for this lofty goal, but nonetheless, the tonics can aid in achieving any state of health desired. According to the Taoists, "radiant health" cannot be achieved through bodily efforts alone. It is necessary to overcome the illusion of "apartness" through direct intuitive perception of one's unity with Nature, and to thence live harmoniously with all beings, contentedly and peacefully. The Chinese called this "cultivating the Way." Chinese tonic herbalism cannot be separated from this grand Way. Though anyone can benefit significantly from the tonics, their ultimate benefit can only be attained through their integration into a path of true physical and spiritual growth. The Chinese developed the system of the "superior herbalism," that is, of the tonics, as a tool to be used wisely on the spiritual path.

According to the basic principle of oneness, it is emphasized that not only must each organ function properly, but all organs must function in concert. Timing and intensity of action and rest must be harmonious. And the organic functioning must be directly and accurately responsive to innumerable environmental changes. The Chinese tonic herbs are used to enhance the adaptive, regulatory powers within the human body-mind which are responsible for maintaining this high level of integration and harmony which results in "radiant health." The herbs are believed by the Oriental people to build the vitality of the body-mind as a whole. Not just the energy of the flesh and muscle need vitalizing, but also the deep tissues, and the mind. And not only need the body-mind be energized, but also harmonized. Especially important is the vitalizing of those functions that have a primary regulatory capacity, those functions that are centrally responsible for the control of our adaptive responses. In this way, all the functions of the body-mind are integrated in the task of maintaining a harmonious relationship among themselves and with Nature.

2.2   First Rule of Chinese Healthcare—Do No Harm

The basic principle of Chinese healthcare is this: health depends upon the internal harmony and vitality of the individual. All actions taken to improve health must aim at establishing and maintaining this condition. Yet the goal of establishing such "radiant health" cannot be attained at any cost. The healthcare arts of the Orient, though generally disciplined and often rigorous, are always pursued with patience and caution. Though the goal of "radiant health" is well worth pursuing, great care must be taken to prevent undesirable side-effects from any methods used. One rule supersedes all others in healthcare: *do no harm.*

In using the Chinese tonic herbs, educated usage will result in benefit without harm. The tonics are favored for the very reason that they are relatively gentle. This has been proven empirically over hundreds, or even thousands, of years. The tonics are so highly prized in the Orient (and more recently in the West) because they have profound effects without negative side-effects, unless grossly abused (*anything* grossly abused is dangerous). In a sense, the tonics are simply highly nutritious foods that are generally not capable of being prepared like normal foods. Some of the tonics *are* used as food in Chinese cooking, but most require special preparation to extract the active agents or to be made palatable. Most of the tonics are prepared by boiling into "soups" and then the soup is drunk. The fact is, most of the tonics are quite palatable and make delicious tea. Pleasantness of flavor is in fact an important criterion for falling into the class of the "superior herbs." The few tonics that do not taste particularly great are blended with other herbs that improve the flavor. In a like manner, the few tonics that may, under certain circumstances, have slight side-effects are blended with other herbs which counteract the negative side-effect but allow the positive actions of the tonic to come through. The tonics can be ground into powder and made into pills or capsules, and in this way taste is of no concern, but in all cases the herbal preparation must be balanced so as to cause no unwanted actions.

In spite of the proven safety of these herbs, knowledge and wisdom are always necessary in life. As discussed previously, imbalance is disharmonizing and anything in excess or improperly used can cause trouble. This is why it is advisable to become familiar with the principles of Chinese healthcare and, in particular, Chinese tonic herbalism, before using the herbs.

The value of study is actually not so much to prevent negative results, but rather, to assure noticeable positive results. The Chinese use thousands of herbs medicinally, and most of these *can* produce negative side-effects if used without a Chinese doctor's supervision. These herbs are called the inferior herbs and the "poisons" and should be used only for medicinal purposes under strict supervision. The tonics are the great exception and are called the "superior herbs" because they are so exceptional in both value and safety (as well as flavor, in most cases). However, if a tonic herb or herbal combination ever seems to have adverse effects, it is not to be continued. There is an excellent selection from which to choose. Simply try another herb or combination of herbs.

Those who explore the Chinese tonic herbal system soon find one or several tonics that work best for them. The tonic most suited to one person may not be perfect for another, so never force a tonic on another person and never let someone force one on you that you do not feel right about. Study the principles well and cultivate your intuition. Never take the tonics lightly—approach and consume them with respect. Most readers are probably familiar with the Japanese tea ceremony which emphasizes "respect." This same attitude should be had by those using the tonics. Respect seems to increase appreciation and sensitivity, two qualities that are necessary for success on the path to, and of, radiant health. Careless, disrespectful use of the tonics will do no good in the long run and may do harm, due to no fault of their own.

Always remember, the first rule of Chinese natural healthcare: Do No Harm!

2.3   See a Person as a Whole, At One with Nature

It is critical that the tonic herbalist see themselves as a whole. Health can be developed and maintained only when all aspects of one's being is functioning properly. This includes both the body and the mind. The tonics should be used to promote internal and external harmony. As the tonics take effect, one should use their new-found energy to clean up and organize their surroundings, as one's environment is both a reflection of and an influence upon a person.

The tonics should not be taken to treat, or even to prevent any specific ailments. Such problems should be taken care of under the guidance of a properly trained medical professional. The tonics have never been used for specifically medical purposes. Other herbs are more suited to treating disease. The tonics should be strictly avoided during a bout of infectious disease, such as a cold or influenza. With continued use of the tonics, such bouts will become much less frequent. It is not that the tonics specifically counteract or otherwise prevent such diseases. They simply bolster the general capacity to handle stress and thus build resistance to disease.

Try to use the tonics in such a way as to benefit your whole being. Do not focus exclusively on one organ or function at the expense of others. The more generalized the action of a tonic herb, the higher is its standing among masters of Chinese tonic herbalism, because in the long run the whole being benefits and in turn the world benefits.

The tonics should be used flexibly and in accordance with natural law. Changing circumstances generally require some change in the usage of the tonics. As the weather changes, the tonics used should be adjusted. Certain tonics are extremely beneficial during one season of the year and less effective at other times. Life-style changes often require a change of tonics. Those who find themselves working very hard physically can benefit more from certain tonics while one who is performing primarily mental exertion should use a different tonic. One who is not working, though losing out on work's benefits, can still benefit from the use of still other tonics. With experience, the herbalist will become an expert in the herbs suitable for different life-style requirements. For example, it would be foolhardy to use herbs that have aphrodisiac qualities unless there is a mate available. In other words, adjust the usage of the tonics to circumstances. This procedure is also valuable training in the general Taoist art of flowing with change.

Remember that the tonics alone cannot assure "radiant health." One must live a generally healthy life-style and maintain a healthy state of mind free from too much emotion and stress, to assure optimal results. Proper diet, harmonious home life, proper sleep, strict hygiene, and appropriate exercise are also essential. If all these aspects of life are on track, the tonics can be of enormous benefit.

Of course, there are many people who lead rather wild, unhealthy lives. Such people may exercise and sleep irregularly, eat without principle or even downright wrong, abuse themselves sexually, and indulge in alcohol and/or dangerous drugs. This is certainly not uncommon. Such a life-style obviously has deleterious effects upon the health. It is generally thought that these people are not destined to attain either "radiant health" or enlightenment in this lifetime. However, these people, too, can benefit from the use of the tonics in that regular consumption of the tonics will tend to slow down the degenerative process. In some cases, such people experience such exhilarating improvement in their condition and/or state of mind that they put their bad habits behind them and renew their life.

Whatever one's condition at the onset of their adventure with the Chinese tonic herbs, if used wisely, there will soon be noticeable benefits.

2.4 Yin and Yang and the Chinese Tonic Herbs

From the traditional Chinese point of view, a working knowledge of Yin and Yang is the basis for understanding oneself as well as to the use of the tonic herbs. It is from this knowledge that one can select the most appropriate herb or herbal combination; blind, unbalanced use of the tonics deminishes the results. The ultimate idea is to create a balanced condition, where both the Yin and Yang energies are in free-flowing abundance and are interacting harmoniously. It is essential that excess is avoided in the intake of either Yin or Yang energies.

Most individuals are imbalanced in terms of their Yin and Yang energies to some degree. This may be due to an excess of either the Yin or Yang element or to a deficiency of one or the other of these primary energies.

There is a time-honored system of characterizing the Yin and Yang nature of both people and the herbs. This is known as the system of the "Eight Entities." The Eight Entities are actually various classifications of Yin and Yang, based upon how the principle is applied. The Eight Entities are composed of four pairs of characteristics, each pair consisting of a Yin and Yang couple. The Eight Entities are:

> Yin and Yang
> Cold and Hot
> Deficiency and Excess
> Internal and External

Yin and Yang Entities: Yin and *Yang* are of course the underlying basis of the Eight Entities. In general, "Cold," "Deficiency," and "Internal" fall under the category of Yin, while "Hot," "Excess," and "External" fall into the category of Yang. In speaking of the Yin Entity, one is referring to the general nature and condition of the Yin energies in the body. Yang Entity refers to the overall condition of the Yang energies in the body. The other Entities are of a more specific nature.

Cold and Hot Entities: Cold and *Hot* Entities do not refer directly to one's temperature. What they do refer to is the *energy* condition of either the whole person or some organ-function. A gross departure from normal human temperature should alert one to some serious problem, in which case the tonics should not be consumed except under medical supervision and medical help should be had.

A person with a Cold constitution or condition* will experience diminished physiological and metabolic functioning, and/or decreased resistance to stresses of either physical or mental types. Thus a person with a Cold condition will be experiencing general malaise, fatigue, and sluggishness.

A person with a Hot constitution or condition will experience physiological and metabolic hyperfunction, and/or over-reaction to pathogenic and other stress factors. Such people tend to be nervous, easily agitated, easily angered and generally over-active.

In terms of the herbs, there are said to be five "atmospheric energies." These are *cold, cool, mild (neutral), warm*, and *hot*. These represent the five therapeutic actions of the herbs. They describe the general physiological and/or metabolic influence of the herbs upon the human body.

Cool and cold herbs are said to "clear the heat," "sedate fire," "cool the blood" and to detoxify. What this all means is that cool and cold herbs sedate excessive physiological activity.

Warm and hot herbs are said to "warm up the internal regions," "disperse cold energy," increase blood circulation, and restore Yang energy. In other words, herbs of this category tend to stimulate functioning.

Hot and warm herbs should form the major part of herbals used by one with a Cold condition, while cold and cool herbs should dominate in herbals used by one with a hot condition. Balance is always the rule, however, and neither hot nor cold herbs should be used alone without the inclusion in the formula of herbs with an opposing nature. Even if a person considers themselves to be of a very Cold condition, for example, requiring Hot energy to create balance in their system, the herbal formula used must contain not only hot and/or warm herbs, but also some herbs that are cool or mild. However, the herbs should be combined in such proportions as to result in a generally warm formula. If regularly consumed, the person's condition will gradually become warmer until a healthy balance is achieved. If just hot herbs are used, one might expect some extreme, and perhaps

---

* One's "constitution" is the energy state acquired at birth and/or through long-term development, while one's "condition" is the current energy state.

unpleasant reactions. Always balance your herbals so that Yang and Yin are both effective and approach your goals cautiously, steadily, and patiently. Again the great Chinese maxim: "Hasten slowly and you will soon arrive."

Mild herbs tend to regulate and to neutralize excess in either extreme. Some of the tonics have this "mild" nature, and others are categorized as either "warm" or "cool," only a few are considered "hot" or "cold." Mild herbs are the most widely used tonics because they correct either extreme and support both Yin and Yang energies. However, mild herbs are generally not as potent as the tonics that have hot, warm, cool, or cold atmospheric energies.

Warm and cool herbs have a relatively gentle affect, while hot and cold herbs are more powerful. It is best to use mostly the cool, mild, and warm tonic herbs at first and to explore hot and cold ones once you have gained some experience. In any case, hot and cold herbs are always used sparingly in comparison with other less extreme herbs. When using hot and cold herbs, *always* balance these in the formula with other herbs that will result in a formula that is, overall, no more extreme than warm or cool. The hot and cold herbs will still have their powerful effect, but the body will not be shocked by the extreme energy and will be much more capable of assimilating it. Once one's condition is balanced, formulas should always be aimed at sustaining balance, under the changing circumstances of weather and other influences.

Deficiency and Excess Entities: Deficiency Entity refers to the "draining of the vital energy," or in other words, the exhaustion of bodily reserves and the subsequent hypofunctioning of the organs. The person will appear weak and low in spirit and they will have a weak pulse and low libido. Their eyes will appear dim and memory will be sluggish.

Excess Entity indicates an excess of energy. Though it is taught that a human being should always have an abundance of energy, it is also emphasized that the energy must not be impeded or blocked in any way. The Ch'i must circulate freely through the entire body. If no blocks exist, there can be no Excess Entity because there is no limit to how much energy a person can have if it is free-flowing. Thus an Excess Entity refers to a condition of excessive energy due to a blockage. This is generally the result of a hyper-reaction of the body-mind to some pathological agent. It is also caused be excessive emotion resulting in imbalanced organic functioning and/or nervous muscle tension. A person with an Excess Entity will appear outwardly strong and willful, and will be easily aroused physically and/or emotionally. The pulse will be strong and quick, and the person may experience an excessive libido. The eyes will appear bright and open and they may tend to talk excessively and show other signs of a hyperactive central nervous system.

In general, people with a Cold condition will also have a Deficiency Entity, and those with a Hot condition will have and Excess Entity.

Internal and External Entities: Internal refers to the realm of the viscera while *External* refers to the surface of the body. Chinese herbs are said to "move" in different directions, generally describing where they tend to act. Some herbs are said to move "upwards," which means that they affect the upper parts of the body such as the chest, shoulders, neck, face and head regions. Other herbs are said to "float," which means that their reactions take place primarily at the surface of the body, in the muscle and skin regions. Herbs that "move upwards and float" are said to influence the External Entity and are of a Yang nature.

Then there are herbs that are said to move "downwards," which indicates that they cause a shift in the balance of energy toward the lower regions of the body, especially the lower abdomen, pelvic region, and legs. Other herbs are said to "sink," indicating that their influence is particularly upon the internal regions of the body, that is, into the viscera. Herbs that either "move downwards" or "sink" are said to influence the Internal Entity and are of a Yin nature.

The Eight Entities thus describe the general action of the herbs. A tonic formula is composed of several herbs combined to establish a balanced condition. If for example, a person feels generally lethargic, they would take a tonic that affects the Yang component, "warming up the system" (increasing physiological activity), and "eliminating the deficiency." Specific herbs may be added so that the effects of the main tonics affect specifically weak areas. Neutral or opposing herbs should be included so that the reaction is not extreme. If a person with a Cold condition prepares an herbal that is balanced to the warm-hot side, and suddenly find themselves flushed soon after consuming it, they most likely included too much of an herb that is of a hot nature and/or moves upward and floats. This should be immediately corrected by consuming something with a slightly cooling nature, and future herbals should include less of the herb(s) that caused the flushing. The feeling one should always have after taking a tonic should be pleasant and without negative side-effect.

2.5   The Five Elemental Energies and the Chinese Herbs

The five elemental energies provide an important basis for selecting herbs. First of all, seasonal influences are of great importance. It has been described how each of the elemental energies tends to dominate during particular seasons. It is therefore customary to use herbs that tonify the elemental component of our system that is dominant during the season that is current. For example, herbs that have a lot of the elemental energy. Water may be used as the dominant component of our tonic formula during the Winter months, when the Water element is also dominant. Of course, other herbs should be used as well to create a balanced formula. It is also customary to include herbs that contain much of the elemental energy of the succeeding season. Thus, the formula used in the Winter months should not only include Water element herbs, but also herbs that provide Wood energy so that when Spring comes, abundant Wood energy has been absorbed by the system and will be readily available when the time comes for it to become the dominant elemental energy in the body.

All five elemental energies exist in everything in different proportions. In the herbs, one or two of the elemental energies will generally predominate, giving the herb a distinctive energy character, and a distinctive *flavor*. It is traditionally asserted that there are five primary flavors that are characteristic of the five elemental energies. These flavors are:

Wood has a *sour* flavor
Fire has a *bitter* flavor
Earth has a *sweet* flavor
Metal has a *pungent* (or *spicy*) flavor
Water has a *salty* flavor

Each of these flavors, indicating the dominant and available presence of an elemental energy, is said to act in a particular manner. The sour flavor is said to be astringent, the bitter flavor is said to be strengthening, the sweet flavor is considered neutralizing and detoxifying, the pungent flavor has a dispersing influence, and the salty flavor is said to be "yielding," or diuretic.

Furthermore, each of the five elemental energies is said to dominate in one or more pairs of major organ systems. These organ systems are understood differently from our Western definitions and will be discussed in some detail in the next Chapter. As the Chinese system goes, the relationships are:

Wood energy dominates in the Liver and Gall Bladder
Fire energy dominates in the Heart, Small Intestine, Circulation-Sex, and
    Triple Warmer
Earth energy dominates in the Spleen-Pancreas and Stomach
Metal energy dominates in the Lung and Large Intestine
Water energy dominates in the Kidney and Bladder

Therefore, the elemental energies present in abundance in the tonic herbs will tend to have significant influence over the organ systems that require those energies to function properly. Thus if one feels that the so-called Kidney system is deficient in vital energy, they might use an herb that is rich in the Water element, since the Water energy is the primary energy of the Kidney system. However, it must be pointed out that every cell in our body requires each of the five elemental energies, albeit in different proportions, and therefore will assimilate some of every elemental energy entering the body.

Besides affecting the organ systems, the flavors, indicative of the elemental energies, have other actions. Pungent and sweet flavors often (though not always) disperse upwards, while the sour, bitter and salty flavors tend generally to flow downward. Some herbs, though, have little or no taste and are said to be of a "mild" flavor. Mild flavor is said to "leak and flow," meaning it has a mild dispersive action.

Herbs with a sweet flavor not only "neutralize," but also may act as powerful tonic agents to the primary energies of the body and mind. They tend to establish organic balance by regulating physiological functions. Sweet herbs are also commonly used to raise one's tolerance to stress and pain, in Chinese tonic herbalism. Most of the tonic herbs do in fact have an over-riding sweet flavor, which accounts for the good taste of the tonics. It further accounts for their ability to eliminate toxins, and improve the general adaptive response to stress.

Herbs with a mild flavor are said to travel quickly through the body and can penetrate where other herbs cannot. They are commonly used to regulate fluid balance in the body. The herbs with a sour flavor have an astringent nature and are therefore used to promote storing, and to prevent leakage and excessive loss of bodily fluids. For example, the Taoists used sour herbs to restrict the flow of seminal fluid during sexual intercourse, thus allowing extended sexual encounters during which yogic techniques were practiced. Herbs with a bitter flavor have the ability to dry out, harden, and sedate. They are used mostly to balance hot and wet symptoms of imbalance. They promote the flow of downstream energy, reduce swelling, relieve the bowels, and tone up the sexual organs.

With experience, you will be able to recognize the various flavors in the herbs. At first it is more difficult because there are often two or three dominant flavors. It is best at first, therefore, to rely upon the information provided in the text as to which elemental energies predominate. However, spend some time tasting the individual herbs to learn to discern the different flavors. You will probably enjoy the taste of the sweetest herbs first. This is as it should be, for these are generally most beneficial and have a cleansing and moderating action; that is, they slow down acute actions. In time, you will come to appreciate and enjoy all of the flavors. You will learn to take the bitter with the sweet, and be a better person for it.

2.6   The Seven Types of Tonics

Tonic herbs nourish and invigorate the Ch'i (energy), the blood, the Yin structures and functions, and the Yang structures and functions. There are also herbs which are specific organ-meridian tonics, herbs which "regulate" the Ch'i and herbs which "regulate" the blood. The tonics can tone up a deficiency or can enhance the circulation of energies already abundant.

There are classically four major types of tonics and three minor types. The four major types are: Energy Tonics, Blood Tonics, Yang Tonics, and Yin Tonics. The minor types are those which are specific organ-meridian tonics and that regulate the blood and energy.

Energy Tonics: Energy tonics are used to increase Ch'i. It is said that the more Ch'i one has circulating within their system, the more *alive* they are. Of course, if there is blockage of the Ch'i, this causes a build-up of Ch'i in the blocked area resulting in over-excitement of the functions related to the area of blockage. This is termed "excess." If the energy pathways are open, there is no limit to the amount of Ch'i one can accumulate.

Most energy tonics act by toning up the functioning of the Lung and Spleen organ-meridian systems. The Spleen governs energy production from food and regulates all energy transformation. It nourishes the flesh, regulates the appetite, controls digestion and assimilation, and provides energy to the entire body. The Lung extracts Ch'i from the air one breathes and distributes the Ch'i to the meridian system and to the skin, where it provides defense energy.

When the Spleen is in optimum health, the appetite is excellent though balanced, the muscles are strong and limber, memory is sharp and one is full of vitality and wisdom. When the Lung is in optimum health, the breath is deep and long, the blood is pure and the skin is radiant (hence the term "radiant health").

Energy tonics also tonify the blood. It is a principle of life that the "Ch'i leads blood." Wherever Ch'i flows, blood follows and thus as the body fills with energy, blood also is produced and circulated.

Energy tonics are generally of a Yang nature and thus energy tonics and Yang tonics are often used supportively or interchangeably.

Yang Tonics: Yang tonics tonify the Yang structures and functions of the body. In the Chinese system, the Kidney is called the "root of life" and provides the fundamental energy of our life. Yang tonics are of vast importance in the tonic herbal system because they can provide Yang energy to the Kidney, which in turn increases the life force of the body-mind as a whole, and this is said to result in a more dynamic and lengthy life.

Tonics that warm up the Yang of the Kidneys increase the general physical energy as well as the energy of the spine and brain. They strengthen the sexual power, increase bone marrow production and thus the blood, strengthen the bones and stabilize the joints. Kidney tonics strengthen the back and protect against injury to the spine. They further provide the energy of courage, fortitude and will power. Virtually every organic and psychic function benefits from the toning up of the Kidney energy, and one whose Kidney Yang is abundant will be able to overcome problems and difficulties with the greatest of ease. Yang tonics increase the adaptive energy and enhance internal defense mechanisms. They provide warmth to the body and keenness to the mind.

Yang tonics may also be used to tone up the Yang of the Heart, Circulation and Spleen. But since Yang tonics are of a warm and dry nature, they must generally be combined with herbs which direct the herb directly to the Kidney or other needy organ and that tend to moisten the organ.

Blood Tonics: Blood tonics build blood. It is explained by the Chinese that the Heart controls the blood, the Liver stores the blood, the Spleen and Kidney produce the blood, and Circulation-Sex conducts the direction of the blood. Blood tonics generally tonify the Yin elements of these organ systems so as to enhance their balanced functioning.

Blood tonics are very widely used in the Orient to promote the sexual functions of women and to maintain healthy reproductive functioning. Blood tonics generally regulate the menstrual cycle and benefit pregnancy. However, blood tonics are not just used by women. Men, too, need an abundant blood supply and the same blood tonics used by women are used by men to build blood and to benefit male reproductive functioning.

The blood, of course, is responsible for many vital processes, including the nourishing of and removal of waste from every cell of the body. Strong, healthy, abundant blood whose constituents are properly balanced is essential to one's health.

As mentioned above, energy tonics also can act as indirect blood tonics, as can Yang tonics by their influence on the Kidney and marrow.

Yin Tonics: Yin tonics nourish the Yin of the body and are most influential over the body fluids and moist tissues. They tend to moisten and "gloss" and provide the necessary body fluids such as blood plasma, spinal fluid, semen, the mucous coating of the lungs and digestive tract, tears, sweat, saliva, urine, lymph, etc.

There are specific Yin tonics for the various bodily fluids and must generally be combined with other herbs which guide them to their target. Yin tonics for the Kidney are beneficial to the entire being if the Kidney Yang is kept in balance. Kidney Yin deficiency is one of the most common of all imbalances, leading to Kidney Yang excess, Liver Yang excess, and excessive Heart fire.

Yin tonics are generally sweet and cold. Blood tonics are generally of a Yin nature and can also be used supportively and/or interchangeably.

Organ-Meridian Tonics: Tonics are also commonly associated with particular organs and meridians. Thus there are herbs which are said to be tonic to the brain, stomach, large intestine, hair, eyes, etc.

These may not have such a profound effect upon the body as a whole, and are thus considered minor tonics. These are often used in herbal formulae as adjunctive herbs to a major tonic with whole-body effects.

Herbs which Regulate the Energy: Besides the major tonic herbs, there are also a number of herbs said to "regulate the energy." These herbs are said to promote the circulation of energy; to prevent stoppages, sluggishness and coagulations; and for moving the energy downward, thus maintaining a clear digestive and eliminative tract. They help maintain a clear mind and happy countenance.

These herbs are often considered to be tonics because they promote digestion, activate the flow of blood and Ch'i, and stimulate cleansing.

The herbs which regulate the energy belong generally to Yang. They are usually warm, aromatic, pungent, and dry and must be used with other herbs that protect the Yin and supplement the energy.

Herbs which Regulate the Blood: There are herbs which are said to "regulate the blood," though some people categorize these under the heading of tonics. These herbs tend to activate the blood by either warming the meridians, preventing coagulations, or regulating the clotting of blood.

Of great importance in the tonic herbal system are those herbs used to maintain proper warmth of the meridians. These herbs are said to protect the blood from attack by cold, and will thus prevent the menstrual and rheumatic pains often caused by the cold.

3 | The Energy System

3.1 The Organ-Meridian System

Relatively little emphasis was placed upon physical anatomy in the Chinese healthcare tradition. The major organs were known, but certainly not in the detailed way that they are today. Instead, the Chinese placed the emphasis on *function*, and on the correspondence between Nature and human life. There's was a vitalistic approach to health, emphasizing energetics and harmony.

When the first yogic practitioners in China became aware of the energetic nature of life, they observed this energy very carefully, both in the Nature surrounding them and within themselves. These apparently extraordinarily sensitive seekers soon became aware that the energy was not chaotically passing through their bodies, but instead seemed to follow a definite circuitry. While meditating, these yogic masters could feel the Ch'i flowing along definite pathways. As time passed, they were able to correlate these energy streams with internal functions and external influences.

Eventually, a complete set of energy channels were recognized. These the ancients called the "Strange Flows," or alternatively, the "Psychic Channels." There were eight primary channels, each felt to regulate major physical and psychic functions. It was soon discovered that one could control the energy flow through these channels through the practice of concentration and guided imagery. Focusing their attention on these Strange Flows, these early yogis found that they could achieve sublime levels of both physical health and spiritual bliss. The psychic and physical manipulation and regulation of these special energy channels became the basis of Chinese Taoist Yoga, *Nei Gung*, as well as such arts as *Tai Ch'i Chuan*, and *Jin Shin Do* Acupressure.

Later, a second system of energy circuitry was discovered. This second circuitry seemed to flow at the level of the flesh, as well as internally, connecting the vital organs to the outside. These energy flows seemed less amenable to psychic stimulation, but were found to have active energy spots located regularly upon them that, when stimulated, caused the energy to move. It was discovered that these points had direct influence upon the organs, and in time the arts of acupressure and acupuncture were developed. It was also discovered during this remote prehistoric period that herbs had profound influence upon these energy flows and upon the vital organs that the flows seemed to unite.

A logical system of energetics was thus developed and became the basis of all the Chinese health arts. Because of their ability to heal themselves and become as "walking gods" among the common people of that time, these early yogis were often approached by the common people for medical help. They became China's first healers, though as a reflection of their primal Taoist philosophy, they always remained humble. They rejected the idea that "they" were "healers," and instead expressed the concept that they were but channels of healing light from a much greater source, Tao, as it manifests through Heaven and Earth. Many practices evolved from the yogic arts which eventually became common arts of the Chinese medical profession, such as acupuncture, acupressure, and herbalism. Some of the original yogic arts were not converted to mundane medical purposes, as useful as these have been, but instead maintained the original idea of promoting a glowing body capable of spiritual growth and possible enlightenment. The higher forms of acupressure, such as *Jin Shin Do*, and acupuncture, such as the Korean *Tae Guk* ("Supreme Ultimate") Therapy and the Chinese Taoist "Internal Duct" Method, have remained relatively aloof from common medical treatment and have emphasized the promotion of "radiant health" through the principle of *Li Ch'i*, the "balance of energy." The tonic herbal system, too, has remained apart from the general category of "medicine" and has remained an art of "radiant health."

The energy system of the Chinese has not changed significantly in over two thousand years. Even today, where skepticism of such old systems tends to disallow all that is not recently "discovered," the Chinese energy system is widely accepted even by hardened modern researchers. Though the exact *modus operandi* has not been clearly explained scientifically, there is a significant amount of evidence that the energy system does exist just as described two thousand years ago, and does in fact have the influence on our health that the Chinese have long claimed it has.

As explained previously, the Chinese saw the body-mind as one within itself and at one with the environment and cosmos. The internal organs communicate with the surface of the body, and thus with the outer environment, by way of the energy circuitry, composed of the twelve so-called "meridians." These meridians travel to and from the internal organs and along the surface of the body through the skin and flesh in an orderly course. In this way, the surface of the body is influenced by, and influences, the internal organs. If a change takes place in an organ or organ system, subsequent related changes will take place at the surface of the body, and vice versa. Organs are also connected by an internal energy circuitry so that change in one organ quickly results in corresponding energetic changes in the other organs.

This energy system is apparently the third major system of communication in the human body, in addition to the nervous system, which transmits information via electrochemical impulses, and the circulatory system, which transmits information through the distribution of hormones and like substances. The Chinese energy circuitry is postulated at this time by respected modern researchers as a primitive but essential healing mechanism that has existed in life-forms since the dawn of life, and continues to be of fundamental evolutionary importance. The energy can be measured by scientific instruments and the entire circuitry has been verified to exist by several different scientific techniques.

It is in vogue today, in some circles, to equate the Chinese meridian system with the nervous system. Many prominent acupuncturists and Western doctors have embraced this view, primarily because an anatomical basis for the system has not been positively identified. The Chinese meridian system was arrived at thousands of years ago by way of meditation, yoga, and paraclinical observation. These are not considered valid forms of proof by Western scientific standards. The fact that stimulation of acu-points by any one of a variety of means can result in observable and reproducible physiological and psychological changes has lead scientists to seek explanation in terms of what modern science knows. The nervous system has been the natural target of hypothesis, study, and research.

But after more than a decade of intense research into the possible correlation of the human nervous system and the meridian system, only slight headway towards true understanding has been made. This has lead prominent researchers to seek in other areas for explanations of the apparent functioning of the acu-points and the meridian system. Suddenly a new field of study has opened up, out of which a number of very significant insights have been gleaned. Most prominent among this wave of researchers has been Robert O. Becker, M.D., research professor and medical investigator at the Upstate Medical Center, New York. Dr. Becker and his team of researchers have established that the portion of the meridian system so far studied by their group *does* have an objective basis in reality and that the meridian system is more primitive than, and to some degree independent of, the nervous system.

For the past fifteen years, Dr. Becker's laboratory has been concerned with the factors that initiate and control healing mechanisms. During that time, they have slowly accumulated evidence for the existence of a previously undescribed or unknown (in the West) physiological mechanism. They believe that they can now describe a complete control system functioning in concert with, but separate from, the nervous system. This primitive data transmission and control system, which antedates and is basic to the nervous system, has been related to several important physiological processes such as: the pattern of *DC* potentials exhibited by living organisms both grossly and within the central nervous system: growth and healing processes of several types: and levels of consciousness such as hypnosis and anaesthesia. The system has been shown to be perturbable in a functionally important fashion by magnetic fields (air ionization). The prime function of the system, according to Dr. Becker, is that of sensing injury and effecting repair. The system has now been shown to correlate almost precisely with the Chinese meridian system.

Dr. Becker postulated that "pain transmission is one of the functions of the *DC* electronic data transmission system. The transmission of *DC* signals via actual current flow over transmission lines is subject to cable constants such as 'resistance,' which serve to reduce signal magnitude with increasing transmission distance. In engineering practice, this is overcome by inserting into the line, at intervals, operational 'booster' amplifiers to restore signal strength and maintain intelligibility over distance. Since our data indicate that the operational signal levels of the biological *DC* system are in the millivolt and nanoampere (very weak) ranges, one can predict the need for structures functioning as operational amplifiers along the channels of *DC* transmission. This analysis leads one to consider the acupuncture meridians as *DC* communication channels and the points as sites of operational amplifier location. If we are correct, the points should show lower resistance and higher conductance than non-point areas of the skin, and both resistance and conductance factors should show an organized field pattern around the point. The points should be discreet sources of direct current. They may demonstrate a polarity indicative of the direction on signal transmission and, when instrumented in series, the points should demonstrate propagation of signal.

"This concept," continues Dr. Becker, "offers an opportunity to objectively assay the system of acupuncture meridians and points in a scientific fashion within the framework of a viable theory. Such analysis has been in progress for the past year and our results indicate that approximately half of the acupuncture points studied exist as real, measurable entities with electrical characteristics as predicted by our theory."

During experimentation, it was found that the meridians did have statistically significant conductance maxima when compared to non-meridian portions of the skin. Marked individual differences were observed between subjects, but repeated scans on individual subjects were highly reproducible. The Becker group's research is highly significant in that it goes beyond the neural theory of the meridian system and supports the classical belief that a primitive energy system is at work in the living body, and that this system is not inherently reliant upon the gross structures of the body, including the nervous system.

According to the Chinese, the energy, or Ch'i, in the meridians both provides energy to, and reflects the internal condition of the viscera. The entire energy system is composed of twelve main "organ-meridian" systems, each relating to major organic and psychic functions. As long as energy in each meridian is abundant, pure, and unimpeded, health is secured. If, however, there is a deficiency of energy, or a blockage leading to excess in an organ or its meridian, imbalance and dysfunction result.

Though the meridians are named after major organs, they must not be confined to those anatomically specific organs as we think of them today. Instead, they should be thought of as *functional* systems. Each "organ-meridian" represents and controls a broad range of generally related physiological activities. At first glance, some of the functions and structures defined as "belonging" to an organ-meridian may seem unrelated. But deeper study has shown an amazing physiological insightfulness by the Chinese in relating activities that are indeed connected, though often at a distance and not anatomically.

In all, the twelve organ-meridians relate to every aspect of our being, physically and psychically. Each organ-meridian controls related physical and emotional functions and as changes take place in the organ or its meridian, peripheral physical and psychic changes also take place. The herbs are each said to affect certain organs and their meridians, so it is essential, if we are to understand the herbs and their actions from the traditional point of view, to understand the organ-meridian systems as the Chinese defined them.

The twelve organ-meridians are organized into six pairs, each pair consisting of one organ-meridian with Yang qualities and one with Yin qualities. Thus there are six Yin organs and six Yang. Each pair also falls into the category of a particular elemental energy. It will be noted that the Fire element contains two pairs of organ-meridian systems while the other elements contain but one pair each.

The following is a discussion of the functions of each of the organ-meridian systems, according to both traditional and modern accountings. It will become immediately clear that the Chinese definition of the word "lung," for example, is not the same as our Western definition. The Chinese concept of the "lung" includes many peripherally related functions as well and is not strictly limited to those organs we refer to today as the lungs. So for the purpose of clarity, when the Chinese term is being referred to, the organ name will start with a capital letter and when the organ as we use it singularly in modern terminology is being referred to, a lower case letter will start the term. Thus we have the Chinese Lung and the Western lung.

The Lungs: The Lungs are a Yin organ system and are dominated by Metal energy. The Lungs are said to govern Ch'i. The Lung system controls the lungs so that under normal conditions one's breathing is long, deep and quiet. Cellular respiration throughout the entire body is also under the control of the Lungs. Ionic particles and free electrons which are inhaled are believed to be passed into the meridian system, which starts with the Lung meridian.

The Lungs also govern the skin, and regulate the opening and closing of the pores so as to produce perspiration, closing of the pores, or shivering, thus protecting and helping to maintain balance of the internal environment. It is said that the skin is the first line of defense against noxious environmental forces such as excessive wind, heat, cold, dampness, microbes, etc. The skin thus facilitates adaptability and protects against external attack of the internal tissues. The breakdown of this system is considered to be the cause of the common cold and of influenza. If the skin is radiant, clear, and elastic, it is a sign that one's respiratory force is strong and that one's primary defenses are powerful.

The Lungs control the voice, which will be low and from deep within if the Lung Ch'i is flourishing. The "voice" is to be distinguished from "speech," which is controlled significantly by the tongue, which is under the energetic control of the Heart. The Lungs "open" into the nose, establishing clear, easy breathing and an acute sense of smell. The Lungs control the larynx and the sinuses.

The Lungs control the diaphragm, the muscle which is in charge of lung movement in breathing. Diaphragmatic movement is an automatic process that takes place without conscious control being necessary. However, it is of tremendous significance that we are capable of conscious control of the diaphragm and therefore of breathing. Because of this control, we can regulate the lungs activity and in turn the entire internal balance. This, of course, has proven to be the physiological basis for virtually all of the yogic and meditative techniques of the world, in which organic and psychological health and harmony are established through breath control. It has now been established that our breathing has a considerable regulatory influence over the autonomic nervous system, which controls all automatic activity in the body-mind. Breathing rhythm and depth have been shown to establish the various balances and strengths of this aspect of our nervous system. Deep breathing strengthens the autonomic nervous system, and balanced breathing balances it.

In addition to these functions, the Lungs control those areas over which its meridian travels.

The Large Intestine: The Large Intestine is the Yang partner of the Lungs under the Metal element. The Large Intestine is largely correlated to the large intestine organ as it is known in the West. The Large Intestine is said to be in charge of transporting, transforming and eliminating solid waste from the system. It plays a major role in water balance in the body and the purity of bodily fluids. Energy may be extracted from the Large Intestine and provided directly to the Kidney where it is transformed into reserve energy. The Large Intestine meridian has special influence in immune response and the opening of the skin to cause perspiration in the case of fever.

The Large Intestine controls those areas over which its meridian flows, with special influence into the throat, face, and head.

The Stomach: The Stomach is the Yang Earth organ-meridian system. The Stomach relates primarily to the organic function of the stomach itself. The Chinese call it the "Sea of Nourishment" and say that it is in the stomach that food is "rotted and ripened," that is, broken down into nutritional constituents. It is in the stomach that the Chinese say Ch'i is extracted from food. In this concept, Chinese theory differs from Western theory. Western science has no theory concerning the extraction of energy from food at the level of the stomach. Instead, it says that food is broken down into basic constituents and then passed on into the small intestine, where these nutrients are absorbed into the bloodstream. The Chinese claim that Ch'i is extracted from the food and transported into the lungs, where it blends with the Ch'i extracted from the inhaled air. This blend of air Ch'i and food Ch'i then enters the Lung meridian and begins its circulation throughout the entire meridian system. It is theorized that this so-called food Ch'i is actually composed of free electrons that result from the chemical breakdown of the food in the highly acidic stomach.

The Stomach has some other important functions. For one, it is considered to play a major role in the building and conditioning of the striated muscle, that muscle which moves our frame. One whose Stomach is functioning properly will have well-constructed, strong muscles. The Stomach is also said to directly influence fluid metabolism, particularly in the abdominal region. The Stomach is also said to control the lips, saliva, and those areas over which its meridian flows.

The Spleen: The Spleen is the Yin Earth organ-meridian system. The so-called Spleen function includes that of the pancreas, as well as that of the spleen. In fact, many of the Spleen's attributes are more accurately recognized as being actions of the pancreas. Therefore the Spleen has a major influence over digestion and absorption of nutritional substances and fluids. It is also said to control the transportation of the nutritional substances and fluids, and is therefore assigned a general regulatory role over the entire gastro-intestinal function. The Spleen is said to influence fluid circulation and distribution and works with the kidneys in controlling the amount of fluid in the body.

Another vital function of the Spleen is its major influence over the blood. It helps regulate the quantity and quality of blood. It is involved dramatically with the female menstrual cycle.

The Spleen is actually responsible for the extraction of Ch'i from the stomach and the transporting of this food Ch'i from the stomach to the lungs. And the Spleen is considered directly responsible for the development and maintenance of the muscles of the limbs and builds flesh throughout the body. The Spleen is held to be generally responsible for physical working power and shares responsibility with the Lungs, which extract Ch'i from the air, for producing vitality for the entire body.

The Spleen controls those areas over which its meridian flows.

The Heart: The Heart is a Yin Fire organ-meridian system. It is the master organ and harbors the Spirit, *Shin* (see next section). The Heart controls the Mind and the emotions. Modern Chinese say that the Heart controls the functions of the cerebral cortex and the Limbic Center of the brain, which controls our emotions. It is said that when the Heart is strong, all other organ systems perform their natural functions harmoniously, and all emotions naturally play a subservient role to the commands of Shin, which can be defined as "all-embracing love."

The Heart system, of course, includes the heart itself, which rules the cardio-vascular system, and is in charge of the distribution of blood. A strong heart is powerful yet calm, and requires a substantial amount of stress to push it to dangerous levels of activity. A calm heart is considered essential to becoming liberated spiritually and in developing radiant health physically.

The tongue is said to receive its ability to cause speech from the Heart. Stuttering or mutism are thus caused by Heart imbalance. The Heart function includes that of two important glands: the thyroid and the thymus. The Heart is the dominant organ system during hot weather, increasing surface circulation of blood to cool the body down. For this reason, the Heart dominates during the summer months.

The Heart controls those areas over which its meridian flows.

The Small Intestine: The Small Intestine is a Yang Fire organ-meridian system. The Small Intestine is said to be in change of the separation of food into its "pure and impure" components, and is in control of the assimilation of these nutrients. The Small Intestine is also the site of bacterial activity by which essential nutrients are produced and absorbed.

Among the functions now ascribed to the Small Intestine organ meridian system, is that of the pituitary gland. The pituitary produces a large number of essential hormones that influence virtually every aspect of our being, and is thus called the "master gland." Among these hormones are ones that regulate our general energy level, our metabolism, resistance, adaptability, sexual functions, emotional reponses, and many more. One of these pituitary hormones, the endorphins, were discussed earlier in connection with emotional stability and raising of the pain threshold. The Small Intestine is said to influence basic emotional balance while the Heart is said to control the higher emotions. The Small Intestine is also said to be in charge of our ability to assimilate ideas and concepts.

The Small Intestine controls those areas over which its meridian flows.

The Bladder: The Bladder is the Yang Water organ-meridian system. Though as an organ it is not one of the most complex, in the Chinese healing arts its meridian is considered to be of considerable importance.

Naturally, the bladder controls the gathering and excretion of urine. Its role in this respect is agreed upon by everyone. Its meridian plays a major role in virtually every function of the body. The Bladder meridian flows from head to heel along the back of the body. It has two main branches flanking the spinal column, and it is this segment that is so highly regarded by all Chinese health practitioners. This zone of the meridian plays a physically and emotionally protective role to the body as a whole and to the individual organs. A special set of acu-points along this segment of the Bladder meridian regulate each of the organ systems and the related functions of the body-mind. These special acu-points lie almost directly above the branch of the autonomic nervous system known as the sympathetic trunk, which is actually a chain of sympathetic nerve ganglia.

The autonomic nervous system (A.N.S.) provides a perfect example of how the principle of Yin and Yang is a realistic basis for understanding the nature of the life process. The A.N.S. is that aspect of the nervous system that controls all functions that operate automatically. It thus controls a multitude of essential life processes, such as our heart beat, digestion, circulation, body temperature, blood pressure, elimination, defense, respiration, etc.

There are two parts to the A.N.S. One part is called the *Sympathetic* nervous system and the other part is called the *Parasympathetic* nervous system. The Parasympathetic and Sympathetic components operate antagonistically to one another and yet in concert, so as to maintain normalcy in the human condition. The Parasympathetic nervous system is in charge of the functions associated with relaxation, rest, absorption of nutrients and energy, peace of mind, etc. Thus it is the Yin component. The Sympathetic nervous system is in charge of discharging previously accumulated energy and the burning of fuel for the purposes of work, defense, aggressiveness, flight from danger, tension, anxiety, etc. Thus it fits the definition of Yang precisely.

Functioning harmoniously, the two branches of the A.N.S. maintain a dynamic balance so that we function healthfully and happily. If circumstances necessitate the dominance of one of these systems over the other for an inappropriate length of time, disease results. If the Parasympathetic nervous system were to become dominant, the person would lack assertiveness and will. They would tend to remain lethargic and passive, even in times of danger, even if their survival is at stake. However, Parasympathetic dominance tends to be euphoric because of the extreme relaxation and lack of paranoia. This state of balance is rare in modern times.

To the contrary, chronic and acute Sympathetic dominance are prevalent throughout society. This has come about as a result of the stress of life, which causes a defensive, aggressive, self-preservation response. Because the nerves that are responsible for these responses, the sympathetic ganglia, lie in the back alongside the spine, the back tends to become chronically or even acutely tense. These ganglia become highly active, thus discharging nervous energy not only to the organs, but to the muscles lying nearby the sympathetic trunk. This is the reason for the chronic back tension. Back tension and pain is the most widely complained of symptom in American society. This is due to our stressful life-style that does not allow time for such arts as yoga and meditation, which counteract the stress response and thus prevent such symptoms as back tension and pain.

Maintaining a balanced, healthy autonomic nervous system is absolutely fundamental to our health and happiness. All the techniques of Oriental healthcare strive to strengthen and maintain a strong and accurately adaptive autonomic nervous system. Western healthcare has sadly neglected and/or ignored this obvious and vital aspect of healthcare. It is for this reason that so many Western people are looking to the East for ways to re-establish and then maintain their health.

The sympathetic trunk is thus highly influenced by the Bladder meridian, especially that stretch of the flow that runs along the spine's periphery. Anything that improves the flow of energy in this region will shift the entire balance of the body back to a more normal state, and thus promote real health. It is said that to achieve radiant health and spiritual illumination, there can be no blocks in this segment of the Bladder meridian.

The Bladder also controls those other areas over which its meridian flows.

The Kidney: The Kidney is the Yin Water organ-meridian system. To many traditionalists, the Kidney is considered the key to life itself. In fact, the Kidney is called the "Root of Life" and alternatively the "Basis of Life." The Kidney is said to be related to the origin of life, referring to the theory that Kidney energy is ancestral, that is, it is passed on from generation to generation. The Kidney is thus associated with the evolutionary transmission of genetic information. It is thus considered immortal. The Kidney is further said to determine the level of our vitality and the duration of one's longevity. In fact, the whole human life cycle is felt to be regulated by the Kidney. Growth, development, maturation, degeneration, and death are the results of the ebb and flow of the Kidney Ch'i. It is no wonder that the care of the Kidney is considered essential and primary to health and longevity by the Chinese, and in particular the Taoists, who know the most about these matters.

The Kidney function includes, of course, that of the renal kidney as described in Western physiology. The kidney filters our blood, removing waste metabolites (by-products of the body's innumerable chemical reactions), and excess water. If this vital function fails, the body quickly becomes dangerously toxic and severe damage can result, and even death. Those who drink too little water often develop kidney stones which can lead to severe impairment of the renal function. Those who drink too much water often find their kidneys weakened, and unable to cope with the excessive work, develop severe cases of edema (bloating). The kidneys also regulate the mineral balance in the body by selectively re-absorbing or passing out minerals in the urine. The kidneys also pass out in the urine selective quantities of unused hormones such as testosterone and estrogen. The overall function of the kidney is to selectively excrete certain waste substances while returning other substances to the blood, so that the composition of the blood and tissue fluids remain constant, within physiological limits and according to environmental factors. For example, the kidney regulates the acid-base balance of the bodily fluids through a complex series of reactions that involve such substances as sodium and potassium, ammonia, bicarbonate and hydrogen ions.

But the Kidney organ-meridian system includes much more than just the kidney itself. The Kidney includes the adrenal glands, which has two parts: the cortex and the medulla. The adrenal medulla produces adrenalin and noradrenalin, and is actually a development of the Sympathetic nervous system. Stress causes the adrenal medulla to release adrenalin and noradrenalin into the blood stream. These substances are not true hormones, but are instead categorized as neuro-transmitters. These same substances are produced by the nerve endings of the Sympathetic nervous system and cause the same biological result, but over a generally more extended time period.

The adrenal cortex is a true endocrine gland, and is among the most important organs in the body. Destruction of the adrenal cortex is fatal. The adrenal cortex is an extremely complex organ which produces a wide range of hormones, all of which are steroids, that are essential in the regulation of metabolic, excretory, reproductive, mineral balancing and defense functions. The adrenals regulate the body's response to stress and help us to adapt internally to the stresses of life such as weather changes, emotional hyperactivity, poisons, injury and trauma, excessive workload, etc. Hormones produced and secreted by the adrenal cortex regulate sugar metabolism through their influence upon the pancreas, and other hormones secreted directly control the reproductive hormone production of the gonads, and thus influence sexual characteristics and activity, including fertility. It has a regulatory control over the production of ova and spermatozoa. Thus the Chinese theory that the Kidney was in charge of the "ancestral energy."

To the Kidney is assigned a number of other vital functions. The Kidney is said to Store *Ching*, the "vital essence," the basic substance responsible for maintaining the vitality of life (see next section). It is a fundamental tenet of the Chinese art of radiant health that preserving the Ching leads to a long, strong life. Ching is reserve energy, the Kidney playing the role as main reservoir for the entire body. The Ching is undoubtedly related to substances produced, stored and secreted by the adrenals and reproductive glands, which are also considered part of the Kidney.

Because the Kidney controls the reproductive glands and secretions, the Kidney is considered to control all physiological aspects of reproduction, including the female fertility cycle, pregnancy, and fetal development. Strong Kidney Ch'i, along with strong Wood energy of the Liver, provides abundant sexual vitality, which to the Orientals is a sign of health. Any sexual or reproductive malady must be traced to the Kidney function. For this reason, Taoists used sexual techniques similar to those used in Tantric yoga to develop the Kidney Ch'i, and in turn the overall life force. However, sexual abuse is a major cause of Kidney degeneration and premature loss of vitality and life. This energy must be developed and preserved. Thus an old Chinese saying: "A fool and his Ching (sexual vitality) are easily parted."

The Kidney also generates the energy of the spinal cord and provides energy directly to the brain, thus promoting clear thinking. Low Kidney Ch'i results in cloudy thinking, weak memory, backache and general fatigue. The Kidney controls, in particular, the lumbar region of the back (the lower back) and determines the strength or weakness of this area. Lumbago, pain in the lower back, is one of modern man's most common maladies, and is attributed by the Chinese to loss of Kidney Ch'i due to excessive stress and/or sexuality.

Also under the control of the Kidney is the skeletal system. This includes the bones, bone marrow and teeth. The life force in these solid tissues is provided by the Kidney. Furthermore, the Kidney provides strength and flexibility to the joints. Injuries, pain and inflammation of the joints are related to Kidney problems. This is particularly true of the spine and knees. Because of its control of the bone marrow, the Kidney plays a major role in blood production and resistance to disease. Bones that are easily broken, or do not mend easily, indicate a deficiency of Kidney Ch'i, while strong bones that rarely or never break even during accidents indicate strong reserves of Kidney Ch'i.

The Kidney also controls the hair on the head, facial hair, and pubic hair. The Kidney is further said to "open into the ears," thus providing the energy of hearing.

The Kidney has a Yin and a Yang component. Together, the Yin and Yang of the Kidney supplies energy to the twelve organs and thus controls the energy of the entire body-mind at a fundamental level. The Yin of the Kidney represents the fluids, tissues, hormones, and other substances of the kidneys, adrenals, gonads and other related organs. The Yang of the Kidney represents the active vitality generated by the various organs in the Kidney system.

Emotionally, the Kidney provides courage and will. A lack of Kidney Ch'i results automatically in fearfulness and paranoia, while a blockage of the Kidney Ch'i, called an excess, results in foolhardy behavior.

The Kidney is considered the most important organ-meridian system, both functionally and therapeutically, since strong Kidney function provides power to all the other organic systems and serves as a reservoir of highly refined stored energy. For this reason, the Kidney tonics of Chinese tonic herbalism are among the most important.

The Kidney controls those areas over which its meridian flows.

Circulation-Sex: The Circulation-Sex organ-meridian system does not correspond well to any particular Western organ. It is a Yin Fire organ-meridian system, like the Heart. However, it is considered subservient to the Heart.

It is often correlated to the pericardium, the heart's protective sack. It is thus sometimes called the "Pericardium" and sometimes called the "Heart Protector." Circulation-Sex is also called the "Minister of the Heart" and the "Abode of the Heart" and the Spirit which resides within, "Shin," organs and is charged with protecting the Heart from attack by the emotions generated by the other organs. Each of the major organs is said to control various emotional aspects of our being. Though each of these emotions is important and has a valid purpose, the over-riding emotional state of Man, according to the Chinese principle, should be universal all-embracing Love, which is called the "Spirit," or "Shin." If an emotion such as fear, generated by an imbalanced Kidney function, or anger, generated by an imbalanced Liver function becomes the dominant driving force of one's personality, Shin recedes and one is said to have lost their original nature. By cultivating Shin, one can regain their original nature and the other emotions naturally become subservient to this all-powerful state of mind. It is the responsibility of Circulation-Sex to protect Shin from the other emotions.

Also under the control of Circulation-Sex is the central circulation of blood, that is, of the major blood vessels. This organ function also has a sexual role. Circulation-Sex has a strong relationship with the Yang energy of the Kidney. The Kidney is a Yin organ as a whole, but of course has a Yang component. They Yang component of the Kidney is in fact quite powerful, providing tremendous vital energy to the body and mind. A major aspect of this Kidney Yang, also called Kidney Fire, is sexual. It is said that the feeling of love that is expressed through sexuality is from Circulation-Sex, which unites physical (sexual) love with emotional love from the Heart (Shin). Circulation-Sex is the link between emotion and physical sexuality, and unifies the physical and emotional aspects of love. One whose Circulation-Sex function is imbalanced may experience a separation of the physical and emotional aspects of love. Thus they may love with their heart, but be incapable of expressing this love sexually. Or, they may be quite capable of the sexual act, but will lack the capacity to feel deep feelings of love. Harmony in this function is considered essential for true happiness.

Circulation-Sex controls those areas over which its meridian flows.

The Triple Warmer: The Triple Warmer is a Yang Fire organ-meridian function. Again, like Circulation-Sex, it is not easily defined in Western terms. This function confuses many Western students initially, but is not really difficult to comprehend after some study and thought. The Triple Warmer integrates the various central functions of metabolism and elimination. The Triple Warmer is responsible for the production of "essential energy," which is of two main types: the nutritive "Ying Ch'i" which flows through the meridians, and the defensive "Wei Ch'i" which flows in the flesh and defends the body against the attack of outside environmental forces.

The Triple Warmer is composed of three divisions known as the three "burning spaces" which basically represent the functional aspects of the three body cavities: the thoracic, abdominal, and pelvic.

The "upper burning space" harmonizes the Lung and Heart functions, and is in charge of the distribution of essential energy (Yang and Wei).

The "middle burning space" harmonizes the Stomach and Spleen, and is thus in charge of the extraction of energy from food and the breakdown of food into basic constituents.

The "lower burning space" harmonizes the Liver, Kidney, Intestine and Bladder functions, and is in charge of absorption of nutrients, elimination of waste, energy storage and reproduction.

Modern Chinese researchers believe that the Triple Warmer is related to the *hypothalamus*, a section of the brain that controls most of the basic life functions such as appetite, body temperature, fluid balance, etc.

Thus, the establishment of a harmoniously functioning Triple Warmer is essential to health. Many of the tonic herbs improve the functioning of the Triple Warmer. Some of the tonics act specifically upon one of the burning spaces or another, though they tend to affect general well-being as a result of their specific activity. Thus, a tonic which is said to affect the upper burning space will improve cardiorespiratory function and the extraction and distribution of blood and energy. A middle burning space tonic will improve digestion and the extraction of energy from food. A tonic to the lower burning space will benefit the assimilative, eliminative, and sexual functions. A tonic to the entire Triple Warmer vivifies and harmonizes all of these functions so that all of the organic functions may be harmonious.

The Triple Warmer takes on those symptoms of the organ functions in its various regions. The Triple Warmer maintains those areas over which its meridian flows.

The Gall Bladder: The Gall Bladder is the Yang Wood organ-meridian function. The gall bladder itself, of course, controls the flow of bile, which is responsible for the digestion of fatty and oily foods. The Gall Bladder organ-meridian system is said to provide muscular strength, in particular the vitality of the legs. It also influences the elimination of muscular fatigue by removing toxins via the lymphatic system. When the Gall Bladder meridian is flowing freely, the body is relaxed and free from muscular aches and pains. Psychically, the Gall Bladder is believed to control the ability to carry out plans. Blockage of the Gall Bladder meridian generally results in an irritable nature, accompanied by a nagging feeling of frustration. One very common result of this condition is the common tension headache, which afflicts millions of people.

The Gall Bladder controls those areas over which its meridian flows. It therefore controls the shoulders near the nape of the neck, the rear of the neck, the occipital region, the top of the head and the forehead. It is clear how blockage of the powerful Wood and Fire energy of the Gall Bladder can results in neck and shoulder tension and headaches.

The Liver: The Liver is the Yin Wood organ. Of course, the Liver system includes the liver itself. The liver is an extremely complex organ physiologically. Blood flowing through the liver is detoxified. The liver also stores large quantities of blood, especially while we are resting or asleep. It also stores large quantities of sugar in the form of glycogen, which is readily pumped into the blood stream whenever work loads require an increase in the blood sugar level. The liver has major control of protein production and breakdown in our bodies. All amino acids absorbed by the small intestine are immediately transported to the liver where they are recombined to meet the body's needs. The non-essential amino acids are produced in the liver. Many substances are broken down in the liver, including all proteins and most hormones. They are then eliminated, or in some instances simply stored in the liver.

But the Liver function, as defined by the Chinese is not limited to the liver itself. The Liver also includes the peripheral nervous system, all the nerves emanating from the central nervous system. The Liver thus plays the very significant role of controlling all neuro-muscular activity. The Liver is therefore directly responsible for all peripheral motor activity and muscular tone. Muscular tension is the result of excessive energy build-up in the Liver meridian. The muscular tissue itself is controlled by the Spleen. But the nerves that control how the muscles function, that is, contract and relax, is under the control of the Liver function. If a person is suffering from general muscular tension, the problem is not in the muscles themselves, but in the nervous system that is dictating the degree of tension. Thus the Liver must be balanced and its meridian free-flowing, if one wishes to experience relaxation. The Liver is also said to control the eyes and vision. This is logically deduced from the observation that the eyes are an extension of the central nervous system. Though Western thought generally holds that the eyes are a part of the central nervous system, a strong argument could be made that they should be categorized as peripheral. In any case, the Liver controls the eyes.

The Liver controls the ligaments and tendons, which also play a major role in sensing and controlling muscular tension. Coordination, especially hand-eye coordination, is said to be under the influence of the Liver, and also the Gall Bladder. The motor center of the brain is believed to be under the control of the Liver system.

The Liver is said to control, due to its Wood elemental energy dominance, the creative drive, sexual drive, birth, and the will to grow. The Liver provides energy to the genital organs and is directly responsible for genital vitality. The internal functions, such as hormone production and germinal cell development are the responsibility of the Kidney, but outward sexual vigor is due to the Liver activity. Sexual activity thus tends to temporarily reduce excess in the Liver meridian and can therefore reduce tension. But it can also deplete the Kidney, which unlike the Liver which is generally excessive due to our over-ambitious drives and desires, is deficient in most people due to chronic or acute stress. It is taught, then, that sexuality is beneficial to the system if it results in relaxation; but if it results in significant fatigue (blurred vision, dizziness, etc.) or exhaustion (knee weakness or aching that does not soon go away, loss of memory, general lassitude, etc.) it is considered to not only be abusive, but dangerous. The Kidneys should never be pushed to their extremes. Instead, sufficient tonics should be taken to provide abundant Kidney energy, and in this way sexuality will not endanger our health. Many of the tonics have aphrodisiac qualities. These often strengthen the Liver energy. However the Kidneys must be built up before using aphrodisiacs. Then, when using the aphrodisiac, a formula should be used that replaces spent Kidney energy in addition to herbs that strengthen the external functions. Balance, as always, is the key to extended success.

Emotionally, the Liver generates the will to grow. It therefore is the root of most of our drives and desires. Curbing our drives and desires so that they do not burden us is the trick to remaining relaxed. The Liver also provides the energy of creativity. A creative individual who does not desire to create more than is possible, can be of great help to his or her fellow Man. Blockage of the Liver results in frustration, anger, and perhaps violent rage. Lethargy results from a deficiency of Ch'i in the Liver.

The Liver controls those areas over which its meridian flows.

* * * * *

In conclusion, it should be obvious that the Chinese had a sophisticated understanding of human function. Though just twelve organs are included in their basic theory, all of the body's functions are actually described. The Chinese system recognizes the integrity of the system as a whole and clearly recognized many of the functional relationships also recognized in Western physiology. The emphasis of the system is upon integration, not the separation of systems into unconnected units. Modern physiology concurs with this view.

The above discussion does not, obviously, describe the multitude of detailed functions of each of the organs and systems. It is advisable that the student study a good Western physiology text in order to understand the details of human function. The bibliography at the end of this book provides some suggestions in this regard. However, with the information provided in this section, one should have an adequate understanding of the Chinese system upon which the tonic herbal system is based.

3.2 The Three Vital Treasures

According to the Taoists, there are three "Vital Treasures" which are the foundation of life and form the basis of the Chinese esoteric system of longevity. The yogic schools concentrated very heavily upon the regulation and maintenance of these "treasures." They are known as *Ching, Ch'i,* and *Shin.* None of the three are easily translated into English, but it is necessary to have a basic understanding of these "vital treasures" to properly utilize and to benefit from the Chinese tonic herbs.

Ching: *Ching* can be translated as "essence" or "basic substance." Ching is the most highly refined *substance* in the human body. The generation of all other energies is dependent upon Ching. Each and every tissue must have some of it to function. It is the living quality in what otherwise would be inanimate matter. Ching is pure vital force. It is both inherent in our living nature and is further made out of the essence of food and air. It is "stored energy."

Though it is stored in all living tissue, probably in small cell organelles known as *mitochondria*, it is considered to be most concentrated in the Yin organs and is thought to be accumulated most abundantly by the Kidney, probably in the adrenals and sex glands. Ching is the energy of regeneration, and is the enormous and highly concentrated energy of the sperm and ova. It is the Ching that gives the embryo the energy to develop and is indeed the driving force of life. Throughout life, it is the basis of our vitality and is the source of mental and physical strength and spiritual power.

Ching is lost through stress and/or loss of sexual substance, depleting the body-mind's overall vitality. Depletion of Ching will lead to weakness, disease, premature aging and death. Increasing the Ching, according to the Taoists, will lead to a long and happy life, free from disease.

The "Seat of Ching" is an energy center known as the *Lower Tan T'ien*, the "Sea of Energy," located internally, two inches below the navel. The center is most likely associated with the *hypogastric plexus*, a major nerve center in the abdomen which provides enervation to major abdominal and pelvic organs. The area of the Lower Tan T'ien is called the *Hara*. Developing the Hara is one of the primary objectives of all of the meditation, yogic, and martial arts techniques of the Orient. Directing one's breath into this region is fundamental to such arts as Zen breathing, Taoist meditation, and Tai Ch'i Chuan, to name a few. By vitalizing the Hara and Tan T'ien, one increases and preserves the Ching stored in the Kidney, leading to radiant health.

Ch'i: The life energy, *Ch'i*, is one of the three Vital Treasures. Ch'i is said to be the offspring of Ching. It is the Ch'i that directly activates all the life functions. Taoist Master Sung Jin Park once said that "if a person can learn the main principle of controlling Ch'i with the Mind and driving Ch'i at will to various parts of the body, they can learn to realize the Way of Immortality."

Ch'i is one of the fundamental concepts in the Orient. All manifestation is the result of this invisible force. Whether it is the growth of a plant, the movement of an arm, or the deafening thunder of a storm, it is all from Ch'i. It is the energy which activates all processes. There is not just one type of Ch'i, but indeed there are innumerable varieties, each with its own specific nature. In the human body, too, there are many kinds of Ch'i. The two main sources of Ch'i are food and air, though we also receive Ch'i through our skin from light and other types of radiation.

When food enters the stomach, its Ch'i, that is, the electrical charge generated by the decomposition of food, is separated off and migrates to the lungs where it combines with the air Ch'i, that is, electrical charge present in the inhaled air. This new blended Ch'i is called *True Ch'i*. True Ch'i tends to be of two types: "clear" and "cloudy," known by the Chinese respectively as *Ying* and *Wei*.

The clear Ying Ch'i enters the meridian system, nourishing all the tissues of the body. The foggy Wei Ch'i wraps around the outside of the meridians and circulates in the subcutaneous tissues providing defense energy for the whole body. Ying Ch'i is relatively Yin when compared to the faster moving, surface-flowing defense energy, Wei. Wei Ch'i is thus Yang.

It is taught by the Taoists that if one has many desires, becomes over-fatigued, cannot control the emotions, and cannot control Ch'i from food (Yin) and from air (Yang), the Ch'i either stagnates or a shortage of Ch'i arises and the Ch'i is weak and disease easily manifests. When disease stays in the body, life is in danger.

The Chinese say that "Ch'i leads blood." This means that whenever and wherever Ch'i flows, blood will soon follow. This is a very important and fundamental principle of the Chinese health arts, and is one of the great secrets of healing and promoting life. By encouraging the free circulation of fresh Ch'i, one also enhances the flow of blood so that cells can perform the functions of metabolism, respiration, elimination, and reproduction under optimal energetic conditions.

When one is in a state of mental and spiritual stability and balance, all the Ch'i in the internal organs is in harmony and disease cannot invade the inner organs. But when one is not in balance and is out of harmony mentally and spiritually, the Ch'i which nourishes the organs can be shaken. When the Ch'i is shaken, the body is unable to protect itself against diseases from the wind, cold, heat, dampness, dryness, etc., and disease can then invade the tissues.

The "Seat of Ch'i" is located in the *Upper Tan T'ien*, located within the brain. It is the area often referred to as the "third eye," and is probably associated with the hypothalamus, which regulates all primal physiological and psychological functions, and/or the pineal gland, which regulates our basic biorhythm.

Tonic herbs are used to promote all the functions of Ch'i in all its human forms, and thus are invaluable in helping to attain radiant health.

Shin: When there is abundant Ching, the veritable "elixir of life" to the Taoists, fresh Ch'i flows abundantly. When this Ch'i enters the heart meridian some of it turns to *Shin*. Shin is not easily translated into English, but can be called "Spirit," "Mind," or "All-embracing Love."

When Ching and Ch'i are out of balance or "dirty," Shin is weak. Shin can be compared to the light given off by a candle. The greater the candle, the greater the light or aura. Shin is indeed the spiritual light and is the source of eternal peace and illumination. Shin resides in the Heart and is infinite and eternal. It is experienced as the bliss of unconditional Love. Shin is developed through compassion and giving from the Heart.

It is the ultimate goal of the Chinese health arts to nourish and experience the three Vital Treasures, Ching, Ch'i, and Shin. The Taoists have taught and demonstrated for thousands of years that those who follow this course of practice will be liberated from the normal human limits. The Taoists used special formulations of the tonic herbs to greatly enhance the development of the three Vital Treasures.

A number of the tonics have strong tonic action on one or more of the Treasures, and the highest levels of herb-combining emphasize the importance of including herbs that develop all three. Such a formulation gives true meaning to the word "elixir."

4 | The Major Tonic Herbs

The special class of herbs known as the tonics are easy to use. Tens of millions of people in the Orient use them regularly to maintain or build their health. A large and rapidly growing number of Westerners have discovered these incredible herbs and are now using them with great benefit.

To apply the system, one need know only a few herbs, understand the basic principles, and use common sense. Different herbs suit different people and are used at different times and under different circumstances. Each of the major tonics will be discussed in this chapter. By reading about each herb, one can select the ones that are appealing, both intellectually and intuitively. As one becomes familiar with the various herbs, the student is advised to obtain a small quantity of the herbs that seem appropriate and attractive. In this chapter, simple ways to use each of the herbs is explained. It is best to use one of these methods. A more complex formulary follows in the Chapter 6. It is best to wait until the various herbs have been explored before brewing up the more sophisticated compounds.

A rule of thumb is that one should experience benefits from the herbs *with no side-effects* within a reasonable period of time. Naturally, different herbs will exhibit their virtues in different lengths of time. Some, like ginseng, may show noticeable results within hours of consumption; whereas an herb like Schizandra may take some weeks before the desired results are obvious. Most herbs, however, will show their stuff within a few days. It will be explained in the text what to expect and when to expect it, approximately. If the results expected do not occur, or if undesirable side-effects are detected, the particular herbal being used should be altered or replaced by another. Guidance is helpful at the beginning, but information provided in this text is more than will be available in most cases and is quite sufficient if studied carefully.

Do not use any herb that results in even minor symptoms without expert advise. And, of course, it goes without saying that if there is doubt as to the safety of any herbals under the conditions of ill-health, consult a physician—preferably one who is familiar with natural healthcare and Chinese herbs. It is a strict rule of Chinese tonic herbalism that the tonic herbs are *not* to be used when acutely ill, even if the acute illness is just a common cold. Correct any acute ailments before starting to use the tonics, and suspend their use if and when you catch a cold or other acute illness.

Tonic herbs are the highest class of herbs, but may vary in quality from batch to batch, and from source to source. One herb may have a wide range of quality, and this will be reflected in the price, taste, and results. It is the author's opinion that, from the beginning, it is wise to use the highest grade herbs available since the initial period of use is quite important and sets the tone for future use. As you progress and become an expert on the herbs, you will automatically be very selective.

The herbs discussed in this text are the most widely used and reputedly beneficial of the Chinese tonic herbs. These herbs have been used over many centuries. Most herbal tonic formulae are composed of these. It is recommended that each herbalist who wishes to become truly expert in the art, try each of the herbs individually and in the suggested combinations in order to truly "know" each herb. Many readers will, however, not be looking to become "experts," but are merely looking for one or two excellent tonics for their own personal usage. In this case, trying just the herbs or herbals that are most attractive is quite sufficient.

GINSENG "The King of Herbs" (*Panax ginseng* C.A. Mey)

Panax Ginseng is one of the most famous and valued herbs used by mankind. It has been used by the Oriental people since the dawn of their civilization and has a rich and extensive history. Ginseng is becoming widely known and used in the West, and like any powerful herb, must be understood in order to be wisely and appropriately used.

Chinese name: *Renshen*
Chinese character: 人参

Traditional Characteristics:

Atmospheric energy: warm energy
Flavor: sweet and slightly bitter
Meridians: mainly Lung and Spleen; but also to some degree, the Kidney, Heart, Liver, and the six Yang organs.
Tonic action: energy tonic

Qualities Attributed to the Root: In the first *Chinese materia medica* (actual date unknown, but written more than two thousand years ago), Shen Nung said of ginseng: "Ginseng is a tonic to the five viscera, quieting the animal spirits, stabilizing the soul, preventing fear, expelling the vicious energies, brightening the eye and improving vision, opening up the heart benefiting the understanding, and if taken for some time will invigorate the body and prolong life." Ginseng has maintained its reputation for over 2,000 years!

The root is said to replace lost *Ch'i* to the meridians and organs. It is used to

benefit all the Ch'i so that one may live a long and happy life. As Louise Veninga says in her excellent book *The Ginseng Book*: "As far as I have been able to determine, ginseng does possess 'non-specific' restorative qualities which strengthen the stress mechanism and, by balancing the body's metabolic equilibrium, increases its efficiency. Those undergoing great physical or mental exertion highly praise ginseng's effect, offering them an alternative to 'pep' pills or caffeine . . . . Many who are spiritually oriented use ginseng while fasting as a valuable aid in obtaining effective spiritual progress. It is for the mind and spirit as well as the body."

Ginseng has been long revered not only by the populace at large, but by spiritual seekers as well. They maintain that ginseng clears perception so that one can understand the deep meanings of the changes which take place. Sages say that ginseng develops the "Center" (the Earth element), gives staying power and stamina, and benefits the three Vital Treasures: *Ching*, *Ch'i* and *Shin*. Because it provides all three of the Vital Treasures, ginseng is revered as a spiritual entity by the Taoists. Ch'an (Zen) Buddhists have said that ginseng speeds up one's karma, and eases the path of spiritual progress. Because ginseng enhances the power and control of the breath and the clarity of the mind, it is invaluable to one who meditates, performs yoga, studies a great deal or performs other like activities.

In combination with other herbs, ginseng can be either a stimulant or a sedative, but will always be tonic. Ginseng is beneficial to both men and women and is used commonly by both. It is a Western myth that ginseng should only be used by men. This is absolutely incorrect. As an energy tonic, it is excellent for women, just as it is for men. Stories about ginseng causing moustaches to grow on women are absurd. Beautiful feminine women take ginseng to maintain their vitality and sparkle, qualities that only enhance a woman's beauty. Ginseng is an excellent tonic to the reproductive systems of men and women alike.

Taoists say that ginseng has the strongest ability of any herb to absorb the energy from the earth. It absorbs the five elemental energies, which are then available in abundance to anyone who consumes ginseng. It becomes a storage vessel of the three Vital Treasures.

Ginseng is capable of extending the powers of adaptability to any who consume it. Those who use it wisely can become radiantly healthy beings, with an adaptive freedom unsurpassed by other men and women.

Varieties and Grading: Ginseng has been the most renowned of Chinese herbs for thousands of years. There are numerous varieties of this herb on the market and innumerable products of which it is an ingredient. The quality and effects vary considerably according to the source of the ginseng, its age at harvesting, and the method of preservation.

Basically, there are three main sources of ginseng: China, Korea, and Japan. There is also a variety of ginseng grown in America, but we will not be discussing that herb here.

Chinese Ginseng: Wild Manchurian Tung Pei ginseng is considered to be the finest of all ginseng, though Korean wild is in the same category. This Chinese variety is fat and white and bears a striking resemblance to the human shape. A wild ginseng root may be up to 200 years old and may be 20 to 30 cm. in length. These roots are of enormous value and sell in China for $3,000 to $10,000 an ounce. Of course, these are now very rare and hardly ever leave China. These wild roots grow only in rugged old mountains in slightly radioactive soil, and are said to glow in the dark. Consume one, it is said, and you are guaranteed a long and healthy life.

However, this is not the herb generally used in Chinese tonic herbalism. The cultivated variety is generally all that is available on the market. The cultivated varieties were, of course, derived from the wild Tung Pei and are in some cases quite excellent, but in other cases, useless.

China produces three main types of ginseng: 1. Yi Sun Ginseng. 2. Shiu Chu Ginseng, and 3. Kirin Ginseng.

Yi Sun ginseng is found growing wild, but is young. So it is transplanted into forest beds very similar to their wild habitat. When old enough, they are picked and sun-dried. These are very close in appearance and quality to true wild Tung Pei roots and cost about $35 per gram. These are available in America from a number of Chinese herb shops and specialty herb dealers.

Shiu Chu is the next grade and these roots are both common and excellent. These ginseng roots are cultivated on ginseng farms from superior stock. They are harvested after six years and preserved by steaming and soaking in date sugar and other herbs. The familiar reddish-brown color is lighter than that of preserved Korean ginseng roots. It is graded according to the size of the roots. The number of roots per "catty" (1.3 lbs.) determines a root's grade. Thus a Shiu Chu 16 root is larger than a Shiu Chu 35 root, because only 16 roots fit into a catty box. The larger the root, the more valuable. At the current time, a Shiu Chu 16 root retails at around $50 per root in the United States. Chinese Shiu Chu ginseng tones up the Yin energy and sedates the Yang. In particular, it is said to sedate "false fire" which manifests as anger, high blood pressure, tension headaches and *excessive* sexual desire.

Kirin ginseng is the lowest grade of Chinese ginseng, but is still of fine quality. These roots are the least expensive and are generally used in patent herbal tonics and commercial extracts, which are often quite useful. The roots are inexpensive and extracts are abundant on the open market. Kirin ginseng, like Shiu Chu ginseng, tonifies the Yin energy and sedates "false fire."

Korean Ginseng: Korean ginseng is not considered to be an import from China. The variety found in Korea appears to have been indigenous to that land and has somewhat different qualities than Chinese ginseng. Korean ginseng is of the utmost quality and in many cases is even superior to Chinese ginseng.

Wild Korean ginseng still can be found in the "old and wild" mountains. In South Korea, where "mountain men," the old Taoist hermits, still survive, these roots are still to be found and used. Wild roots found in these remote regions are virtually priceless in the city marketplaces of the Orient, especially if found by one of these hermits. Wild roots found in less rugged mountains are less valuable, but are still expensive and very effective in their actions.

The Koreans cultivate large amounts of high quality ginseng. This ginseng is sold throughout the world. There are two varieties: red and white. The best roots are steamed and preserved, which turns them a dark reddish-brown. White ginseng roots have been peeled and sun dried without further steaming or preservation. Korean roots are graded into three main categories: 1. Heaven grade, 2. Earth grade, and 3. Man grade. Heaven grade is the highest grade. "Heaven grade 15" is the best Korean red ginseng available. North Korean red Heaven 15 is considered to be next only to wild roots, but are rare in the United States for political reasons. South Korean Heaven 15 roots cost around $50 an ounce. Heaven 20, 25, and 30 are all considered to be superb roots. Earth grade roots are considered effective, but a small Heaven grade root is superior to a large Earth grade root. Man grade roots are of low quality and are rarely used by anyone using ginseng as a tonic. Smaller Heaven grade roots are fairly reasonably priced and well worth the price.

Korean white ginseng roots are fine for daily use as a light general tonic and "pick-up." However, many of the "instant" ginseng products available are suspect. Many of these products have very little ginseng of low quality, and are often composed primarily of fillers such as lactose. Whole white roots, on the other hand, are good. White ginseng has a less long-range tonic effect, but are very good and much less expensive than red ginseng. Large, Heaven grade white roots are truly excellent.

Korean ginseng is different in its effects than Chinese ginseng. It is quicker in its action and is generally more blatant. It tones up the Yang as well as the Yin, so it will increase the fire energy, thus stimulating sexual drive and assertive, willful behavior. It is therefore not recommended for people with Yang, hot conditions, but is excellent for those who lack Yang energy.

Japanese Ginseng: Japanese ginseng has a bad reputation because of its generally low quality, though Japanese roots look very good. However, some Japanese roots are excellent and are prized by ginseng connoisseurs who can recognize good ginseng. If the ginseng has little taste, it is probably quite weak. Good Japanese ginseng has the same rich flavor that is associated with Korean ginseng. Like Korean ginseng, good Japanese ginseng is effective in toning up both the Yin and Yang.

Selecting a Root: In selecting a root, use your knowledge of ginseng and Chinese herbalism wisely. Also let your intuition guide you, as a root that appeals to you will do you the most good. The author generally picks his roots by source, grade, price and the look on the face of the head of the root. Some roots have such wonderful countenances, however, that when you get it home you never want to use it!

In selecting a Korean ginseng root, one must be very careful not to be sold a counterfeit product. Counterfeit roots are weak roots that are often quite large.

These are generally sold at "bargain" prices, but are in fact no bargain. You cannot buy a Heaven 15 or 20 ginseng root for $10. If someone tries to sell you one at such a price, look elsewhere. It is imperative that you know your ginseng dealer and that the dealer knows his business. The sources listed in the appendix are reputable experts and are thus good sources of ginseng. Many other excellent sources also exist, but one must always be careful.

Modern Knowledge: Because of ginseng's reputation, considerable research has been conducted into its chemistry and pharmacology. Most of the claims for ginseng have been confirmed.

Ginseng contains saponin, ginsenin, panoxic acid, panaxin, panaquilon, volatile oils, vitamins B_1 and B_2, calcium, potassium, iron, sodium, silicon, magnesium, titanium, barium, strontium, aluminum, manganese, sugar, starch, mucilage, and several steroids.

Saponin affects sugar metabolism. Ginsenin acts somewhat like insulin. Panoxic acid regulates metabolism and the functioning of the cardiovascular system, and helps prevent cholesterol buildup. Panaxin is a direct central nervous system stimulant and is a cardiovascular tonic. Panaquilon is a general endocrine tonic and has regulatory actions on the endocrine system, probably at the hypothalamic and pituitary levels. The volatile oils seem to be direct stimulants to various brain centers.

The steroids in ginseng are responsible for many of it effects. These steroids are similar to the human sex hormones testosterone and estrogen, as well as being closely related to cortisol (cortisone) and other adrenalcortical hormones. The adrenal hormones regulate many of our most important metabolic and adaptive functions.

A great deal of research has been done to determine the mechanisms of action of ginseng. Space does not allow us to pursue this subject in detail in this volume. There are several excellent books available that are entirely devoted to ginseng, and these texts detail a tremendous amount of scientific research. It is important to emphasize here, though, the most interesting finding in this research. Most research conducted in China, Japan, the United States, the Soviet Union, and elsewhere in recent years points to ginseng's ability to allow its consumers to handle stress much more efficiently. Ginseng seems to bolster the functioning of the adrenal cortex and the central nervous system in their functions of adaptation.

Ginseng also contains what are known as "ginsenosides." Behavioral studies in rats have shown that some ginsenosides can decrease fatigue and promote learning in rats. Studies done in the U.S.S.R. have shown that ginsenosides have gonatrophic effects, increasing the weight of the testes in test animals. Japanese research has shown that ginseng can increase the number of active sperm. Ginseng has been shown to have beneficial effects on the adrenals, the thyroid, and in particular the pituitary.

One of the potentially most important studies conducted on ginseng has confirmed that an alcoholic extract of ginseng can increase the anti-radiation capability in rats. Rats were fed ginseng and then exposed to lethal levels of radiation. The ginseng-fed rats' survival time was extended 100% as compared to the control group.

Ginseng has become a prime example of an "adaptogenic" agent. Scores of research projects have been conducted which have shown that animals given ginseng as a regular part of their diet are able to function normally, or more normally, under stressful conditions than animals fed normal diets but no ginseng. Animals fed ginseng consistently outperform animals not fed ginseng and can survive under conditions normally intolerable to that species. Ginseng seems to relieve what is known as the "stress syndrome" which occurs after prolonged stress of either physical or mental origin. Laboratory animals given ginseng do not develop enlarged adrenals (a dangerous sign), high blood pressure, neurosis, or deficiency of ascorbic acid (vitamin C) in the adrenals even when exposed to stresses that normally would cause these reactions. Experimental animals fed ginseng have been shown to have significantly greater physical endurance than animals fed a normal diet but no ginseng. Laboratory animals fed ginseng have been shown to outlive animals not fed ginseng by 14% of a lifetime.

Ginseng has been shown to be an excellent tonic to pituitary and adrenal deficiency syndromes and is used as a standard therapeutic agent for these syndromes in Chinese and Japanese hospitals.

Preparation and Dosage: Ginseng may be taken raw or cooked. A common way to use ginseng is to buy a root, steam it until it is soft enough to slice and then slice into pieces the thickness of a penny. Suck and chew on one or several pieces a day.

Ginseng may also be used raw by grinding it to a powder in a coffee grinder. It should be prepared as above before putting in a home grinder. The powder may be mixed with other ground herbs or taken alone in capsules, which can be purchased at the health food or drug store. Take several capsules a day. Capsules of powdered ginseng are widely available on the market in a variety of grades. Pills of ground and pressed ginseng are also available, such as "Four Ginsengs Dragon Eggs" by East Earth Herbs.

Ginseng extracts are also very popular. There are several excellent brands on the market. "Panax Ginseng Extract" from China is good and is also inexpensive. Many other excellent extracts are produced in Korea. Or you may make your own. Place a root in any preferred spirit (wine, vodka, brandy, etc.). Though not essential, it is considered sound practice to place several jujube dates in the jar with the ginseng. Allow this to sit for several weeks, then consume one shot a day at bedtime or in hot water after dinner. This is a very common and excellent method of consuming one's daily dose of ginseng. Taoists often perferred alcoholic herbal tonics, but *never* abused the method by over-imbibing.

Generally speaking, however, ginseng is usually *cooked* in combination with other herbs. Many formulae using ginseng are given in the Chapter 6. Ginseng goes well with many other well known Chinese herbs, such as Zizyphus jujube (jujube dates), Polygonum multiflorum (Ho Shou Wu), Angelicae sinensis (Tang Kuei), and Astragalus membranaceus (Huang Ch'i).

A very famous formula for ginseng commonly prescribed as a tonic by Chinese herbalists is a combination of equal parts of the following herbs: Ginseng, dried ginger, Atractylus, and Glycyrrhizae (licorice root). This combination, known as "Ginseng Soup," is especially beneficial to the digestive and metabolic functions and provides warmth and energy to the muscles.

Ginseng must never be cooked in a metal pot, and actually should not even be sliced with a steel knife, though this is generally not practical. Cook ginseng, and for that matter all Chinese tonic teas, in an enamel or glass pot. Bring two ounces (total) of herbs in four cups of water to a boil, then simmer for one hour or until one or two cups of brew remain. Drink while warm, before meals. The herbs may be recooked twice more before being ground into the dog food or otherwise composted. Many herbalists feel that it is the *second* cooking that is actually the most potent; so by all means, do not waste these valuable herbs by discarding them prematurely.

Actually, the best way to prepare ginseng teas is in a "ginseng cooker," which is a porcelain double-boiler unit. No waste occurs with this method. With a ginseng cooker, good ginseng essence is not lost in steam, and less of the herbs yields a richer final product. Again, the herbs should be used over several times. In fact, a "ginseng cooker" is the best way to prepare practically all of the tonic brews. These"ginseng cookers," which are quite lovely and reasonably priced, are available from herb suppliers (see *Sources* in the Appendix).

In summary, select your ginseng wisely, prepare it with respect and use it properly, and you will experience the full effects of the "King of Herbs."

TANG KUEI (*Radix Angelicae sinensis*)

Tang Kuei is very highly praised and widely used in the Orient. It is known to be an excellent blood tonic and, though beneficial to men and women alike, is considered to be the ultimate woman's tonic herb.

    Chinese name: Tang Kuei
    Chinese character: 當歸

Traditional Characteristics:

    Atmospheric energy: warm energy
    Flavor: sweet-pungent
    Meridians: Heart, Liver, Spleen, and Kidney
    Tonic action: blood tonic

Qualities Attributed to the Root: Tang Kuei is very important in Chinese herbalism. It is the most highly praised blood tonic used in the East. Tang Kuei is used by women to regulate the menstrual function and as a sedative. Though this root is extremely popular with women, men too can use Tang Kuei to build blood with no problems. It is said to clean the blood, and to act as a hematonic.

Tang Kuei is used by millions and millions of Oriental women to tonify their sex organs and to maintain normal reproductive functioning. Tang Kuei can be used before, during, and after pregnancy. It has been proven to benefit the entire female hormonal system.

When cooked, it is a powerful blood tonic. It is said to warm up the inner organs, improve circulation, beautify the skin, hasten healing of cuts and wounds, and to act as a sedative. Since most women have a tendency to be slightly anemic, Tang Kuei is popularly used in its cooked form to build blood.

The root eaten raw also has a blood tonic effect, though slightly less than when cooked. However, it has been shown that raw Tang Kuei has a stronger regulatory effect on the female reproductive system and is also used raw to heal the reproductive and vascular tissues.

The whole root is said to "harmonize" the blood, meaning that it contributes to healthy blood composed of a proper proportion of elements. The middle part of the root is said to preserve the internal organs and to nourish the blood. In general practice, the whole root is used.

Varieties and Grading: Tang Kuei mostly comes from the Chinese provinces of Szechuan and Kansu in southwestern China. The root is grown for one year, then harvested, peeled and dried in the shade. The larger the root and the sweeter the taste, the better the quality. If it is very sweet (Tang Kuei is never purely sweet, but always has a pungent flavor as well), it is of high quality. If, on the other hand, it is very bitter, it will not be of much benefit, if at all. Most Tang Kuei available is of "average" grade and is mildly sweet-pungent. If you get to know your source, they may favor you by selling you a higher grade if you request it. In any case, do not purchase very small roots. Also, you might ask the source. Korean Tang Kuei is considered to be very weak. As with ginseng, "bargain" Tang Kuei should be passed up. Tang Kuei is relatively inexpensive (a few dollars an ounce), so go for the best.

Modern Knowledge: *Radix Angelicae sinensis* contains volatile oils which give it its distinctive action and aroma. It also contains Vitamin B_{12}, Nicotinic acid, Vitamin E, and Sucrose. Laboratory tests have shown that Tang Kuei consumed raw or with alcohol relaxes the uterus. Used with water, it will tonify the uterus and can stimulate its contraction. It has been found to cause an increase in circulation of blood in the uterus and can result in developing an undeveloped uterus. It has been found to be laxative and to relieve congestion of the tissues of the pelvic cavity.

It has been shown to aid both males and females to absorb and utilize Vitamin E. Tang Kuei has been found to lower blood pressure, slow down the pulse rate, and relax cardiac muscle. It has been demonstrated that *Angelicae sinensis* has bacteriacidal action against such bacteria as *Bacillus Dysenteriae* and *Staphylococcus*. Extracts of this herb have been show *in vitro* and *in vivo* antiviral and antifungal activity. It is known to stabilize blood sugar levels, and is used by both Eastern and Western-style physicians in the Orient to treat all symptoms of menopause.

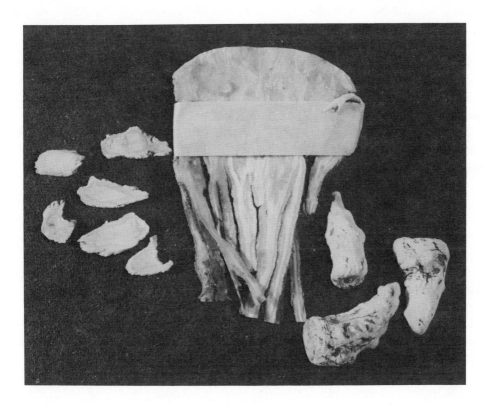

Preparation and Dosage: Tang Kuei, like ginseng, may be consumed raw or cooked, alone or in combination with other herbs.

To eat it raw, as a blood purifier, steam *slightly* (for just a few minutes) to soften and slice into pieces the thickness of a penny. Allow these to dry in a flat basket in a warm dry place not in direct sunlight. When dry (usually around 24 hours), put in a dark jar to store. Eat a piece or two each day. The taste of Tang Kuei raw is definitely palatable, though it will take a few days before you actually start *liking* it. However, most people who eat raw Tang Kuei *do* acquire a real liking for its unique flavor and become quite attached to their Tang Kuei routine.

Tang Kuei is a main component (25%) of a very famous and widely used commercial tonic called "Shou Wu Chih" which also contains several other famous tonics. It is a superb blood tonic, beneficial to the circulatory and reproductive systems. It comes in liquid form, the highly concentrated extract of several great tonic herbs. This is taken by adding one tablespoon (or more if so desired) of "Shou Wu Chih" to a cup of boiling water, letting it steep for five minutes and then drinking. It is traditional to drink this tonic tea twice a day: once before breakfast and again at bedtime. This amazing concoction adds energy to our day and helps us sleep deeply at night. Consumed in this manner for a few weeks, "Shou Wu Chih" will prove to have remarkable tonic effects on sexual functioning. Beware; 'tis powerful stuff!

To prepare a Tang Kuei root for drinking, cook one root with six Chinese red jujube dates in 3 cups of water. Simmer until one cup remains and drink one half cup. Repeat twice a day for three days. Due to the very pleasant taste of the red jujube dates, this is the most popular way to prepare Tang Kuei.

Or, prepare chicken soup using three Tang Kuei roots in addition to whatever other vegetables you would normally add. Consume the soup over a four-day period. This popular method of preparing Tang Kuei is considered extremely tonic and nourishing. It is the most highly recommended way of taking Tang Kuei when *recovering* from an illness. It is also recommended for those who are overly thin, pale and weak. Chicken soup with Tang Kuei will build blood and flesh. For convenience, a chicken soup extract with Tang Kuei is available in Chinese markets. Of course, chicken soup itself is recognized the world over as a tonic.

A very famous brew known as "Four Things Soup" is composed of equal parts of Tang Kuei, *Rehmannia glutinosa*, *Peonia albiflora*, and *Rhizoma Ligusticum*. This is the most widely prescribed woman's tonic by Chinese herbalists. It is the great standard, used by all Chinese herbalists to help their female patients balance their reproductive systems, especially to regulate the hormone balance and menstrual cycle.

Tang Kuei is also widely combined with *Radix Astragalus* to improve the blood circulation in both men and women. If one's flesh is stiff, pale, or chilly, or if the feet and hands are often cold, this brew will improve circulation and warm up the outer regions of the body. It is excellent during the winter months, especially for those who have to spend much time out of doors. Those using "Shou Wu Chih" will not need this brew.

There are also concentrated extracts of Tang Kuei available which may simply be added to tea or other beverage.

CHINESE LICORICE ROOT (*Glycyrrhizae uralensis*)

Licorice root stands next to ginseng in importance in Chinese herbalism. It is the most widely used of all Chinese herbs. It is known as the "Grandfather of Chinese herbs," as the "Great Adjunct," and as the "Great Detoxifier." It is used as a harmonizing ingredient in a large number of Chinese herbal recipes and is itself an excellent tonic and longevity herb.

Chinese name: Kan Tsao
Chinese character: 甘草

Traditional Characteristics:

Atmospheric energy: neutral energy
Flavor: very sweet
Meridians: enters all twelve meridians, though it is especially beneficial to
　　　　　　the Spleen, Stomach, Kidney and Lung
Tonic action: energy tonic

Qualities Attributed to the Root: Chinese licorice root is said to revitalize the
"Center," referring to the "middle burning space." It supplements the energy
and strikes a balance into the internal regions of the body. It is believed to drive
out all poisons and toxins from the system and to eliminate side-effects from
other herbs used with it. Thus it is called the "Great Detoxifier" and the "Great
Adjunct."

It is said to be especially tonic to the Spleen and Kidney, and regulating
to the Stomach. It acts as a blood tonic through its effect on the Kidney (bone
marrow) and Spleen. It sedates and soothes excess fire, generally called "false
fire," and moistens the lungs and throat.

The "Great Adjunct" is said to aid all other herbs in entering their respective meridians and is thus of tremendous importance in the Chinese tonic herbal system. It is also believed that licorice will clean the meridians and allow *Ch'i* to flow smoothly. It is also widely claimed that licorice root builds flesh (muscle) and beautifies the countenance.

Licorice root is also used throughout the Orient simply because it builds energy. It is now known that this is at least partly due to its remarkable power to regulate blood sugar balance. It is also widely used to sharpen the power of concentration. Licorice root relieves abdominal pain and congestion and benefits the functions of the abdominal organs. It has been used successfully for a thousand years in cases of anorexia, a symptom now a growing health problem in the West.

It is said that licorice root is effective in relieving the intoxication due to bad food, drugs and alcohol. An old Chinese herbal classic says that "licorice is the cure for thinness and can change the weak into the strong." The same classic states that "licorice is the master of toxic *Ch'i* of the world and the mountains and rivers and the fog and dew; it eliminates the toxins of the earth and miasma."

Shen Nung, China's first great herbalist, said: "licorice root is the master herb of the hot and cold evil *Ch'i* of the viscera. It fortifies the sinews and bones and muscle growth, and doubles our strength; it cures swollen wounds due to wrenching and cutting, and detoxifies the blood and energy."

Another old herbal text says that "licorice root is the master of acuteness, and relieves pain and tension due to stress."

Licorice root is obviously quite highly regarded by those who know and use the Chinese tonic herbs. When used over a long period of time, Chinese licorice root is said to produce radiant health and to prolong life.

Varieties and Grading: Chinese licorice root is a very different herb from the Western variety of licorice, *Glycyrrhizae glabra*. The Western variety can cause nervousness, an obviously undesirable side-effect. To the contrary, Chinese licorice, *Glycyrrhizae uralensis*, is energizing but calming, and does not have the side-effects associated with Western licorice. Be *sure* to use *Chinese licorice* root.

Licorice grows widely in northern China. Larger roots with smooth pulpy texture are most desirable. If the root, when cut in cross section, is a rich yellow, it is of high quality. The sweeter the taste, the more effective the herb, since the sweetness reflects the quantity of ist most important active ingredient, glycyrrhizin.

Modern Knowledge: *Radix Glycyrrhizae* contains glycyrrhizin (6–14%), glycyrramarin, liquiritin and other flavinoids, mannitol, glucose, sucrose and starch, etc. Glycyrrhizin is the substance responsible for the sweet taste. Glycyrrhizin binds 50 molecules of sucrose. This molecule, with its load of sucrose flows through the blood stream. Upon commands from the adrenal cortex due to sudden energy requirements, the bound sucrose is detached and utilized for the energy needs of the body and mind. It thus acts something like a time capsule. Because of this activity, blood sugar levels can be stabilized, eliminating the manic hypoglycemic syndrome.

In pharmaceutical tests, it has been found that glycyrrhizin has a function similar to that of adrenalcortical hormones. It is almost identical to the adrenal steroids. Laboratory tests in China have demonstrated that extracts of *Radix Glycyrrhizae* can help to eliminate or detoxify over 1,200 known toxins. This remarkable capacity as a detoxifying agent is virtually unparalleled in the realm of pharmacology.

Licorice has been shown to increase intestinal peristalsis and regulate the bowels. Recent studies have shown that licorice combined with ginseng is a specific pituitary tonic, improving overall hormonal functioning. Compounds isolated from this herb have been found to have anti-inflammatory, antibacterial, and antitussive activity.

Preparation and Dosage: Licorice root may be chewed raw, or may be cooked and used as a tea. Children have long been encouraged to chew slices of the root, which is believed to encourage growth and muscular development. It is thus known as "wood candy" and is a favorite of children who come to know it. Once they have discovered it, children need no coaxing to chew on this delicious herb. Whenever the author's son (aged 10) can get his hands in the herb jar, he fills his pockets with licorice root. Chewing the "wood candy," he seems much less attracted to gum and candy.

Licorice, like many other Chinese tonic herbs, may be extracted in alcohol. Place 8 to 12 slices of licorice root in a jar of alcohol such as vodka. Allow to sit for a few weeks. The result is a delicious liqueur. However, only one or two shots a day, after dinner, is sufficient to improve health. Excessive drinking defeats the purpose.

Most commonly, licorice root is used as an *adjunct* to other herbs, which are either boiled or ground into a powder and taken in capsules or pills. See "Ginseng" for the recipe for "Ginseng Soup."

A very excellent way to use licorice was taught to the author by Master Sung Jin Park. Combine four or five slices of licorice root with a slightly larger portion of Dendrobium (discussed later), bring to a boil and simmer for about 20 minutes. This combination has long been used by the Taoists to replace Kidney energy spent in handling stress, and is recommended for those who have endulged in excessive sexual activity. This combination, which we call "Suk Gok and Licorice" (*Suk Gok* is the Korean name for Dendrobium, a type of orchid), quickly replaces the lost energy. Suk Gok and Licorice is *delicious*, simple to prepare, and can be used as a safe and excellent daily tonic tea. This combination is excellent for those involved in the healing arts, as it provides "healing energy." The author, for many years, operated a large acupressure school and clinic in Santa Monica, California. At the "Acupressure Workshop," Suk Gok and Licorice was always brewing so that the teachers, practitioners, clients and students could drink it as they wished. It was ever popular, and many thousands of people swear by its rejuvenating power, not to mention its good taste.

As mentioned above, licorice may be combined with a commercial grade of ginseng in equal proportions and consumed on a daily basis as a tea. This is an excellent whole-body tonic via the endocrine system. It is considered a particularly excellent tonic for postpartum mothers.

   In counteracting an anorexic tendency or frailness and weakness after an illness, decoct licorice root with Codonopsis, Atractylus, and Poria, in equal proportions and drink two or three times daily. These other herbs will all be described in detail later. This combination should regulate the appetite and metabolic processes. It will also improve energy and build blood, confirmed through clinical use in Chinese hospitals.

HO SHOU WU (*Polygonum multiflorum*)

Ho Shou Wu is a very famous herb in the Orient, used by millions regularly to help develop *Ch'i*. It is China's most renowned "longevity herb." It has acquired a broad reputation as a youth preserver, rejuvenator and sexual tonic. It is an extremely important herb in the Chinese tonic system.

   Chinese name: Ho Shou Wu
   Chinese character: 何首烏

Traditional Characteristics:

   Atmospheric energy: warm energy
   Flavor: bitter-sweet
   Meridians: Liver and Kidney
   Tonic action: energy tonic

Qualities Attributed to the Root: The roots are tonic and nutritious. Ho Shou Wu is said to build strength in the Liver and Kidney, and also in the muscles and bones. It is said to preserve, or even rejuvenate, the original color of one's hair and to increase the "generative energy," increasing the sperm in men and fertility in women. It will calm the nervous system and clear the eyes. Its strength comes from its remarkable ability to cleanse the body by cleaning the kidney and liver, which in turn clean the blood. By virtue of its ability to accumulate tremendous quantities of *Ch'i* into its root, this herb will tonify these organs and will fortify the blood. Though Ho Shou Wu provides abundant *Ch'i*, it is not a stimulant, and is in fact slightly sedative.

   "The root, when old," says Li Chih Shen, a great Ming Dynasty herbalist, "is said to have mysterious properties. At fifty years it is as large as a fist and is designated 'mountain slave' and if taken for a year will preserve the color of the hair and moustache; that at a hundred years is as large as a bowl, is called 'hill-brother' and if taken for one year, a rubicund and cheerful countenance will be preserved; that at 150 years is as large as a basin, is called 'hill uncle' and if taken for one year the teeth will fall out and come afresh; that at 200 years is the size of a one peck ozier basket, is called 'hill father,' and if taken for one year the countenance will become like that of a youth, and the gait will equal that of a running horse; and that at 300 years is the size of a 2 peck ozier basket, is called 'mountain spirit' and has a pure ethereal substance, and if taken for some time, one becomes an earthly immortal. Wonderful restorative and reviving powers are ascribed to the ordinary root."

Varieties and Grading: The tuberous root generally comes sliced. The larger the tuber, the more efficacious and valuable the herb. Most of the Ho Shou Wu on the market is of average to good grade. Very old roots are very rare, though the author is told that they are occasionally obtainable in China. Dark slices are the most potent, while those heavily streaked with white are of lower quality. If the tuber is neatly sliced, this is an indication that the root is of higher grade.

Modern Knowledge: Extracts of *Polygonum multiflorum* have in animals shown antitumor activity. It has also shown sedative and antipyretic effects and anti-progestational activity. *Polygonum multiflorum* has been shown to have anti-inflammatory activity, to decrease blood coagulability, to have cardiotonic, hypotensive, and vasodilatory activity.

Preparation and Dosage: Ho Shou Wu is a basic ingredient in many tonic herbal preparations. It may be eaten alone, raw. Sugar coated pilled of raw 100% Ho Shou Wu are popular. These are marketed as "Shou Wu Pian."

Ho Shou Wu is a main constituent of a great formula known as "Longevity Herbal." Longevity Herbal is a formula developed by Grand Master Moo San

Do Sha, Sung Jin Park's master. Moo San Do Sha is an herbalist of the highest order. Longevity Herbal is a perfectly balanced combination of well known and rare tonic herbs designed to develop the three Vital Treasures, *Ching*, *Ch'i* and *Shin*, and thus to enable one to attain "radiant health" and spiritual bliss. The formula is too complex to elaborate upon here and contains several rare herbs, but Longevity Herbal is available already prepared (see *Sources* in the Appendix).

Ho Shou Wu is also the other main ingredient in "Shou Wu Chih." The very popular and potent commercial tonic imported from the People's Republic of China. "Shou Wu Chih" was discussed under Tang Kuei, which is the other major ingredient.

If you wish to prepare your own tonic brew, cook Ho Shou Wu with an equal amount of ginseng. This is what Li Ch'ing Yuen did, and he lived to be 252 years old. Or extract these two herbs together in a jar of alcohol. Consume one *sake*-cupful daily, after dinner or just before bedtime.

SCHIZANDRAE FRUCTUS (*Schizandra chinensis*)

Schizandra is a very special herb. It was for a great while highly favored by the wealthy classes of China, especially by the emperors and royal women. Its fame is due to its reputation as a youth preserver, beautifier and as a powerful sexual tonic. The part used is the small fruit which has a delicious flavor.

Chinese name: Wu Wei Tza or O Mi Cha
Chinese character: 五味子

Traditional Characteristics:

Atmospheric energy: warm energy
Flavor: sour-salty, with sweet, pungent and bitter overtones
Meridians: Lung, Kidney, and Liver
Tonic action: Yin and Yang tonic

Qualities Attributed to the Fruit: The name Wu Wei Tza means "five flavors herb," associated with the five elemental energies. However, its main taste is sour and salty. It is said to increase the functioning of the Lung, Liver and Kidney.

It increases the Water Ch'i in the Kidney and increases the "water of the genital organs" considerably, referring to sexual fluids. It relieves sexual fatigue and is quite famous for increasing the sexual staying power in men. It causes the female genitals to feel warm, healthy, extremely sensitive, with a healthy amount of "female elixir." Wu Wei Tza provides abundant Ching energy, the energy of the Kidney. It is well known as an aphrodisiac when used properly and combined with other herbs, for both men and women, and has thus been a popular herb in the wealthy households of China, including those of the emperors. It would have undoubtedly been widely used by all classes of Chinese but for its relative scarcity until recent times.

Wu Wei Tza drives out "false fire" Ch'i (anger and neck-shoulder tension) from the body. It is also widely used to beautify the skin and to protect the skin from the sun and wind. For this reason, it has been very popular with China's wealthy women. It is also used to drive out mucous and to protect the lungs and to build the Wei Ch'i (the defense energy which flows in the skin).

Wu Wei Tza develops the basic energy of life and is thus of great use to all, even to those who are not sexually active. It is mildly sedative (calming) and is said to have pain-alleviating properties. It generates vitality and radiant beauty when used regularly for some time. If used for 100 days successively, Wu Wei Tza is said to purify the blood, rejuvenate the Kidney energy (especially the sexual energy), brighten the mind, and cause the skin to become radiant.

Due to the fact that all five classical flavors can be detected in Wu Wei Tza, it is believed to contain the quintessence of the five elemental energies as the basis of its properties.

Varieties and Grading: All Wu Wei Tza on the market is of good grade and quality. However, the fresher the better. All are dried in the preservation process, but fresher Wu Wei Tza has more luster and is fuller than an older batch.

Modern Knowledge: Schizandra chinensis contains shisandrin, schisandrol, volatile oil, chamigrenal, malic acid, citric acid, tartaric acid, Vitamin C, etc. Extracts of this plant have shown *in vitro* activity against Mycobacterium tuberculosis. Extracts also are able to induce non-specific resistance in man, comparable to similar effects well established for Panax Ginseng.

Preparation and Dosage: Wu Wei Tza contains tannin, which can be difficult on the digestive system, especially if the person's stomach and digestive system is weak. Tannin is water-soluble, so Wu Wei Tza must be soaked in pure water for at least several hours before using. If the berries are soaked and the tea is not overcooked, there should be no difficulties. A few sources sell the berries pre-soaked (see *Sources* in the Appendix).

Soak a handful of Wu Wei Tza in a pot of water for several hours, or preferably overnight. Throw out the water and rinse the berries. Add three fresh cups of water and a few slices of licorice root. You may also add an equal quantity of lycii berries. Simmer about 15 minutes (be careful not to make the tea too strong). Drink this tea daily for 100 days to cleanse the blood, build Ching energy of the Kidney, to beautify the skin, and to build superb sexual stamina. Besides being a marvelous tonic, it is very delicious. This is one you may wish to serve to friends.

LYCII FRUCTUS (*Lycium chinensis*)

Lycii (pronounced Lee-Chee) is a widely used major tonic herb. It has great renown as a longevity herb since it was used by Li Ch'ing Yuen who lived to be over two hundred and fifty years old. It is also very popular because these berries are easy to use in cooking and are quite delicious. Lycii brightens the spirit.

Chinese name: Kou Chi Tza
Chinese character: 枸杞子

Traditional Characteristics:

Atmospheric energy: mild energy
Flavor: sweet
Meridians: Liver, Kidney, and Lung
Tonic action: blood tonic

Qualities Attributed to the Berries: Lycii berries are well known as a Liver tonic and also as an excellent blood tonic. Prolonged consumption of Lycii is said to promote cheerfulness. Consumption of Lycii is said to increase vitality and brighten the eyes, especially improving night vision. Regular consumption of Lycii is said to lead to a long life.

It is said that Lycii strengthens and invigorates the legs. Lycii berries are also said to be constructive and otherwise beneficial to the complexion. Lycii is mildly sedative and calms the heart and nervous system.

Varieties and Grading: Lycii berries should be a vibrant red color. If they are brown or brownish-red, they have been in storage too long. They should also be pleasantly sweet and tender. If they are anything but sweet, or are dry and crunchy, they are too old.

Modern Knowledge: Lycium chinensis has shown central nervous system stimulant and autonomic effects in laboratory animals. It has shown hypoglycemic, hyperglycemic and antifungal effects, and is being used in modern Chinese hospitals for hypertension, nephritis and for cancer.

Preparation and Dosage: Blend with other tonic herbs or use in cooking as did Li Ch'ing Yuen. Consume daily. The berries are quite edible,
Make a brew with equal parts of Lycii and Schizandra. This is one of China's most famous tonic brews.
Or, decoct with Rehmannia as a Kidney tonic, especially if sexual vitality is desired. Cook with ginseng for the same purpose.

ASTRAGALI RADIX (*Astragalus membranaceus*)

Astragalus is one of the most popular tonic herbs used in the Orient. It is a tonic to the essential energy and is a favorite of young adults as an energizer.

> Chinese name: Huang Ch'i
> Chinese character: 黄耆

> ### *Traditional Characteristics:*

> Atmospheric energy: warm energy
> Flavor: sweet
> Meridians: Spleen, Lung and Triple Warmer
> Tonic action: energy tonic

Qualities Attributed to the Root: Huang Ch'i is said to strengthen the primary energy and to tonify the three burning spaces. It is famed as a specific energizer to the outside of the body and is therefore beneficial to younger adults, who tend to be physically active. Some people consider *Astragalus* to be a tonic superior to ginseng for younger people.

 Astragalus is believed to be strengthening to the legs and arms, and is traditionally used by people who work outdoors, especially in the cold, because of its strengthening and warming nature. As an energizer to the outside of the body, *Astragalus* is used to tonify the protective energy (*Wei Ch'i*) which circulates just under the skin. *Wei Ch'i* is the Yang counterpart of the more Yin nutritional energy (*Ying Ch'i*) which flows through the twelve meridians and supplies the organs with vital energy. Wei, like Ying, is generated in the Lungs and after the Lungs have extracted *Ch'i* from the air and the Stomach and Spleen extract *Ch'i* from food. The air and food energies are united in the Lung to generate the "essential energy." Ying and Wei are the two components of the essential energy. *Wei Ch'i* circulates in the subscutaneous tissues providing suppleness to the flesh and adaptive energy to the skin. It is the *Wei Ch'i* which provides the energy to perspire, produce goose flesh or shiver. If *Wei Ch'i* is deficient, exhausted or blocked, environmental forces such as heat, cold, humidity, wind, etc. (the so-called "vicious energies") will penetrate through the flesh and injure the flesh, blood and inner organs. *Astragalus*, in tonifying the Lung, especially its Yang component, helps the body build an abundance of free flowing *Wei Ch'i*, thus fortifying the defense mechanism.

 Astragalus is also a blood tonic (*Ch'i* leads blood). It helps to regulate fluid metabolism, and those who consume it regularly are said to rarely suffer from fluid retention and bloating. It is also now considered an excellent regulatory

tonic to the sugar metabolizing functions, especially when combined with licorice root.

Used with *Tang Kuei*, it is said to be of great value in improving blood circulation. Used with ginseng, it is claimed to build respiratory endurance, especially for those who work physically or are involved in sports. Many experts recommend that younger people use *Astragalus* where older people should use ginseng because *Astragalus* effects the outer energy more while ginseng effects the inner energy. Of course the two combined make a balanced herbal that effects both inner and outer energy, warming up the entire body, inside and out.

Varieties and Grading: *Astragalus* is a very popular herb and appears on the market in many varieties and grades. The highest quality *Astragalus* are large roots, usually cut into long, thin slices. These slices will reveal a yellowish core to the root. Pale, crooked, or thin roots are of lower quality. *Astragalus* is one of the more expensive Chinese tonic herbs, ranking with ginseng in demand by those "in the know."

Modern Knowledge: Extracts of *Astragalus membranaceus* have shown *in vitro* antibacterial effects as well as hypoglycemic activity in animals.

A recent article published in *Cancer*, a publication of the American Cancer Society, reports that the aqueous extract of *Astragalus membranaceus* restored the immune functions in 90% of cancer patients studied. The article states that the cellular immune response is usually impaired in cancer patients, especially in those with advanced disease. Immune response is further compromised by radiation and/or chemotherapy. *Astragalus* has been found to be a "response modifier" which favorably modulates the subnormal immune apparatus of cancer patients. In studies performed at the National Cancer Institute and five other leading American Cancer Research Institutes over the past eight years, it has been positively shown that *astragalus* strengthens a cancer patients immune system. Researchers believed, on the basis of cell studies, that *astragalus* augments those white blood cells that fight disease and removes some of those that make the body more vulnerable to it. There is clinical evidence that cancer patients give *astragalus* during chemotherapy or radiation, both of which reduce the body's natural immunity while attacking the cancer, recover significantly faster and live longer. It is evident that nothing is *astragalus* directly attacks cancers themselves, but instead strengthens the body's own immune system.

In these same studies, both in the laboratory and with 572 cancer patients, it also been found that *astragalus* promotes adrenal cortical function, which also is critically diminished in cancer patients. *Astragalus* also ameliorates bone marrow depression and gastrointestinal toxity caused by chemotherapy and radiation therapy.

Chinese researchers, conducting parallel research, have found that *astragalus* enables mice to resist highly infectious viruses and to produce larger amount of interferon. Interferon is a vital cellular protein that inhibits viral growth and is believed to be effective against virus-related cancers.

Because of astragalus' ability to strengthen the immune system, it is now being looked into as a possible treatment for the acquired immune deficiency syndrome, better known as AIDS. *Astragalus* reduces the so-called "T-Suppressor Cells" which inhibits one's immunity, and are found in high numbers in AIDS patients. T-Suppressor Cells also are more prevalent in the elderly, making them more succeptible to disease. Thus *astragalus* is being studied for its potential ability to prolong life.

A group of researchers in Texas recently reported that when *astragalus* extract is added to a culture medium in which human lung cell mass is grown, the cellular aging process appears to be significantly postponed. In two identical groups of cultured cell mass, one treated with *astragalus*, and one not, the untreated cells survived 61 to 66 reproductive generations, while the cells treated with *astragalus* survived an average of 98 generations—a 50% increase in life expectancy.

Astragalus membranaceus contains a number of active ingredients, including: glycosides, choline, betaine, linoleic acid, linolenic acid, isoamnitine, and kumatakenin.

Preparation and Dosage: *Astragalus* combines well with many herbs. Combine with ginseng in various proportions in order to attain stamina and strength. Or blend with *Tang Kuei* to encourage *Astragalus'* warming and blood tonic qualities. It also combines to form a fantastic tonic with *Ho Shou Wu* and/or licorice root. Another choice: brew with ginseng *and Ho Shou Wu* or brew with *Tang Kuei* and *Ho Shou Wu.*

All of the above combinations should be simmered for ½ to 1 hour. Drink one cupful from one to three times a day before meals on a regular basis.

To build strength and muscle, combine with *Codonopsis, Atractylus* and licorice root. This formula is diuretic.

For older people who suffer from arthritis pain and numbness, there is a tonic composed of *Cinnamomun cassia, Zingeber officional, Paeonia lactiflora,* and Jujube dates. Decoct and drink once or twice daily. This formula is supposed to improve peripheral circulation and limber up the joints and tissues. This formula is used in Chinese hospitals and by outpatients of the hospitals.

REHMANNIAE RADIX (*Rehmannia glutinosa*)

Another commonly used tonic herb, *Rehmannia* stands out as one of the most effective Chinese blood and Kidney tonics.

Chinese name: Ti Huang
Chinese character: 地黄

Traditional Characteristics:

Meridian: Kidney
Tonic action: Yin tonic and blood tonic

Qualities Attributed to the Root: Traditionally, it is used as a blood tonic when it is cooked. If it is consumed raw or has not been steam processed, it is said to be purifying and cooling to the blood.

It is said to prolong life, "quiet the soul and confirm *Shin* (The Spirit)." It is equally beneficial to men and women. *Ti Huang* is used also as a diuretic and heart tonic. It is said to strengthen the bones and tendons and to nourish the marrow. It is also considered to be tonic to the eyes and ears. *Ti Huang* has been used for centuries to reduce fever in any illness.

Ti Huang is sold either raw or steam processed. The two varieties have different pharmacological actions.

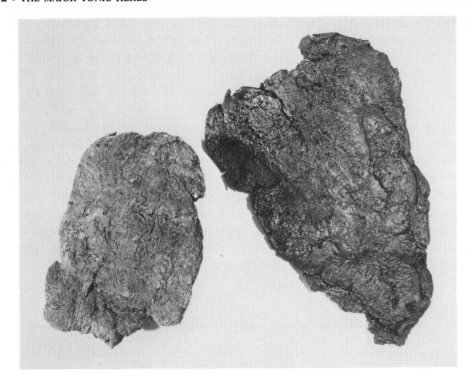

Steamed Ti Huang:

(*Traditional Characteristics*)
Atmospheric energy: warm energy
Flavor: bitter-sweet
Meridians: Heart, Kidney and Liver
Tonic Action: blood tonic

Qualities Attributed to the Steamed Tuber: Steamed *Rehmannia* is said to supplement the blood and nourish the Yin. It tones up the marrow, supplies the necessary food to the kidneys. It helps circulate the blood in the legs and is used after childbirth as a tonic which strengthens the female reproductive organs and relieves abdominal pain.

Raw Ti Huang:

(*Traditional Characteristics*)
Atmospheric energy: cold energy
Flavor: bitter-sweet
Meridians: Kidney, Small Intestine, and Heart
Tonic action: Yin tonic

Qualities Attributed to the Raw Tuber: It is claimed to be "the Kidney's own leading herb." It increases the Yin of the Kidney and thus promotes Kidney functions and "preserves life." It cools the blood and moisturizes dryness. It keeps the heart cool, regulates the Yin and Yang in the Lung, and regulates the dampness and heat in the Stomach and Spleen (the middle burning space). By improving blood flow to the liver, it purifies and tonifies that organ.

Varieties and Grading: As described, *Ti Huang* comes steamed or raw. Most available *Ti Huang* is of good grade. Both raw and steamed *Ti Huang* are superb Kidney tonics, but because the raw has a cold atmospheric energy and moistens the system while cooling the blood, it is the herb of choice for hot weather, especially in the summer months. Steamed *Ti Huang*, being warming and tonic to the blood, is best used in the cold seasons as an excellent Kidney tonic.

Modern Knowledge: Ten years of laboratory and clinical research with humans in China has demonstrated that *Ti Huang* has antihypertensive activity, prevents renal failure, and is cardiotonic.

Preparation and Dosage: *Rehmannia* may be eaten raw, straight from the herb jar. Eat a small piece each day. Select raw or steamed *Rehmannia* according to condition and the weather.

It is combined with *Tang Kuei*, *Paeonia*, and *Ligusticum* in "Four Things Soup," the most famous of all women's tonic brews, discussed under *Tang Kuei*.

It is also a constituent of many tonic herbals, including "Shou Wu Chih." It is the main constituent of an herbal known as "Lui Wei Ti Huang Wan," which tonifies the Kidney and calms the Heart, relieving nervousness and Kidney problems associated with high blood pressure. It is also used by the Chinese elderly to ward off senility.

CODONOPSITIS RADIX (*Codonopsitis lanceolate*)

Codonopsitis is another widely used major tonic, used in much the same manner as ginseng. It is considered an excellent substitute for ginseng in any formula calling for ginseng. It is considered more mild than many varieties of ginseng so is often favored over ginseng where ginseng's energy may be too strong.

Chinese name: Tang Shen
Chinese character: 党参

Traditional Characteristics:

Atmospheric energy: neutral (mild) energy
Flavor: sweet
Meridians: Lung and Spleen
Tonic action: energy tonic and also a Yin tonic

Qualities Attributed to the Root: *Codonopsitis* is a general tonic used to restore bodily vigor, just like ginseng. However, because *Codonopsitis* has a *mild* energy, it is called for in many formulae where the warm or hot energy of ginseng is not wanted.

Codonopsitis is very effective as a tonic to the "middle burning space" which includes the Stomach and Spleen's unified function. It is excellent as an energy tonic, providing energy to the Lung and Spleen, those organ systems that extract *Ch'i* from environmental sources, and thus helps to generate energy for the entire body.

It is said that this herb tones up the energy of the Spleen without making it too dry, and nourishes the Yin of the Stomach without making it too wet. The ability to balance the primary metabolic functions is one of this herb's great qualities. It also lubricates the Lungs and its passages, but always appropriately and not in excess. *Codonopsitis* stimulates the production of blood, and is considered an excellent nutrient. It clears the lungs of excess mucous and detoxifies the blood so that the skin becomes elastic, smooth and radiant.

Nursing mothers use *Codonopsitis* to increase milk production and to build strong blood. *Codonopsitis* is an excellent tonic herb for all those in a weakened condition, as well as for the healthy, as it is known to have no side-effects and provides benefits equal to all but the best ginseng. Indeed, a high grade *Codonopsitis* root will generally be superior to average commerical-grade ginseng. However, the effects of *Codonopsitis* are not as long lasting as those of ginseng. It is, on the other hand,

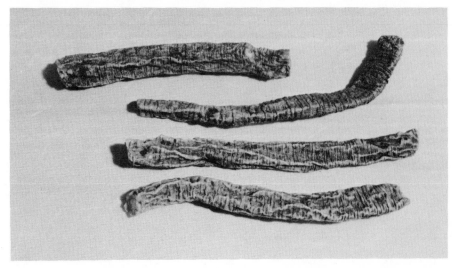

less expensive than ginseng and thus often more appropriate for daily use. It is also more suited to people who have "false fire" symptoms: stiff neck and shoulders, headaches, high blood pressure, glaucoma, easily enraged, etc. Ginseng, when properly balanced can be used by anyone, but *Codonopsitis* might be just as useful without the slight risk of overstimulation.

Varieties and Grading: *Codonopsitis* comes in a wide range of varieties and grades. Excellent *Codonopsitis* comes from Szechuan and Shansi provinces. Long, straight, large roots are the sign of high quality.

Modern Knowledge: *Codonopsitis* contains saponin, inulin, starch and alkaloids. The saponin is similar to that of ginseng.

Preparation and Dosage: Use as you would ginseng. Any formula that calls for ginseng can use *Codonopsitis* as a formidable substitute.

Codonopsitis is a part of a famous, popular and excellent tonic brew known as "Change of Season Soup" which contains equal parts of *Codonopsitis*, *Lycium*, *Astragalus*, and *Dioscoria*. It is used whenever major shifts in the weather occur, or at *any* other stressful time, to build the adaptive energy of the body-mind, and thus to ward off diseases due to rapid change. "Change of Season Soup" is the perfect example of an "adaptogenic" herbal; that is, an herbal that helps the body to adapt to stress by the reinforcing of the body-mind's own adaptive mechanisms.

Codonopsitis also is a constituent in a powerful tonic known as "Dragon Herbal," developed by Moo San Do Sha. It contains equal parts of *Codonopsitis*, *Poria cocos*, *Atractylus*, and honey-fried licorice. It is one of the best energy tonics ever developed and is also *quite* delicious. This is an extremely energizing tonic, perfect for hard workers and those involved in the martial arts or other active sports.

"Change of Season Soup" and "Dragon Herbal" can be purchased premixed (see *Sources* in the Appendix).

Codonopsitis with a little licorice root is considered a major tonic for those tending toward *anorexia*.

ATRACTYLUS (*Atractylodis ovata*)

Atractylus is an important general body tonic which acts generally upon the digestive system and balances the appetite. It is widely used in Chinese weight control programs.

Chinese name: Pai Shu
Chinese character: 白朮

Traditional Characteristics:

Atmospheric energy: slightly warm energy
Flavor: sweet-bitter
Meridians: Spleen and Stomach
Tonic action: energy tonic

Qualities Attributed to the Rhizome: *Atractylus* is a renowned tonic widely used in many formulae. It has warming properties and is a mild stimulant. As a tonic to the Spleen and Stomach, it is said to benefit the digestion and to help regulate fluid metabolism. It is well known and widely used as a very safe diuretic. Upon continued use, *Atractylus* will help regulate the appetite, so it is widely used as a weight control herb.

Atractylus is also used to strengthen the legs, and the muscles in general. By regulating the Spleen, it helps build energy which is distributed to the entire body. *Atractylus* is considered one of the best energy tonics by Chinese herbalists.

Varieties and Grading: All grades on the U.S. market are of approximately equivalent grade, which is generally excellent.

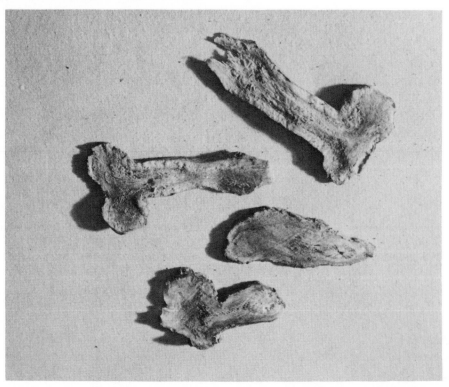

Modern Knowledge: *Atractylus ovata* contains 1.5–2% volatile oil, and other chief components: atractylol, atractylone, eudesmol, and hensol. It has shown stomachic and diuretic effects on laboratory animals, and has shown *in vitro* antiviral activity. It has also shown estrogenic activity in animals.

Preparation and Dosage: *Atractylus* is often used in tonic formulae designed to adjust metabolism. Ground into a powder, or cooked with a little licorice root, it will regulate the appetite. If one overeats habitually, consuming this herb will, after a few days, tend to reduce the appetite. It is also mildly diuretic.

   Atractylus is one of the four components of "Dragon Herbal," the delicious and extremely powerful energy tonic designed for athletes.

   For *anorexia,* the Chinese combine *Atractylus* with *Poria cocos,* licorice, and *Codonopsitis,* and take this either as a brew or powdered (four capsules a day). Or combine with *Citrus aurantium* (orange peel) and either decoct or grind into a powder and take orally (four capsules a day).

   As a powerful Lung tonic, combine *Atractylus* with *Cinnamomum* (Chinese cinnamon), licorice root, and *Poria cocos.* Decoct and drink twice daily.

   As a blood tonic during pregnancy, combine with *Tang Kuei, Paeonia, Ligusticum,* and *Scutellaria.* Decoct and drink twice daily.

SUK GOK (*Dendrobium hancockii*)

Suk Gok has been used by the Taoists as a daily tea. The stems of Chinese orchid are an excellent and delicious tonic and longevity herb. It is especially useful in quickly replacing spent adaptive energy.

   Chinese name: Shih Hu (Korean: Suk Gok)
   Chinese character: 石斛

Traditional Characteristics:

   Atmospheric energy: cool energy
   Flavor: mild-sweet and lightly salty
   Meridians: Kidney, Lung, Stomach
   Tonic action: Yin tonic, especially to the Kidney

Qualities Attributed to the Stems and Leaves: *Dendrobium* has been traditionally used as a daily tea to replenish spent *Ching* energy, especially the *Ching* stored in the Kidney. The Kidney is considered to be the whole body's reservoir of *Ching,* so replenishing the Kidney replenishes the whole being.

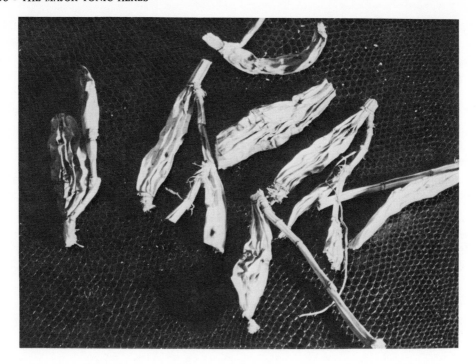

In replenishing and increasing *Ching*, *Suk Gok* increases the generative force. *Suk Gok*, being a Kidney Yin tonic, is said to increase the sexual fluids in men and women. It strengthens the lower back and knees (areas controlled by the Kidney). *Suk Gok* is famous for relieving fatigue from over-indulgence in sex. For those who maintain a balanced sex life, *Dendrobium* is said to build superb sexual vigor.

This herb fills the Kidney meridian up with new vitality and strengthens muscles. It nourishes the Yin of the Kidney and nourishes the saliva, which the Taoists call the "Precious Fluid." *Suk Gok is* used to balance hot conditions, replace damaged or lost fluids and to relieve thirst, depression, and deficiency fever after illness.

Suk Gok has also been considered to be a perfect tonic for those who are themselves involved in the healing arts. It is said to provide "healing energy" which one gives up in service. It therefore prevents the fatigue and breakdown sometimes prevalent among people who give much of themselves to others.

Varieties and Grading: Large, golden, well preserved stems and leaves indicate good quality. If the stems have much pulp, they are most excellent. If the *Suk Gok* is dry and brittle to the point of crumbling when gently squeezed, it is probably too old to be very potent. It is the white pulpy insides that have the tonic action.

Preparation and Dosage: Prepare as a tea. Rinse the herb, then mix with licorice root. Use four or five pieces of licorice root and about twice as much *Suk Gok*.

Simmer for about twenty minutes or until the tea is rich and tastes good. Drink a couple of cupfuls a day, or even as much as desired. It is a very pleasant tasting tea and can be used daily. This is the tea that Master Sung Jin Park himself drank as his basic beverage and which the author served at his school-clinic for many years with great success. It is an excellent way to get a daily dose of licorice, as well. This tea will prove especially useful during and after heavy stressful circumstances or after endulging in sexual play to the point of fatigue. Those who perform one form or another of the healing arts will find that a cup or two a day will increase their power and endurance.

"*Suk Gok* and Licorice" is simply a perfect daily tea and can be used by anyone, young or old. It can be served to guests since it is quite delicious. Tell them they are drinking "orchid and licorice tea."

RED JUJUBE DATES (*Zizyphus jujube*)

Red jujùbe dates have been used since ancient times as a tonic nutrient, a cleanser, and as an important adjunctive herb to other tonics.

Chinese name: Ta Tsao
Chinese character: 棗

Traditional Characteristics:

Atmospheric energy: neutral (mild) energy
Flavor: sweet
Meridians: mainly Stomach, but also to all twelve meridians
Tonic action: Yin tonic and energy tonic

Qualities Attributed to the Fruit: This common Oriental fruit is said to purify the twelve organ meridians and especially the Stomach, which is the body's "center" and is of the element Earth. Red jujube dates "clear the 'nine openings,'" including the eyes, ears, sinuses, nose, throat, bowels and urinary tract. Red jujube dates enhance the efficacy of other tonics and improve circulation.

Red jujube dates are universally believed in the East to build strength and extend life. They are nourishing, beneficial to the viscera, slightly sedative, and mildly laxative. Red dates tone up the Stomach, Heart and Lung functions. They dry up excessive mucous while properly moistening the tissues.

This herb plays an important role in Chinese tonic herbalism. It is often used as a "dispersive" agent or Yin counterpart to Yang tonic herbs such as ginseng. Since red dates remove obstructions to *Ch'i* flow, they are very useful when using

Yang herbs, whose energy should not be allowed to dam up. By preparing a warm or hot herb with red dates, the Yang herb's Ch'i will pass smoothly through the meridian system and organs. For example, ginseng (especially Korean ginseng, which has a warm-hot energy) cooked and consumed in significant quantity without an adjunctive balancing herb has been known to create mild "false fire," that is, shoulder tension or headache. The condition is always temporary and passes in a matter of hours, but is non-the-less uncomfortable and needless. By simply adding a few jujubes, the effects of the ginseng are maximized and there are no negative side-effects at all, plus one gets the advantage of the jujube's own tonic qualities.

Varieties and Grading: Fresh dates can sometimes be purchased in Korean, Japanese, and Chinese markets in late summer, even in America, especially in warmer climatic zones. Red jujube dates can be purchased dry and packaged in most Oriental markets. The trick to picking out good jujubes is in noting their size. In the case of jujubes, smaller is better. So where several varieties are available, which will be the case in many Oriental markets, choose the smallest variety; then the market owner will exclaim: "Oh, you know Chinese herbs!"

Modern Knowledge: *Zizyphus jujube* extracts have been shown to have sedative, hypotensive, cardiotonic, laxative, and smooth muscle relaxing properties in animals.

Preparation and Dosage: Use with ginseng or *Tang Kuei* as described above, or with any Yang tonic.

CINNAMON (*Cinnamomum cassia*)

Chinese cinnamon is a strong Yang tonic. Its unique taste has made cinnamon a favorite culinary herb throughout the world, but the Chinese variety has unique and powerful tonic actions.

Chinese name: Kuei Pi
Chinese character: 桂皮

Traditional Characteristics:

Atmospheric energy: hot energy
Flavor: sweet-pungent (spicy)
Meridians: Kidney and Circulation-Sex
Tonic action: Yang tonic, especially to the Yang of the Kidney

Qualities Attributed to the Bark: Chinese cinnamon promotes good circulation and enables *Ch'i* to circulate freely. Its hot energy is responsible for its famed warming qualities. As a Yang tonic, especially Kidney Yang, it is famed in China as a strengthener and sexual tonic.

Its energy moves upwards and floats. Prolonged use is said to result in a more youthful, rubicund complexion, and is said to clear the skin of blemishes. In moving upwards it disperses energy blocks in the neck and shoulders and thus relieves tension in this area. In moving outward, it warms the flesh. Cinnamon is used to warm up cold visceral organs and to calm the nerves. It is also used medicinally to treat headaches, colic and fever.

Varieties and Grading: Cinnamon is highly prized and premium grades are very large (over a quarter-inch thick) whole pieces up to a foot long and forming a tube several inches in diameter. Such cinnamon is quite expensive. Excellent cinnamon is available that is almost as thick but is broken up into chunks. The larger and spicier, the better. Chinese cinnamon is much richer tasting than the thin culinary cinnamon commonly used in the West. Good cinnamon should be pleasant to chew raw.

Modern Knowledge: Cinnamomum cassia extracts have shown *in vitro* antifungal and antibacterial activity. The volatile oil from cinnamon has shown antiviral activity as well as hypotensive and cardiovascular effects. Cinnamaldehyde, an active ingredient in cinnamon, has been shown to have sedative activity in mice, and has shown hypothermic and antipyretic activity as well.

Preparation and Dosage: Cinnamon is usually an adjunctive herb. Its taste is bitter if boiled, so do not boil cinnamon for more than a few minutes. It is best to use an herb cooker, since the herb brew will not quite boil and yet will thoroughly cook the essence out of the herbs. In any case, use very small amounts of cinnamon, as its flavor and effects are very powerful.

Many people chew small pieces raw. Its flavor is hot and sweet, like "red-hot" candies, and is usually delicious if you enjoy spiciness. The author's son (aged ten) discovered that chewing a piece of cinnamon and a piece of licorice root together tastes just like "Dentine" chewing gum.

Add to cool herbs when a more mild action is desired, or add to mild herbs when a warmer action is desired.

As a Kidney tonic, especially for older people, combine a little Chinese cinnamon with *Rehmannia, Dioscoria,* and *Cornus officionalis.* Decoct and drink twice daily. Add cinnamon, as always, just a few minutes before the rest of the brew is finished (20 minutes to an hour), then let steep for five minutes. If an herb cooker is used, add the cinnamon 15 minutes before the brew is finished.

As a Stomach tonic, decoct with *Codonopsitis, Atractylus* and dried ginger.

To tonify the female reproductive organs, decoct with *Tang Kuei* and *Cyperus rotundus.*

Most tonics are not used when one has a cold, but cinnamon can be. A replacement formula is composed of equal parts of *Paeonia,* licorice, dried ginger, jujube dates, and a small amount of Chinese cinnamon. Decoct for 20 minutes and drink three small cupfuls a day until fever and headaches are relieved, then twice daily until the cold has ceased and regular tonic regimen can be resumed. Or prepare with *Ma Huang* (see *Ma Huang* for details.) These formulae will open up the skin and let off heat through perspiration and are very beneficial at the early stage of a cold or flu.

As a sexual tonic, add a little cinnamon to *Suk Gok* and Licorice or to *Suk Gok* and a little ginseng.

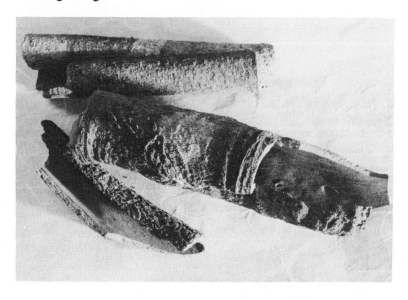

WILD ASPARAGUS ROOT (*Asparagus lucidus*)

Wild Asparagus root was credited by holymen as a *Shin* developing herb. *Shin* is the Taoist "vital treasure" that resides in the heart and manifests as unconditional and all-embracing Love. Wild asparagus has been used by the sages and seekers of the Orient to open up the Heart Center and to tonify the Kidney energy, and thus to prolong life.

Chinese name: Tien Men Tong (Korean: Chung Moon Dong)
Chinese character: 天門冬

Traditional Characteristics:

Atmospheric energy: cold to cool
Flavor: sweet-bitter
Meridians: Kidney, Lung, and Heart
Tonic action: Yin tonic

Qualities Attributed to the Root: Sages in the Orient say that *Chung Moon Dong* is a very special herb. They say that it generates *Shin* energy, our Spirit. It is said to develop peace of mind, a strong mind, good memory, and is recommended to prevent stress from taking its toll. It is said to calm the heart and balance the seven emotions, allowing love to rule our nature.

As a Lung tonic it is said to make the skin supple, soft and smooth and to increase the lung's ability to extract *Ch'i.*

Asparagus root promotes the production of Kidney Yin, and prolonged use is recommended in impotence and frigidity. It has slight diuretic action and removes heat and pains in the feet, chest and neck.

Use of wild Asparagus root is said to lead to a happy, mild manner, excellent vitality and beautiful skin. It is said to strike a balance into the internal functions of the body. It is said that one who consumes *Chung Moon Dong* for a long time will feel so light that they can fly. This is of course a spiritual description, referring to the freedom of spirit one experiences when one has attained at-one-ment-with Tao and is guided by universal love, *Shin.*

Varieties and Grading: Asparagus root is often eaten raw. Connoisseurs know that good *Chung Moon Dong* is soft, chewy and the sweeter the better. At its best, its consistency is like that of a jelly bean. A good batch of *Chung Moon Dong* rarely stays on the herb shop shelves very long as knowing herbalists buy out the stock of this wonderful herb.

Modern Knowledge: *Asparagus lucidus* has been found in animals to have diuretic, anticancer, anthelmintic, antipyretic, cardiotonic, smooth muscle relaxant, antioxytocic, galactagogue, and *in vitro* antibacterial activity.

Preparation and Dosage: Eat one wild Asparagus root daily, raw. Chew well and breathe deeply. *Chung Moon Dong* is a component of Master Moo San Do Sha's "Longevity Herbal" (see *Ho Shou Wu* and also *Sources* in the Appendix).

TIENCHI (*Radix Pseudo-ginseng*)

Tienchi, also called Tienchi ginseng because of its close biological similarity to Panax ginseng, is also called by the Chinese "the miracle root for the preservation of health." It stands as one of the most excellent health preserving herbs known to man.

Chinese name: Tienchi or San Chi
Chinese character: 三七

Traditional Characteristics:

Atmospheric energy: neutral (mild) energy
Flavor: bitter
Meridians: Heart and Kidney
Tonic action: blood tonic and Yin tonic

Qualities Attributed to the Root: China's most famous herbalist, Li Chih Shen, said that "*Tienchi* is more valuable than gold." Since ancient times *Tienchi* has been taught as a premier life-preserver and general tonic, building the blood and strengthening the primary energy. It has long been recognized as one of China's best blood tonics, and has been used to improve circulation and to prevent anxiety.

Modern Knowledge: Like Panax ginseng, a tremendous amount of scientific research has been done on *Tienchi*. As a matter of fact, *Tienchi* now seems to be even more valuable, with the research bringing to light a number of actions of this herb that make it of special interest in these modern times.
   Tienchi is distributed in either its raw form or steam-processed, each with different pharmacological activity. Let us review what is now known about these two forms of *Tienchi*.

Raw Tienchi: A great deal of scientific research has been conducted on raw *Tienchi*. *Tienchi* contains three particularly important substances: Saponin A, Saponin B, and flavinoids. It appears that these substances provide raw material for the human synthesis of major adrenal hormones such as cortisol and reproductive hormones such as testosterone, estrogen, and progesterone. It has been found to promote non-specific RNA to deploy amino acids to form gamma globulin which acts as an antibody for the control and prevention of general diseases.
   The most astounding and significant research findings, however, revolve around *Tienchi*'s ability to positively affect the heart and its tributaries. Chinese research

indicates that *Tienchi* increases blood flow in the coronary artery (the artery that supplies the heart itself with blood) and increases the consumption of oxygen in the middle muscular layer of the heart. This results in the lowering of blood pressure and in improving regularity of the heart beat. This has led to the finding that *Tienchi* can prevent insufficiency caused by stagnation of blood in the heart. Research further indicates that *Tienchi* can relieve chest pain and/or the feeling of oppression in the chest due to angina pectoris induced by coronary insufficiency. *Tienchi* has also been found to arrest both internal and external bleeding, while being able to disperse blood clots. *Tienchi* has been distributed to members of the armed forces of several Asian countries to be used in case of injury.

Tienchi has further been demonstrated to significantly reduce the cholesterol levels in the blood and coating the arteries. Research has also confirmed the ancient precaution that *Tienchi* should not be used during pregnancy. *Tienchi* has the capacity to cause the expulsion of blood clots lodged anywhere in the system. It has been found that *Tienchi* treats an embryo as a blood clot, and can therefore result in abortion

Steamed Tienchi: Like raw *Tienchi*, the steamed variety is rich in iron, calcium, proteins, saponins, flavinoids, etc. However, steamed or otherwise cooked, *Tienchi's* effects are somewhat different from those of the raw variety. It becomes a very efficacious blood tonic, strengthening the body and promoting growth. Like the raw variety, steamed *Tienchi* reduces blood cholesterol levels.

Varieties and Grading: *Tienchi* is more scarce in Chinese markets than most of the other major tonics. It comes either as a whole, unprocessed root, a sliced unprocessed root, or powdered in either the raw or steamed form. For cooking as part of an herbal recipe, the sliced variety is best since the whole root is very hard to slice.

Preparation and Dosage: For those who wish to use raw *Tienchi* to benefit the cardiovascular system, capsules packaged by the Po Chien Company of Los Angeles are the best since they are easy to take, and Po Chien uses the best *Tienchi*. This particular company is highly reputable and all of their products are excellent. All instructions for use are provided (see *Sources* in the Appendix).

The Chinese cook *Tienchi* to make a blood tonic. They cook it with chicken. Steamed *Tienchi* comes as a powder from the Yunnan Paiyao factory, and in capsules from Po Chien. Complete instructions are provided for its usage.

Among the tonics, *Tienchi* is one of the least pleasant tasting. It has a bitter flavor that is difficult to get used to. For this reason, capsules and pills are most palatable and are overall the best way to take *Tienchi* unless it is a minor ingredient in an herbal formula that overwhelms its flavor. The capsules and pills are easy to take.

ROYAL JELLY (*bee secretion*)

Royal Jelly, the natural food of the Queen bee which is produced from honey by special worker bees, is a remarkable super-nutrient. This substance has etched its mark on the world health market in recent years. A relatively recent discovery, Royal Jelly is already one of the most important and widely used tonics in China and around the world.

Chinese name: Fengwang
Chinese character: 蜂蜜

Traditional Characteristics:

Atmospheric energy: neutral (mild) energy
Flavor: bitter
Meridians: Triple Warmer, Kidney
Tonic action: Yin tonic and energy tonic

Qualities Attributed to the Glandular Secretion: Royal Jelly is a thick whitish substance produced by worker bees. This glandular secretion is made from honey and serves as the sole diet of the Queen bee. Royal Jelly has been the subject of intense research in recent years, being recently discovered—it is not a *traditional* Chinese tonic herb.

It is known that the Queen outlives all other bees in the hive by about twenty-fold, the common bee living from four to five months and the Queen living five to six years. This longevity has been positively attributed to her consumption of Royal Jelly. Without this food, the Queen would live only as long as other bees.

Royal Jelly is as close to being a complete food as is known to man. It contains a full range of amino acids, vitamins, minerals, enzymes, etc. It contains virtually all the essential amino acids. It contains Thiamine Hydrochloride, Riboflavin, Pyridoxine Hydrochloride, Vitamin A, Vitamin B_{12}, Vitamin E, Vitamin C, and Pantothenic Acid, among others. The list of nutrients goes on and on.

Because Royal Jelly is used by the Queen bee, and has been found to stimulate the Queen's incredibly productive fertility, it is generally considered to be especially beneficial to women. This has been confirmed by the finding of important female hormones present in Royal Jelly.

Varieties and Grading: All Royal Jelly is of excellent quality. It is possible to obtain *pure* Royal Jelly only from a very few sources (see *Sources* in the Appendix). Most Royal Jelly comes blended with other products and those range in quality depending on the quantity of Royal Jelly used and the other substances used.

Preparation and Dosage: Many excellent products are currently available which use Royal Jelly as a main ingredient. Any trip to one's local health food store will provide ample selection.

As mentioned above, Royal Jelly can be obtained from a few sources in its fresh, whole, jelly-like state. In this form, it is bitter tasting. However only a drop or two, literally, is necessary each day to do its wonders. Some women who have used this pure fresh Royal Jelly have claimed truly miraculous results, such as becoming pregnant after many years of being unable to do so, or having their hair grow nine inches in nine months after the hair had stopped growing many years before. Keep fresh Royal Jelly refrigerated.

Royal Jelly can be obtained dried and powdered and/or blended with other products in pills. Many such products are available.

Royal Jelly also is blended with honey and the extracts of one or two other Chinese tonic herbs and sold in boxes of ten glass vials. This is the most popular form in which Royal Jelly is marketed. These tasty extracts are readily available at many health food stores. They contain such tonic herbs as ginseng, *Astragalus*, *Codonopsitis*, *Schizandra*, etc. These small glass vials are opened when needed and the sweet juice is sucked through a straw that is provided. Read the labels to see what herbs are blended with the Royal Jelly. All varieties are delicious and highly beneficial. Besides the long term effects of the herbs, these elixirs provide quick energy. Most people take one or two vials a day.

PORIA (*Poria cocos*)

Next to Licorice, *Poria cocos* is the most widely used herb in Chinese herbalism. Poria is a superb Yin tonic, and is a great balancing agent to Yang tonics such as ginseng. It is one of the most respected herbs in the Chinese herbal system.

>   Chinese name: Fu Ling
>   Chinese Character: 茯苓

Traditional Characteristics:

>   Atmospheric Energy: neutral
>   Flavor: mildly sweet
>   Meridians: Primarily Spleen, Lung, Kidney, Triple Warmer, and also the
>   Bladder, Heart and Gall Bladder
>   Tonic action: Yin tonic and energy tonic

Qualities Attributed to the Herb: This herb has been found to have so many beneficial actions that it has long since established itself as China's premiere Yin tonic. The ancients said that Fu Ling "restores and refreshes the body and the mind, and when used regularly will prolong life."

Poria cocos is a solid pulpy fungus which grows on the roots of fir trees. The Chinese use Fu Ling both as an herb and as a food in traditional cooking. The part used is the white inner part of the fungous mass.

Poria cocos has several major actions for which is valued. First, it is the perfect example of a Yin tonic, which is defined as an herb which tonifies the Yin structures and functions, and benefits fluid metabolism. Poria does regulate the metabolism of bodily fluids, and strengthens the Bladder and Kidneys in particular so that the urinary system functions optimally. *Poria cocos* is a superb diuretic tonic.

Secondly, *Poria cocos* is considered to be especially excellent for benefiting the circulation of Ch'i in the Triple Warmer which is vitally important in maintaining a healthy condition in all the internal organs. The Triple Warmer regulates the production of energy from food and air as well as the elimination of wastes.

A third excellent quality attributed to *Poria cocos* is its action as a nervine. Poria is considered a Heart tonic, and all Heart tonics are tranquilizing. Poria is said to relieve anxiety and to mitigate "heart pangs." This calming quality of *Poria cocos* is said to contribute to the lengthening of life. Poria is also said to be soothing to the lungs and is widely used in Lung tonics. Poria is helpful in regulating blood sugar.

Poria cocos is considered the perfect herb for people recovering from a debilitating disease, as it strengthens the Spleen and general metabolic functions and has secondary blood tonic effects. *Poria cocos* is often used as a tonic for weak and/or nervous people, and also for frail, nervous children. *Poria* and *Licorice* are China's two most widely used children's tonic herbs.

Varieties and Grading: The bulbous fungus comes sliced in the herb shops. The pieces should be very white. If the pieces are fairly firm and maintain their shape, and they are white, the Poria is of high quality.

Modern Knowledge: *Poria cocos* has been found to have tranquilizing, diuretic, and hypotensive actions in laboratory animals. An anticancer agent has be isolated from *Poria cocos* and is being studied with great interest at several research centers.

Preparation and Dosage: *Poria cocos* is not generally used as the primary herb in an herbal recipe, but is very widely used as a secondary herb. Combine with *Atractylus*, *Licorice* and *Codonopsitis* to regulate the metabolism, to rapidly increase vitality, and to build up the system in general. This is especially good for weak people and those recovering from illness.

5 | The Minor Tonic Herbs

A number of valuable herbs fall into the category of "tonics" which for one of several reasons may be called "minor tonics." Some of the herbs fall into this category not because they are weaker or of less lofty character than the herbs described in the previous chapter, but because they are so much less common that they play only a minor role in Chinese tonic herbalism. Others are termed "minor" because they simply have not gained the broad reputation of the major tonics and are therefore used less often and in smaller quantities. Still others are called "minor" because they are in fact less potent as tonics.

In this chapter, we will be discussing more or less briefly a number of these minor tonics. They cannot be ignored because they do play an important role in Chinese tonic herbalism. They are in essence the "journeymen" of the system. Though *ginseng* and *Tang Kuei* and the like receive most of the attention of the masses, many tonic formulas utilize less well known and yet powerful tonics to support the actions of the more famous leading herbs. Though one could practice the art of tonic herbalism with just the major tonics, or even just a few of those, one who wishes to know the subject in its depth or who wishes to use prepared herbals and would like to know what the actions of the formula will be, must be familiar with the minor tonics. These tonics deserve much respect. They are not a whole lot different from their more famous cousins, the major tonics, but are simply lower profile.

TU CHUNG (*Eucommia ulmoides*)　杜仲

Since the dawn of Chinese herbalism, the dried bark known as *Tu Chung* has been recognized as one of China's pre-eminent tonic herbs. It was discussed second only to *ginseng* in the first pharmacopia of China, that of Shen Nung written about three thousand years ago. Though it has always been regarded with esteem equal to any of the major tonics, it has not been used nearly as much as other tonics such as *Astragalus*, *Codonopsitis*, or *Atractylus*. This is primarily because of its relative scarceness. The bark of a temperate zone rubber tree, this herb has recently received tremendous attention in China and by American drug companies.

It has been found that *Eucommia ulmoides* contains an active principle which

may be the most effective drug yet discovered for treating, and perhaps preventing high blood pressure. Absolutely no side effects have been discerned, which is quite an improvement over reserpine, the current drug of choice in most cases of hypertension (*note*: reserpine was originally extracted from another Chinese herb, *Rauwolfia*).

Because of the value of this new drug which can be extracted from *Tu Chung*, China has recently severely limited the quantities of the herb that can be exported from China. Therefore, less is available in the West, and what is available is being sold at premium prices. However, the *Tu Chung* that is reaching the American markets is generally of superb quality.

Besides its activity in treating hypertension, *Tu Chung* is considered a superb tonic to the Kidney and Liver. It is very popular as a sexual tonic and is used by those who are impotent or suffer from lumbago. *Tu Chung* has also been found to have anti-inflammatory effects.

DEER ANTLER (*Cornu Cervi parvum*) 鹿角 or 鹿茸

Deer antler is one of the most renowned and respected tonics from China. It is a first class tonic, but is listed here as a minor tonic because it is of animal origin and is used more rarely than most of the major tonics. *Deer antler* has been used since ancient times for its superb energy producing quality. It is said to tonify the Kidney, Liver, Heart, and brain and to increase blood circulation.

Young deer horn in particular is used for producing pure energy, toning up the marrow, sharpening the mind, benefiting the blood, strengthening the heart, and as a Yang sexual tonic. *Deer antler* is a common component of many expensive elixirs and combinations claimed to be aphrodisiac. It is said to strengthen the mind and to increase longevity. *Deer antler* is very popular among wealthy old Oriental gentlemen.

Like other popular Chinese tonic herbs, *deer antler* comes to the market in many forms. It comes whole, sliced, in pills, and in patent medicines. The deer themsevles are not killed for their antlers, which fall off naturally each year and are collected. These antlers play a major part in the male sexual role of the deer. They contain powerful hormones. Larger antlers indicate that the deer was involved in more sexual activity and was generally more powerful and potent. Such antlers are worth more than smaller antlers.

Whole and sliced *deer antler* is expensive, but is undoubtedly worth the price. It may be added to practically any tonic formula.

A large variety of pills are also available at Chinese markets and herb shops. These pills usually blend *deer antler* with *ginseng* and/or other tonic herbs to create "virility pills." Those imported from China and Japan are almost all excellent. An example of such a pill is the "Ching Pill" discussed in Chapter 8, which utilizes the highest grade Deer Antler in the world.

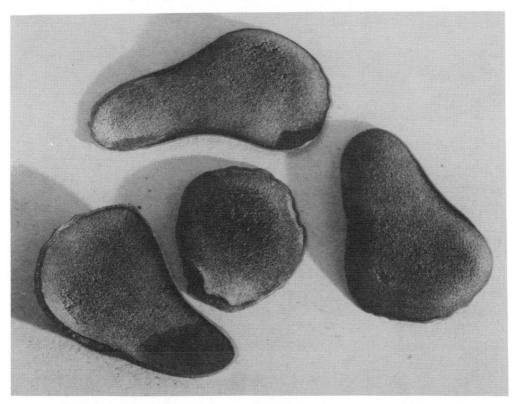

A Chinese product known as **"Pantocrin"** is also available in Chinese markets. It is the extract of *deer antler*. This is one of the finest products available at a very reasonable price. A few drops of this sweet liquid under the tongue provides great energy both physically and psychically. It tastes very good and has no negative side-effects. On the positive side, Pantocrin is said to increase physical stamina, sexual vitality and clarity of mind. Many people in the West who had previously used stimulants such as coffee, amphetamines, or cocaine have switched to the harmless Pantocrin for quick substantial energy. Pantocrin has been found to be a healthful central nervous system stimulant.

Pantocrin can also be added to other tonic brews to enhance their energy boosting potential.

HSIN-I (*Magnolia liliflora*) 辛夷

Simply put, one Chinese source says that the unopened flower of the Magnolia tree "corrects the energy." This herb is reputed to "give lightness to the body, brightness to the eye, added length of life, culminating in great old age." It is further said to warm the three burning spaces, lubricate the muscles, benefit the nine body cavities, open up the nose, expel mucous, reduce facial swelling, and promote the growth of hair.

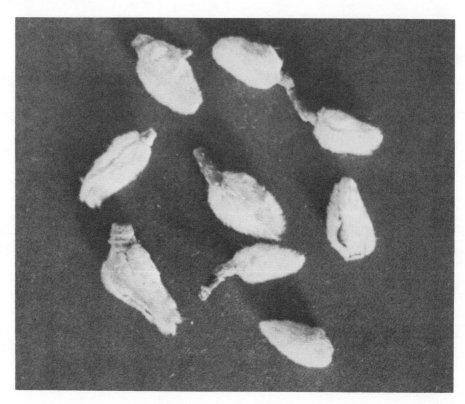

SHAN CHU-YU (*Cornus officinalis*) 山茱萸

Cornus is a Yin tonic which acts upon the Kidney and uro-genital system. It is slightly warm in nature, and is sour and biting to the taste. Like other sour herbs, this herb controls sperm ejaculation and retards perspiration. A quinol glucoside has been isolated which acts as a urinary antiseptic. Extracts have also shown antibacterial activity against *Staphylococcus aureus*, *Salmonella typhula* and *Shigella dysentarae*. Extracts have also shown anti-allergenic effects.

Combine with *Rehmannia*, *Dioscorea*, *Poria*, and *Alisma plantago*, and decoct as an excellent Kidney and Bladder tonic and to strengthen the lower body.

BUPLEURUM (*Bupleurum chinense*) 柴胡

Bupleurum is traditionally used to strengthen the Stomach and Intestines, and to promote blood circulation of the liver. It is said to warm the trunk and to pull fresh *Ch'i* into the upper part of the body. It is also said to strengthen the Lungs, head, sense organs of the face, and limbs. *Bupleurum* is especially recommended for toning up the leg muscles. *Bupleurum* is traditionally said to regulate the Liver energy and to clear up stagnation in the Liver.

Experimentally, *Bupleurum* has been found to have choleretic, antipyretic, hypoglycemic, anticancer, smooth muscle relaxant, strengthening of the capillaries, anti-inflammatory, and analgesic activities. The active principles appear to be a mixture of triterpene glycosides, referred to as saikosides, which have been shown to have the following pharmacological activities in animals: hypotensive, cardiotonic, anti-inflammatory, sedative, stimulant, and anti-ulcer effects. Extracts have also shown antibacterial activity and a volatile oil extracted has shown antiviral activity *in vitro*.

Though *Bupleurum* is listed here as a minor tonic because it is not as widely recognized by the masses, it is highly tauted and widely used by herb doctors in the Orient, particularly in Japan. As a Liver tonic, decoct with *Paeonia*, *Citrus aurantium*, and *licorice root*. As a female reproductive tonic, decoct with *Tang Kuei, Paeonia* and *Atractylus*.

SCUTE (*Scutellaria baicalensis*) 黄芩

Scutellaria, called *Pan-chih Lien* in Chinese, is said to equalize the vital principle. It is tonic to the Bladder, quieting to the pregnant uterus, and mildly stimulant to the respiratory organs. It is tonic to the sexual organs when combined with certain herbs. It has a slightly cold energy, so it relieves heat congestion and detoxifies the blood.

Three active ingredients have been isolated: baicalin, wogonin, and bicalein, all of which are diuretic. Extracts of *Scutellaria* have shown *in vitro* antibacterial effects. Extracts have shown sedative and cardiotonic activity in animals. Flavinoids in *Scutellaria* have shown antihistaminic activity.

As a tonic during pregnancy, used by the Chinese to stabilize the fetus, decoct with *Atractylus* and *Tang Kuei*. As a diruetic bladder tonic, decoct with *Atractylus*, *Poria* and *licorice root*.

PAEONY ROOT (*Paeonia albiflora*) 芍藥

Paeonia is a famous and highly prized "women's herb," which is used traditionally to balance the female hormonal system and to improve blood quality. It is said to purify the Yin energy, and is an excellent blood tonic. *Pai-Shao*, as it is called in China, has a cool atmospheric energy and a bitter-sour flavor. It enters the Liver and Spleen meridians primarily, but to some degree also the Stomach and Small Intestine meridians.

Herbalists say that *Paeony root*, if consumed for a long time, will add vigor to the body and lengthen life. They say that this herb restores liver balance, neutralizes the blood, and raises the pain threshold. It relaxes the muscles and relieves spasms and cramps, and is famed for relieving menstrual cramps and pain.

Paeonia is also said to help regulate intestinal peristalsis and to promote the digestive function. It is said to control sweating, act as a diuretic and reduce excess heat.

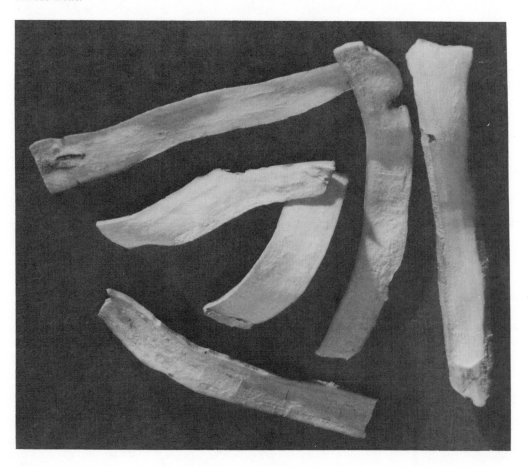

Perhaps *Paeonia* is most famous because it is believed that a woman who consumes *Paeony root* teas on a regular basis will become as radiant and beautiful as the famed peony flower itself. The herb is said to make the flesh elastic and silky smooth. It is also used as a tonic during pregnancy.

Pharmacological studies indicate that *Paeonia* has antitumor activity in laboratory animals. An active principle paeoniflorin, has been isolated from *Paeonia albiflora*, which has been shown in animals to have antispasmodic, anti-inflammatory, hypotensive (peripheral vasodilator), and smooth muscle relaxant effects on rat stomach and uterus, and has also been found to have diuretic activity.

The root slices are nearly white with a very slight pinkish hue. *Paeonia* is a component in the very famous women's regulatory tonic, **"Four Things Soup"** (see *Tang Kuei*). A simple way to use *Paeonia* is to blend three parts of *Paeonia* with one part of *licorice root*. Bring to a boil and simmer for 15 minutes. Drink one cup, twice a day on an empty stomach to purify the system, beautify the skin, to build blood and benefit the female functions.

CYPERUS ROTUNDUS 香附子

This rhizome is tonic and stimulant. It is said to correct poor circulation of the *Ch'i* and to relieve congestion. Extracts of *Cyperus rotundus* have shown extensive antifungal and antibacterial activity. It has shown prolonged hypotensive and vasodilating effects, as well as diuretic, tranquilizing, smooth muscle relaxing, antipyretic, anti-emetic, and analgesic activity.

Cyperus is forbidden during pregnancy.

Besides being used in many tonic formulae, it is a main ingredient in a sexual tonic brew composed of equal parts of *Cyperus* and *Poria cocos,*, and a spoonful honey. This brew is said to prolong virility and produce fertility.

As a Lung and Spleen tonic, combine with *Citrus aurantium (orange peel)*, *Paeonia*, and *licorice root*. Decoct and drink twice daily on an empty stomach.

CORDYCEPS SINENSIS 冬虫夏草

Cordyceps is considered by many to be a first-class herb. It is said to be restorative and tonic in nature. It was said by Li Chih Shen, the great sixteenth century herbalist, to be equivalent to *ginseng* in invigorating and toning up the systems of the body. It is said to be efficacious in enriching the marrow and in building *Ch'i*. Being tonic to the Lung and Kidney, it is often used as a tonic during recovery from cases of serious injury or disease. *Cordyceps* is a form of fungus.

Cooked in a soup with chicken or duck, its powers are said to be very much enhanced. This is the most common way of using this excellent herb. Use ten slices (*Cordyceps slices* are small) for each pot of soup and cook until the fowl is done.

CITRUS AURANTIUM 橙皮

The dried peel of oranges and tangerines is considered a precious herb by many Chinese and is actually quite popular. Though it is not specifically a tonic in the classical sense, it finds its way into many tonic formulae because of its excellent adjunctive qualities.

Mainly, it prevents the clogging effect of some strong tonics and is therefore used to balance such herbs as *ginseng*, in much the same way that *licorice root* and *red jujube dates* are used as adjunctive herbs. It discharges excess fire and removes obstructions, dispersing energy coagulations of the Liver, which cause a person to feel frustrated, angry, depressed, and generally unhappy.

Essential oil isolated from *Citrus aurantium* has shown antibacterial and antifungal activity, and three flavonoids from this herb are antifungal. These flavonoids are also anti-inflammatory. The flavonoids have shown antitumor activity in cell cultures.

Found in all Oriental markets, these dried peels can be cooked with *ginseng* as a sexual tonic, or with *Atractylus* and *Scutellaria* as a tonic to the three burning spaces.

ACORUS CALAMUS 水菖蒲

Acorus is said to be "the strengthening and life-prolonging herb." It is specifically tonic to the Spleen and Stomach, is said to detoxify the blood, relieve intestinal blocks, and has aphrodisiac qualities.

Acorus has been shown in the laboratory to relax smooth muscle, and has insecticidal, antifungal, antibacterial, CNS depressant, hypotensive, and hallucinogenic activity. It also affects respiration in rat brain, and has anticonvulsant activity, due to sesquiterpene aconic acid.

Acorus is used in many common commercial tonic preparations.

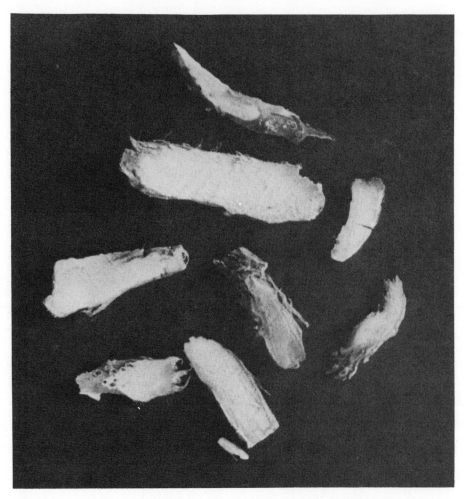

DIOSCORIA BATATAS   山藥

Dioscoria is widely used as a secondary tonic. *Dioscoria*, a type of yam, is an important Yin tonic that is said to benefit the spirit, promote flesh, and when taken habitually, to brighten the intellect and prolong life. *Dioscoria* serves as a Stomach-Spleen tonic, as well as nourishing the Lungs and supplementing the Kidney *Ch'i*. This white, brittle herb has cooling properties. Its energy is classified as neutral and it is sweet tasting.

    Dioscoria has been found to contain steroid precursors.

    Dioscoria is part of "Change of Season Soup" (see *Codonopsitis*). As a Kidney tonic, decoct with *Rehmannia*, *Cornus*, and *Schizandra*. This formula is also tonic to the Lung.

ZINGIBER OFFICINALE 乾薑

The dried ginger used in Chinese herbalism is a mild and excellent product. It adds a zesty, yet smooth flavor to any herb tea and has a wonderful warming quality. It is said to warm up and be tonic to the Stomach and Spleen, aiding digestion and dispelling cold energy. For the body as a whole, it tones up the Yang.

Ginger is the perfect adjunctive herb to use when a brew is cool or mild in nature and it is desired to up its atmospheric energy.

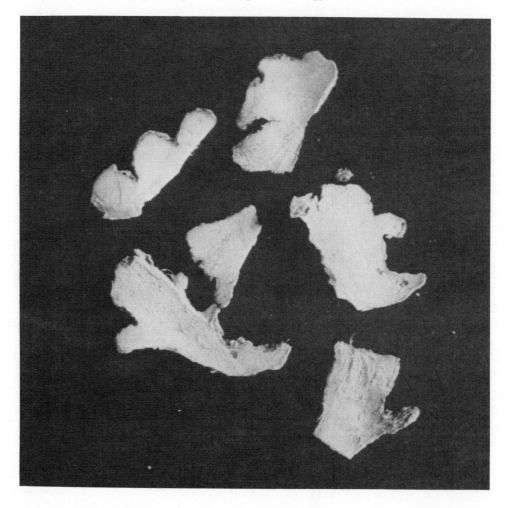

ALISMA PLANTAGO-AQUATICA 澤瀉

Alisma is a truly excellent and ancient tonic, but has not always received the attention due it. The classics say that if "taken for a long time, the eye and ear become acute, hunger is not felt, life is prolonged, the body becomes light, the complexion becomes radiant, and one can walk upon water (a reference to spiritual powers)."

It is further claimed that *Alisma* "renders labor easy. Stimulates the female generative apparatus, and promotes fertility." *Alisma* is a pure Kidney tonic of the first order.

A large amount of modern research has centered around the serum cholesterol lowering constituents of *Alisma plantago-aquatica*. The active principle is a triterpene, Aliso A. Extracts of *Alisma plantago-aquatica* have shown anticancer activity. Extracts have been shown effective in repairing carbon tetrachloride-induced fatty liver degeneration, and to reduce blood sugar in diabetic animals.

One excellent tonic formula using this marvelous tonic herb contains equal parts of *Alisma*, *Cornus*, *Paeonia*, and half a portion of *Rehmannia*. This is an excellent Kidney tonic, especially for those with weakness in the lower back and weakened sexual functions.

MA HUANG (*Ephedrae Sinensis*)　麻黃

Ma Huang is one of the most famous Chinese herbs. It is primarily known in the West as a medicinal herb, used for clearing Lung conditions and as a central nervous system stimulant. However, used properly, it can act as a special tonic and has been used in this context by Chinese monks for a thousand years.

Ma Huang has a warm energy and a sweet flavor. It enters the Lung and Kidney meridians and acts as an energy tonic. *Ma Huang* is used as a tea to keep awake and alert, and to clear the perceptions. It has long been used by Taoists and Chan (Zen) monks before meditation since it sharpens the awareness without causing agitation or a "come-down" effect. It also clears the respiratory system and is said to benefit the energy of the Lung and Kidney, and thus the whole body.

Though *Ma Huang* is considered a "stimulant," which it definitely is, because of the acute alertness it brings, it is said to help relieve stress because it *calms* the mind. *Ma Huang* is said to clean up the meridians and is tonic to the Kidney, supplying *Ching* energy.

Its energy is said to move upwards and float. Thus it is used to clear fevers, blocked-up ears, headaches, to clear the sinuses and to relieve colds. It is a mild diuretic and keeps the eyes bright and clear.

Ma Huang is most famous for its effects upon the Lung functions. When one drinks a mild brew of *Ma Huang*, the person will feel a sense of controlled power in the lungs. Breathing will be long, full and calm. This deep breathing, the basis of all yogas and meditative techniques, results in a wonderful sense of well-being. Thus *Ma Huang*, used properly, is the perfect meditator's herb. It also is excellent for the purposes of studying, staying awake on the road, playing music, or any other activity which requires alertness and mental control.

It is a desert herb and is therefore very drying. It must therefore be used in very small quantities to prevent a loss of Yin elements and should be balanced with Yin herbs.

Most Chinese *Ma Huang* is of similar grade. Twigs are dried and brown. *Ma Huang* can also be found growing wild in the deserts of the Western United States. The fresh plant, however, is slightly toxic. Too much fresh *Ephedrae* may result in respiratory hyperactivity and heavy expelling of mucous. For this reason, it is not generally categorized as a "superior herb." The sun-dried Chinese variety is, on the other hand, mild and safe, especially when blended properly with other herbs.

Ephedrae sinensis contains a total of 1.5% alkaloid, the main component being l-ephedrine. Minor components are d-pseudo-ephedrine, N-methyl-ephedrine, N-methyl-pseudo-ephedrine, nor-ephedrine, nor-pseudo-ephedrine, etc. Laboratory tests have shown ephedrine to be diaphoretic, diuretic, and antitussive. Ephedrine hydrochloride, originally extracted from Chinese *Ephedrae*, is now used worldwide

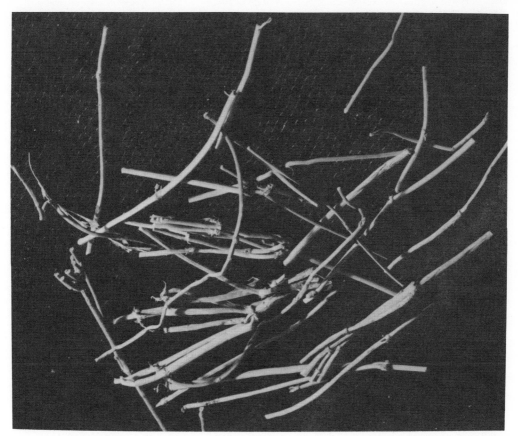

as an anti-asthmatic drug and is commonly used by Western pharmaceutical companies in many commercial medicines.

To prepare *Ma Huang*, blend ten one-inch twigs of *Ma Huang* with a small amount of *cinnamon*. Boil the *Ma Huang* first for 15 minutes then add the *cinnamon* for another 5 minutes. Let steep for a few more minutes. This tea promotes circulation, warms the skin, hands and feet, and in the case of fever, will promote perspiration.

Ma Huang is used with *licorice root* to strengthen the Lung energy and warm the body. Used with *cinnamon*, *licorice root*, and *ginseng*, it is known as "Genghis Khan Alertness Tea" since it was used by the guards of Genghis Khan to stay awake (they were beheaded if they were caught dozing off while on guard duty).

Use with *Suk Gok*, *Astragalus*, and *licorice root* to stay awake and for physical energy. Be sure to use very little *Ma Huang*—it is very powerful.

Ma Huang should not be used continuously by people who are in a weak condition. These people should use the classical tonics to build up their energies. A strong person, however, will find *Ma Huang* simply amazing.

LIGUSTICUM (*Ligusticum lucidum* or *wallichii*)   川芎

Ligusticum is an important Chinese herb, especially in women's tonics, but also blood tonics in general. This highly aromatic herb has a neutral energy and a bitter-pungent taste. *Ligusticum* is most widely used because it is very effective in increasing and improving the circulation of blood and *Ch'i*. It is also said to warm the meridians, protect the blood and to cool excess fire. *Ligusticum* nourishes the Yin, supplements the Kidney *Ch'i*, strengthens the muscles and bones, and promotes clear vision and hearing. Because *Ligusticum* is so effective in improving circulation, it is very useful as a cleansing tonic. It discharges toxins from the liver, and is in fact considered to be primarily a Liver tonic (Liver tonics always purge the liver of toxins and improve the functioning of the peripheral nervous system). *Ligusticum* is one of the ingredients in the very famous women's tonic called "Four Things Soup" (see Chapter 4, *Tang Kuei*). Shen Nung, China's first herbalist, said of *Ligusticum*: "It is tonic to the vital centers, brightens the eye, strengthens the Yin, quiets the five viscera, nourishes the vital principle, makes vigorous the loins and navel, expels the hundred diseases, restores grey hair, and if taken for a long time will increase the firmness of the flesh, giving sprightliness and youth to the body." *Ligusticum* has a strong flavor similar to that of *Tang Kuei* but stronger. It combines well with almost any other tonic herb and may be added to almost any formula.

Ligusticum has been found to contain an extremely powerful immune system stimulant. It has, in this respect, properties identical to those found in *astragalus membranaceus*. Extensive research is being done on *Ligusticum* as an agent that may be used in the treatment of cancer, AIDS, and to counteract some of the symptoms of old age. (See *Astragali Radix*, page 98)

TREE PEONY (*Moutan*)   牡丹皮

This herb is the bark of the tree peony and is widely used in Chinese herbalism. *Tree peony* has as slightly cool energy and a mild flavor and is often used in women's tonics because it is believed to be very beneficial to the female fertility cycle. It is tonic to the Liver (and thus is detoxifying), energizing, and if used for a prolonged period of time is supposed to strengthen the body and lengthen life.

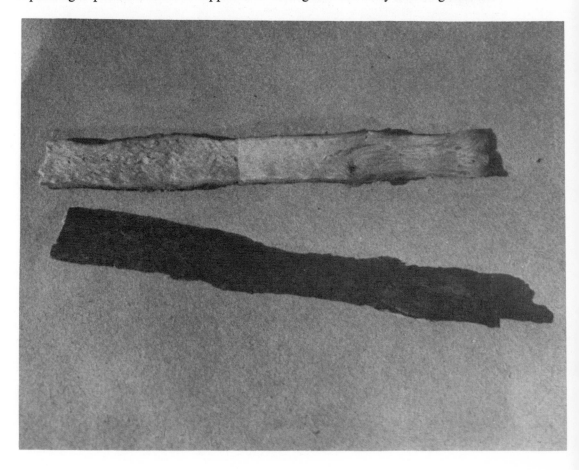

PRINCE GINSENG (*Radix Ophiopogonis*)　麥門冬

Though *Prince Ginseng* is not actually related to *Panax Ginseng*, it is always listed in Chinese herbal texts right next to the original "King of Herbs." This tiny root (about one inch long) looks like a miniature *ginseng* root, and acts as though it was a mild variety of their more famous namesake. *Prince Ginseng* is a gentle energy tonic that can be taken over an extended period of time, yielding approximately the same results as true *ginseng*: vitality, a happy spirit, and long life. Like *Panax Ginseng*, this little herb is considered to be especially beneficial to the Lung and Spleen functions and is thus considered an energy tonic.

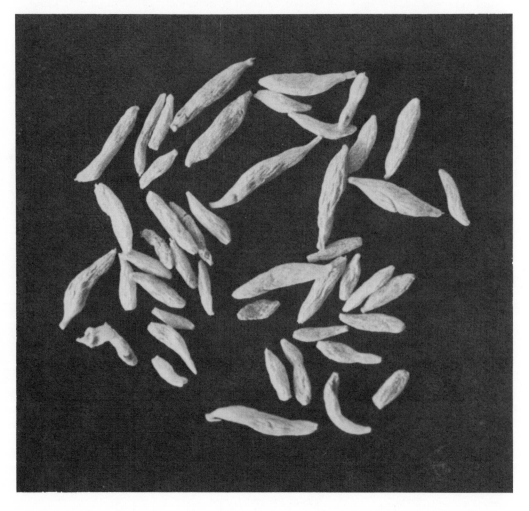

6 | Herbal Preparation and Traditional Tonic Recipes

6.1 Techniques of Herbal Preparation

There are several standard methods of herbal preparation, each of which has its benefits. Some herbs may be chewed or consumed raw. Other tonics are prepared by boiling into teas, while still others are cooked up as soups with broths of chicken or other stock. Another popular method is to make alcoholic tonics. The recipes presented in this chapter will include each of these types of preparation.

Generally, if several herbs are combined and are, as a unit, more beneficial raw, they should be ground into powder and consumed in capsules. This is generally done by breaking and chopping the herbs into fine pieces. If very hard herbs, such as red *ginseng*, are used, these should be softened by slight steaming first so as not to clog up or break the grinder. In most cases, a good kitchen coffee grinder will suffice quite well in this task. The resulting powder can be encapsuled and stored. It is best to store powdered herbs, encapsuled or not, in a dry dark jar and kept away from direct sunlight or excessive heat. This protects the potency of the tonic. Take the capsules according to the recommended dosage or as needed.

There is a simple and traditional way of making pills, as well. After grinding the herbal combination into a powder, blend in enough honey and arrowroot powder to transform the powder into a thick paste. With the fingers, make small pea-sized pills. These should be firm and hold their shape. Allow to dry in the open air in indirect sunlight, or place the still sticky little pellets on a baking pan and bake for a few minutes to harden the pills. These hardened pills should be stored in a dark jar and stored in a cool dark place.

By far the most popular technique of herbal preparation is by boiling. Generally, combine the herbs so that their total weight is around ½ to 1 ounce. This mixture is added to approximately four cups of water in a pyrex or procelain tea pot. Do not use a metal pot. It goes without saying that pure water is preferable to tap water, which in most locations in America is chemically polluted. Either bottled water or water passed through a high quality water purifier is recommended. There are water purifiers available at a reasonable price that remove virtually *all* contaminants (see *Sources of Recipes*). Different herbs must cook different lengths of time to extract their essences. Generally, soft, light herbs such as *Suk Gok* and *Shizandra* and herbs with a strong flavor such as *licorice* or *cinnamon* need short cooking time; whereas hard, heavy herbs such as most of the roots need extended cooking. Each recipe will give a recommendation in this regard.

The tea should be brought to a boil, at which time the flame should be turned down so that the brew continues to simmer (a low boil). Unless otherwise stated, the tea should be allowed to slowly cook until only ⅓ to ½ of the liquid remains. This should take from ½ to 2 hours. After the tea has been boiled down to this amount, allow it to cool somewhat and drink half of the remaining tea before a meal. Save the other half for later, at which time it should be reheated. Usually, the herbs can be cooked at least one, or possibly several more times before discarding. The spent herbs are puréed by people who have pets and mixed in with their food or are allowed to dry and, when dry, ground up and sprinkled on plant soil as fertilizer.

By far the *best* way to prepare the herbs by cooking is to use a "ginseng cooker." A ginseng cooker is a specially designed ceramic bowl. It has two lids, one flat and one domed which goes on top. Ginseng cookers come in a variety of sizes, the smallest being capable of holding about 1 cup of liquid and the largest being capable of holding several cups. The herbs are placed in the ginseng cooker along with enough water to fill the cooker up to the holes in the handles.

Place the cooker with its contents into a pot of water. The water level in the outer pot should come up to the bottom of the handles (see illustration). Turn on the burner and bring the outer water to a boil. Allow to simmer until the water has half boiled away from the outer pot. The liquid inside the cooker remains just below boiling and, because of the lids, does not evaporate. When half of the outer water is gone, fill the pot back up to the original level with hot water and continue to cook. This process is repeated several times, depending upon the time available and the strength of the tea desired. The tea, prepared in this manner, will be very rich. Drink as directed and save the remainder of the brew in a jar for reheating later. Meanwhile, the herbs should be refrigerated. Herbs cooked in a ginseng cooker can be recooked several times. If a root such as *ginseng* has been used, after the first cooking it is wise to break up the root into smaller pieces so that its inner tissue can be cooked in subsequent cookings. Many herbalists feel than it is the second cooking in a ginseng cooker that will yield the most potent tonic brew. This method has two great advantages. First, none of the elixir is lost in evaporated steam; and secondly, since the water remains slightly below boiling, some vitamins and enzymes remain intact that might otherwise be broken down during boiling. Ginseng cookers are all hand painted and are quite lovely. Antique ginseng cookers can also be found occasionally. New ginseng cookers, which are produced in the Peoples Republic of China, are very inexpensive (see *Sources of Recipes*). This is the recommended way to decoct Chinese tonic herbs.

Another very popular method of preparing tonics is to place the herbs in a jar of liquor so as to produce a tonic liqueur. Many people who enjoy this approach pay a visit to a liquor store in an Oriental neighborhood and use a Chinese, Japanese, or Korean spirit. Rice wine is very popular, but other liquors will suit different tastes. Western liquors can be used as well, vodka and tequilla being

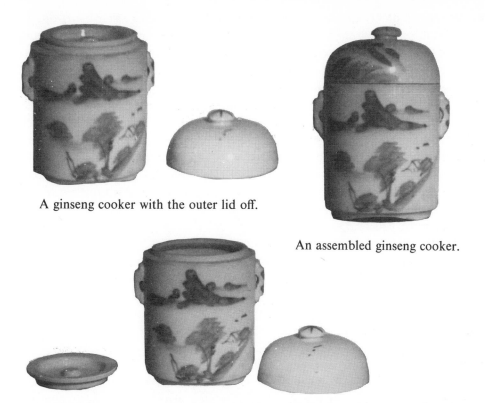

A ginseng cooker with the outer lid off.

An assembled ginseng cooker.

Ginseng cooker, showing the inner lid (left), bowl (center) and outer lid (right). This lovely cooker is handpainted, yet only cost a few dollars. It is the best method of cooking Chinese tonics.

The ginseng cooker, which is filled to the handles with water and herbs, is immersed in a pot of boiling water. This double boiling yields the purest extract and without waste.

commonly used. About one ounce of herbs should be placed in a quart of spirit. This should be allowed to sit in a dark place for two to six weeks before using. When this tonic has matured, one or two sake-cupfuls of the tonic liqueur, called a "chiew" in Chinese, can be consumed each day, usually after dinner or at bedtime. The tonic effects of this brew are destroyed by over-imbibing, so use it for what it is—a tonic. Of course, tonics prepared as liqueurs will have a slight immediate sedative effect but tend to show the tonic effects more quickly than tonics prepared by other methods. Of the techniques for preparing the tonics, this is the most convenient because it requires little effort and yields a potent tonic that, once mature, will last some time. Therefore time spent preparing the tonic is minimized. Be certain, if this is the method chosen, that a new tonic liqueur is prepared in time for it to mature (preferably six weeks or more) before the previous batch runs out.

Preparing the Chinese tonic herbs is an art, much like gourmet cooking. It requires careful attention to details and timing. As time goes by, the herbalist will know exactly how much of each ingredient to use, which method is most suited to their needs and to their life-style, and exactly how much preparation time is required. One of the great secrets of Chinese tonic herbalism lies in regularity; that is, arranging one's preparation time so that the tonics can be consumed rhythmically, each day at the same times.

Approach preparation as though it were a holy service. Maintain clean utensils and an orderly herb stock. Keep herbs tightly sealed to protect their freshness and to prevent invasion by vermin. Use only pure water. Obtain a tea cup that has a special feeling about it and use this cup just for your tonics. Though not necessary from a pharmacological point of view, Taoists or people of high consciousness usually give thanks before and after consuming their tonics. In this way, the greatest benefit from the tonics may be achieved.

6.2   Traditional Tonic Recipes

Chinese tonic herbalism has been a going concern for three thousand years. The tonics have been combined and recombined innumerable times, creating innumerable tonic formulae, and a vast formulary currently exists. Though many people prefer to use simple combinations, such as those described in Chapters 4 and 5, many people also enjoy preparing more complex or more specific tonic formulations.

There are incredible tonic combinations well suited to all the various needs of men and women, the young and old, the weak and strong. There are more great tonics than one could ever consume in a lifetime. But as the months and years pass, one who uses the Chinese tonics will find many occasions to change their tonic to suit new situations and needs.

Many formulae were developed long ago which have been passed on from generation to generation and age to age. Those formulae that have survived the test of time are now considered classics. These traditional recipes have been used thousands or millions of times and have proven their worth. The following collection of traditional tonic recipes is a representative cross-section of this great herbal tradition. A more complete collection of traditional recipes will be forthcoming in a future book, but the recipes that follow should provide the serious practicing tonic herbalist with some truly excellent choices.

6.3 Sources of the Recipes

The author has been collecting and testing recipes for over a decade. The recipes come from a wide variety of sources. Some were passed on to him by Master Sung Jin Park, who had in turn received knowledge from Grand Master Moo San Do Sha. These are generally ancient formulations, though some were developed by Moo San Do Sha.

Other sources include traditional and modern Oriental herbal texts and pharmacopias. Still other recipes were passed on to the author by various Oriental herbalists. Some of these were teachers, some were herb shopkeepers, and some were herb doctors.

In fact, the author has collected recipes from virtually every source available in the English language. All of the recipes presented in this chapter except for "Teeguarden's Shou Wu Chih" are traditional Chinese, Japanese, or Korean formulations. Of the several thousand recipes in the author's collection, this selection seemed to be most appropriate to this text.

Essentially, the recipes in this section are directed to the "intermediate" or "advanced" student of Chinese tonic herbalism; that is, one who has tested most of the basic recipes presented in Chapters 4 and 5 and is familiar with most or all of the major and minor tonics. However, if any of these recipes are especially appealing to the relative beginner, they should certainly be used, as long as instructions of preparation and dosage are followed scrupulously, and understanding of the actions of the tonic is clear. If one of the recipes is used by the novice, the individual herbs should be researched in Chapters 4 and 5. The tonic recipes listed here are all safe and will not result in negative side-effects if instructions are followed. But intelligence, good judgment, and common sense are necessary to assure optimal results. If you have any doubts, or suffer specific ailments, consult a physician or certified health practitioner. Do not continue using a formula if you believe there may be negative side effects.

6.4 Chinese Herbal Tonic Recipes

The following recipes utilize the major and minor tonics. The numbers next to the herbs indicate the proportion of the herb to be used in the formula. If no numbers are present, an equal amount of each herb should be used. The tonics may be prepared by any of the standard methods, unless otherwise stipulated. If cooking is the method of choice, longer cooking will result in a stronger tonic. Children may use these tonics, but the tonic should be diluted by half. Weak people or those recovering from illness should also use a weaker or diluted brew. However, specific tonics are presented for children and weakened adults and these are generally indicated for these people.

Ginseng and Tang Kuei Formula

Ginseng	2
Tang Kuei	2
Atractylus	1
Paeonia	1
Poria	1
Licorice	1
Cinnamon	1

This traditional tonic is said to tone up the muscles, build vitality, improve blood circulation, improve fluid metabolism, tone up the reproductive system, act as a blood tonic, strengthen metabolism, improve the appetite, and tone up the Kidney and central nervous system.

Li Shih Chen's Tonic Decoction

Ginseng
Atractylus
Poria
Licorice
Ginger
Red Jujube Dates

Li Shih Chen is China's most famous and respected herbalist. This seventeenth century master spent his entire lifetime collecting and compiling all the information on Chinese herbs and all the formulae available from all over China. His great classic on Chinese herbalism is the standard text of all Chinese herbalists to this day. This tonic decoction is one of his most highly recommended formulae. It is a general tonic for all conditions.

Mind Tonic

Tang Kuei	2	
Red Dates	2	
Ginseng	1	
Lycium	1	
Schizandra	1	
Astragalus	1	
Suk Gok	1	
Ma Huang	1	(optional)

This is a mental tonic. Used without the *Ma Huang*, it will gradually over a short period of time help to sharpen the memory, quicken the mind and clear the perceptions. It will help establish sound sleep and serve as a general tonic because of its tonic action on the Kidney system. Used with *Ma Huang*, its effects of sharpening the mind are powerful and immediate. This is an excellent tonic for any who are involved in strenuous mental activity. This formula also serves as a blood tonic, and without the *Ma Huang* is slightly sedative. The amount of *Ma Huang* used determines its stimulative effects.

Kim's Complete Tonifying Formula

Ginseng	
Atractylus	
Poria	Energy tonic
Licorice	
Rehmannia	
Paeonia	
Ligusticum	Blood tonic
Tang Kuei	
Astragalus	
Ginger	
Red Dates	Supplementary tonic
Cinnamon	

Dr. Se Han Kim is one of the great living masters of Oriental medicine. He is a true genius and a marvelous teacher. The author has met many great Oriental doctors and teachers, but none have surpassed the knowledge and skill of Master Se Han Kim. Master Kim received his training in a Taoist mountain temple in Korea. This formula is a prime example of Chinese tonic herbalism. This formula is composed of three groups of herbs. The first four herbs when prepared together make up one of Chinese herbalism's most famous and effective energy tonics. The second set of four herbs make up China's most famous blood tonic (see next recipe). The final four herbs are supplementary tonics that enhance the action of the overall concoction and have their own powerful tonic effects. A very small amount of each herb is used so that the total weight does not exceed one ounce. This is a perfect Chinese herbal tonic for anyone.

Four Things Soup

Tang Kuei	(double in the Fall)
Rehmannia	(double in the Winter)
Ligusticum	(double in the Spring)
Paeonia	(double in the Summer)

This is probably Chinese tonic herbalism's most famous and widely used tonic recipe. It is a superb blood tonic and is used by women to regulate their menstrual cycle and to tonify the reproductive system. It is also given to children, mixed with honey, to develop strong bones and teeth. It is highly recommended for teenagers who suffer from acne. *Cinnamon* may be added to increase circulation, and some women substitute *orange peel* for *Tang Kuei*. As noted, it is traditional procedure to double one of the ingredients, according to the time of the year. All women could benefit from this tonic, though it is also beneficial as a blood tonic for men and as a Kidney tonic to the young.

Cinnamon and Atractylus Formula

Cinnamon	1
Atractylus	2
Poria	1
Red Dates	3
Ginger	1
Licorice	1
Paeonia	1

This formula is used to fortify the entire system. It is said to improve circulation, strengthen the muscles and viscera, improve the appetite, tonify the Stomach, Heart and Kidney, and to act as a general blood tonic. If not cooked too long, this brew will be pleasant tasting and is an excellent children's tonic. Adults should drink it full strength.

Ginseng and Astragalus Formula

Ginseng	2
Astragalus	2
Tang Kuei	1
Atractylus	1
Orange Peel	1
Ginger	1
Red Dates	1
Licorice	1

This herbal tonic is used to supplement the vigor by tonifying the Stomach, improving the appetite, relieving fatigue, strengthening emotional stability, improving respiration, regulating the blood pressure, increasing resistance to stress and disease, tonifying the blood, sharpening the mind, and building muscular strength. It is currently being used in China as a post-operative tonic and to build strength after a disease. It can be used as a tonic for those who have experienced physical, mental or emotional fatigue. It can be used by those who are underweight and undernourished, as this is said to improve the absorptive ability of the body's cells. It is good for children when diluted.

Complete Tonic Formula

Ginseng

Tang Kuei
Atractylus
Poria
Ligusticum
Cinnamon
Astragalus
Rehmannia
Paeonia
Licorice

The Complete Tonic Formula is a well known tonic to strengthen body and mind. It helps build blood and beautify the skin, while toning up the muscle and adding sparkle to the eye. It is an energy tonic, a blood tonic, a Yang tonic and a Yin tonic; thus it derived its name. Consumed regularly, it will strengthen the constitution and lengthen life.

Teeguarden's Shou Wu Chih

Ho Shou Wu	3
Tang Kuei	3
Rehmannia	2
Orange Peel	2
Red Dates	2
Licorice	1

The commercial product known as Shou Wu Chih is one of the great tonic formulations known to man. However, it is sometimes not available, so we can make our own. Some of the herbs used in the commercial product are rare or unavailable, so this formula differs in some of its details from the commercial product, but the major herbs are the same and the overall effect is virtually identical. It should be cooked until it is very strong (preferably in a ginseng cooker).

Longevity Tonic

Ginseng
Ho Shou Wu
Lycium
Schizandra
Asparagus

This is a classic longevity tonic used by the Taoists. It is said to build the three Vital Treasures, *Ching*, *Ch'i* and *Shin*. It is believed to create a jovial personality and an open heart. It has a powerful tonic effect, in particular, on the Kidney and Liver.

Defense Energy Formula
Cinnamon
Red Dates
Licorice
Ginger
Paeonia
Ma Huang

As a tonic, this formula is used to replace other tonics when resistance is low and sensations are felt indicating a cold may be imminent, or even during a cold. This formula will increase circulation and build the *Wei Ch'i*, the defense energy that circulates in the subcutaneous layer of the skin. If a fever is present, this formula will cause perspiration, which should break the fever. This formula is by no means restricted to times of low resistance. It can be used any time as a mental tonic and stimulant and to relax the joints and tendons when one is under stress.

Shoulder Relaxing Fourmula
Tang Kuei	2
Atractylus	2
Paeonia	2
Licorice	1
Cinnamon	1

This recipe is used to improve blood circulation, to tonify the lumbar region, to strengthen the legs and hips, to strengthen and regulate the joints, and to relax the shoulders.

Vitality Combination
Poria
Ginger
Atractylus
Paeonia

This combination is used to tonify and regulate metabolism.

Recovery Tonic
Ginseng	3
Asparagus	5
Schizandra	5
Rehmannia	2
Ligusticum	2
Paeonia	2
Orange Peel	1

Licorice   1

This tonic is recommended by Chinese herbalists for those who are recovering from acute diseases to help restore vitality and to quicken the process of recovery. It improves metabolism, acts as a blood tonic and Kidney tonic, increases energy and rids the body of toxins.

Major Kidney Tonic

Rehmannia   6
Dioscoria   3
Cornus   3
Poria   3
Paeonia   3
Alismatus   3
Cinnamon   1

This formula is tonic to the Kidney system. It builds vitality, regulates the renal system, strengthens the brain, tonifies the reproductive organs, helps build strong bones and strengthens the spine, and is tonic to the eyes and ears.

Antler Energy Tonic

Deer Antler   1
Atractylus   1
Tienchi   1
Ginseng   1
Rehmannia ⎫
Paeonia   ⎬ 1
Poria   ⎭

Antler Energy Tonic is usually ground into a powder. One teaspoonful, or three capsules, of this tonic powder is taken with water twice daily for one month as a very powerful and effective energy tonic.

Tang Kuei Gin

Tang Kuei
Rehmannia
Paeonia
Astragalus
Poria
Licorice
Codonopsis
Ligusticum

Tang Kuei Gin is a famous excellent women's tonic formula. It is renowned as a blood tonic and for improving the functioning of the menstrual function. This formula is often prepared as an alcoholic extract.

Li Shih Chen's Aphrodisiac Pill
Cyperus
Poria
Honey

Grind the Cyperus and Poria into a powder and mix with honey to make pills. China's great herbalist considered it aphrodisiac.

Preserving Youth Pills
Atractylus
Ho Shou Wu
Red Dates
Lycium
Black Beans
Honey

This formula works best in pill form. It is said to benefit the Spleen and Kidney functions. Those taking these pills will retain their youthful appearance until seventy, according to the Chinese classic from which this recipe was derived.

Vital Essence Formula
Lycium	2
Schizandra	2
Ginseng	1
Deer Antler	1

This is one of the most potent tonics in the Chinese system. This formula is said to be an energy and blood tonic, to stengthen the mind and body, to build a powerful Kidney force which enlivens the entire body and mind, to benefit the vision and hearing, and is a powerful sexual tonic, suited to those who wish to be highly active sexually. This formula derives its name because it is said to enhance the "vital essence."

Poria Tonic
Poria	2
Ginger	1
Atractylus	1

Used in tea form to tone up the sexual organs.

Bupleurum Sedative Formula

Bupleurum	2
Scutellaria	1
Ginger	1
Paeonia	1
Red Dates	2

This tonic is recommended for those with a Yang constitution (broad jaw, strong muscles). It regulates the Liver and Gall Bladder, improves the appetite and alleviates muscle tension.

Paeonia Analgesic Tonic

Paeonia
Red Dates
Ginger
Licorice

This formula acts as a general tonic, building strength and blood, while improving blood circulation. It is also a Stomach and Blood tonic. It also has pain alleviating qualities, and is therefore often used as a tonic by women who have difficult menstrual periods.

Barefoot Doctor's Blood Tonic Formula #1

Ho Shou Wu
Tang Kuei
Red Dates
Soy Beans

This tonic soup is said to supplement and restore the energy and blood.

Barefoot Doctor's Blood Tonic Formula #2

Astragalus	3
Steamed Rehmannia	2
Tang Kuei	1

Used to regulate and restore the blood and energy.

Barefoot Doctor's Thyroid Tonic

Ho Shou Wu
Sea Vegetable

Used as a thyroid tonic and to regulate metabolism.

Athlete's Tonic

Ginseng	3

Astragalus	3
Atractylus	3
Bupleurum	2
Citrus	2
Ginger	2
Red Dates	2
Licorice	2

This tonic builds stamina. It will put weight on an underdeveloped athlete and will build blood. This famous body building and nourishing tonic formula builds strength and stamina quickly. It is a Stomach tonic and strengthens the intestines.

Nerve Tonic #1

Paeonia	3
Bupleurum	3
Atractylus	3
Poria	3
Ligusticum	3
Ginger	2
Licorice	1

This combination serves as a nerve tonic. It builds energy while relaxing the nerves. It is especially beneficial to those whose necks and shoulders are stiff. It will increase the appetite in those who refrain from eating because of a nervous stomach. This tonic is especially good for those who become easily flushed or who have hot flashes.

Nerve Tonic #2

Poria	3
Cinnamon	2
Atractylus	2
Licorice	1

This formula will strengthen the nervous system. It is tonic to the Heart and Kidney functions. It is especially beneficial to one who becomes dizzy easily.

Lycium Elixir

Lycium	4
Red Dates	1
Licorice	1

This tea is said to be a general tonic as well as being a sexual tonic, nerve tonic, and Kidney tonic.

Body Warming Formula

Atractylus	2
Paeonia	2
Red Dates	2
Ginger	2
Licorice	1

This tea warms the body and increases the metabolism of fluids. It improves fluid circulation and has diuretic actions. It is a Spleen-Kidney-Triple Warmer tonic.

Dioscorea Virility Wine

Dioscorea
Cornus
Schizandra
Ginseng

Extract these herbs in a good wine for six weeks. This tonic wine is strengthening to the virile powers, and beneficial to the Spleen and Stomach, therefore building muscle and energy.

Lycium-Rehmannia Wine

Rehmannia
Lycium

Allow to extract in good wine for six weeks. This is known as a fine tonic, especially as a sexual tonic.

Ho Shou Wu Wine

Ho Shou Wu
Atractylus
Lycium
Asparagus

Extract in Chinese glutinous rice wine. The resultant tonic is nourishing, tonic, aphrodisiac, and reconstructive.

Orange Peel-Ginger Formula

Orange Peel
Ginger

Decoct and drink. This simple tonic warms the hands and feet as well as the belly.

Atractylus-Tang Kuei Blood Tonic

Atractylus	3
Tang Kuei	3
Red Dates	2
Cinnamon	1

This is an excellent blood tonic.

Blood Cleanser

Paeonia	2
Tang Kuei	2
Rehmannia	1
Burdock root	3

Burdock root can be bought at any market that sells Oriental vegetables. Dried burdock root is available at any herb shop and at health food stores that carry herbs. This is a blood purifier and blood tonic.

Heart Tonic

Rehmannia
Tang Kuei
Poria
Cinnamon

Liver Tonic

Ho Shou Wu	2
Lycium	2
Paeonia	2
Ligusticum	1

Stomach Tonic

Poria	10
Atractylus	5
Ginger	1
Licorice	1

Renal Tonic

Ho Shou Wu
Poria
Astragalus
Rehmannia
Licorice

Sexual Tonic
Ginseng
Ho Shou Wu
Poria
Schizandra
Asparagus
Rehmannia
Licorice

Taken over time, this formula will tonify the Kidney system and the sexual function in particular.

Drinker's Formula
Atractylus
Cinnamon
Poria
Alismatus

This formula is recommended by the Chinese for those who have drunk too much alcohol.

Urinary Tonic
Rehmannia
Cornus
Astragalus
Paeonia
Dioscoria
Poria
Alismatus
Cinnamon

Make into capsules, and take three cupsules, three times a day. This outstanding formula is a general tonic with diuretic properties.

Weight Loss Tonic
Poria	10
Atractylus	5
Ginger	1
Licorice	1

This formula is a fine Kidney tonic with diuretic actions. The formula is especially useful as a weight loss tonic.

Anti-Anxiety Tonic

Licorice	3
Red Dates	10
Wheat	10

This is a famous remedy for hysteria, anxiety, and emotional disturbances of all sorts. It is also a great tonic for anemia, general weakness, and constipation.

7 | Compounding The Chinese Tonic Herbs

In Chinese herbalism herbs are rarely used alone. They are almost always "compounded" so as to bring about a desired effect. The tonics, however, are a very special class of herbs and this rule does not always hold. Many of the tonic herbs may be taken regularly by themselves without compounding. *Ginseng, Tang Kuei, Asparagus root, Licorice root, Ho Shou Wu* and many others can be used alone with great benefit and without problems.

Yet the art of compounding is fundamental to Chinese tonic herbalism, as it is to medicinal Chinese herbalism. In many cases, the effects of herbs can be enhanced or altered by combining with other herbs. This is why such a vast formulary exists, not only in the realm of medicinal herbalism but also in that of the tonics, as exemplified in the previous chapter. For this reason, the basic rules of compounding hold true in all branches of Chinese herbalism.

Those who use the Chinese tonic herbs invariably find themselves compounding their own formulas. This is a natural response to the desire to create tonics perfectly suited to the individual. Unlike the medicinal herbs, the tonics lend themselves well to this creative compounding. In order to develop excellent tonics, it is simply necessary to know the rules of compounding and the principles upon which they are based.

The basic principles of compounding are based upon the laws of Yin and Yang and upon the actions of the herbs individually and combined, and upon the fundamental principles of the Chinese health arts. The herbal compound must bring about energetic balance—this is the basis of the principle of *Li Ch'i*, "balancing the energy," upon which all Chinese health arts are based. All tonic formulae should have purely beneficial results, and should *never* have negative side-effects. This is based upon the principle of "do no harm." If the tonics are properly compounded, there will be no negative side-effects, but only improved health.

7.1 Traditionally Recognized Combinations

Often among the tonics, two or more herbs may be combined simply because they are known through experience to mutually benefit one another and have gained popular renown as excellent tonic compounds. A few examples of this are:

Ginseng and *Red Dates*
Lycium and *Schizandra*
Tang Kuei and *Astragalus*
Ho Shou Wu and *Tang Kuei*
Ginseng and *Ho Shou Wu*
Royal Jelly, Tang Kuei, and *Astragalus*
Lycium, Schizandra, and *Deer Antler*
Suk Gok and *Licorice*
Etc.

There are many such simple combinations that are accepted *a priori* by the Chinese after thousands of years of testing. Many such basic combinations are suggested in Chapters 4 and 5.

7.2   The "Four Responsible Positions" Method of Compounding

Chinese herbs are often compounded according to the various roles different herbs may play in the formula. This is known as the "Four Responsible Positions" method of compounding. According to this method, there are four positions in a formula: King, Minister, Assistant, and Servant. Each position plays an important role in the formula that assures its proper balance and effects.

According to this method, there is a principle herb which is basic to the formula. This herb, called the *King*, is selected according to the purpose of taking a tonic and upon the primary effect desired. It is also, like all the herbs, selected according to the person's condition and according to atmospheric conditions such as the weather and season. Generally, a powerful herb is used as the King which has whole-body tonic effects as well as more specific tonic action. Ginseng, for example, is very commonly used as a King herb in Chinese tonic recipes.

Another herb is added as the primary assistant to the King. It is known as the *Minister*. This tonic herb reinforces the actions of the King. There may be more than one Minister, and occasionally there can be more than one King. In the tonic herbal system, the King and Minister are always of the "superior herb" class. If a tonic compound is to have more than one primary action, say to build *Ch'i and* Blood, two Kings may be used: one which is an energy tonic and one which is a blood tonic. Each of these Kings will then be supported by a Minister with like action. The Minister, however, may have a different atmospheric energy and may enter different meridians, in order to balance the energy of the formula.

A third responsible position is called the *Assistant*. This herb, or herbs, is included in order to counteract any possible actions that may be brought about by the King and/or Minister herbs which are not desired, or to tone up areas and functions not within the scope of the King and Minister. Thus if the King and Minister are primarily energy tonics, the Assistant may be a blood tonic. Or if the King or Minister cause energy to rise and this is not desirable, the Assistant may be chosen because it counteracts this effect. The Assistant serves to bring balance and harmony to the formula.

The fourth position is called the *Servant*. The Servant acts to harmonize the various ingredients and to insure proper absorption into the meridians, blood stream and organs. In medicinal herbalism, the Servant is often used to treat pain and to give quick symptomatic relief of symptoms, while the King and Minister attack the disease at the root. In tonic herbalism, however, the Servant mainly acts as the harmonizer and serves as a guide. The servant may also have its own tonic effects which must fit properly into the compound.

Let us take a look at a couple of examples of this method. A well known ginseng formula is composed of four herbs: *Ginseng, Atractylus, Ginger,* and *Licorice.* In this formula, *ginseng* is the King. It acts to tone up the spleen and to enhance the production of essential energy (Ying and Wei). *Ginseng* thus sets the tone of the compound. It also has whole-body tonic effects and is, of course, of the "superior herb" class. The *Atractylus* is the Minister. *Atractylus* is an tonic herb of the highest order and is itself often used as the King. The *Atractylus* is used in this formula to support the energy tonic actions of the *ginseng*, which acts upon the Spleen. *Atractylus*, too, has Spleen tonic and energy tonic action and further regulates the energy in this region (the middle burning space). It also adjusts the fluid balance and regulates the appetite. The Assistant is the dried, sliced ginger used in Chinese tonic herbalism. It also supports the action of the King by warming up the middle region and the intestines. *Ginger* improves circulation, and good circulation is necessary if ginseng is to work properly. If circulation becomes blocked up, *ginseng's* powerful effects may become too concentrated in certain areas and may not be distributed to the whole body as it should. *Licorice root* plays the role of Servant in this formula, a role it plays quite well and quite often. *Licorice* is well known for its ability to harmonize various herbal ingredients and to enhance their absorption. *Licorice* is, in addition, tonic to the Stomach, Lungs and Kidney and helps regulate sugar and fluid metabolism. Licorice is called the "Great Adjunct" because of its abilities to harmonize all other herbs. *Licorice root* is also known as the "Great Detoxifier" because it harmlessly rids the body of toxins and removes toxins, if there are any, from herbal compounds. *Licorice* assures a smooth ride for the King and Minister herbs and prevents negative side-effects.

The above described tonic formula acts as an energy tonic. It will tone up the metabolism, developing the Central *Ch'i* and nourishing the flesh. It also has blood tonic effects, because *Ch'i* leads Blood, and because good digestion leads to strong blood. It builds the essential energy, will be slightly stimulating, and will have diuretic effects. All of the effects associated with the King herb, *ginseng*, will result from use of this tonic.

As a second example of compounding according to this method, let us formulate a tonic designed to fortify the organism while concentrating on improving vision. We will call it the *Eye Tonic*. First we will use a major herb as King which will have whole-body tonic action via the Liver, which controls the eyes. An excellent choice is *Ho Shou Wu*, which is said to calm the nervous system, tonify the Liver and clear the eyes. As the Minister we will use *Lycium*, which is famed for its benefit to the eyes as well as to the system as a whole. *Lycium*, too, is a Liver tonic. For an Assistant we will use *Red Dates* because of their general buffering action and also because it is a Liver tonic. The *Red Dates* play their role as Assistant in this formula perfectly since it is also a Blood tonic, in contrast to its King, *Ho Shou Wu*, which is an energy tonic. *Red Dates* are also known to combine well with *Ho Shou Wu* and *Lycium*. The *Red Dates* also play something of a Servant role in this formula because, like *Licorice*, it helps the body to absorb the tonic and rectifies negative side-effects. But playing the official role of Servant in this formula is a non-tonic herb that is highly reputed for its benefits to the eyes. This herb is the small Oriental chrysanthemum flower. These flowers are used in Chinese herbalism to directly and quickly benefit the eyes and vision by clearing obstructions and allowing energy to flow freely through the eyes. This herb also helps to clear up eye congestion and eye infections in medicinal herbalism. The formula thus reads:

> *Ho Shou Wu* (King),
> *Lycium* (Minister),
> *Red Dates* (Assistant and Servant),
> *Chrysanthemum flowers* (Servant).

This combination of herbs may be decocted, or it may be extracted in alcohol for a few weeks, after which time one *saké*-cupful may be consumed before bed each night. An alcohol extract is indicated here because alcohol goes to the Liver, carrying the herbs with it. The alcohol thus acts as a guide to the herbs. This so-called "Eye Tonic" is much more than just that. The first three herbs are marvelous longevity tonics. This brew, with or without the chrysanthemum flowers, is a virtual "Liqueur of Longevity."

In creating your own tonics, follow these principles and all the other lessons and advice offered in this text. Within a relatively short time you will master Chinese tonic herbalism and will be on the High Road to Immortality!

8 | Commercially Prepared Tonics

For those who do not wish to be bothered selecting individual herbs and with the subsequent preparation, there is an excellent alternative. On the market today in America are commercially prepared Chinese herbal tonics of every description and for every need. It is not possible to describe all of the tonic preparations available. This would require a volume in itself. Many of the tonics are composed of a long list of common and rare herbs and some are prepared by complex and sophisticated processes. Others are less complex, or use traditional recipes handed down in a family of herbalists for generations. And there are tonics that are newly developed.

Products come in many forms. There are extracts, oral liquids, pills, capsules, and liquors. In this chapter, a selection of these tonic preparations will be described in some detail to give the student of Chinese tonic herbalism an idea of what is available and what to look for. A listing of the tonics readily available in American Chinatowns and Koreatowns, as well as in healthfood stores will be presented as well. Those products that will be discussed in some detail are those with which the author is personally familiar, has used, and of which he is confident.

By using these commercially prepared tonics, the student of Chinese tonic herbalism will not only be using the tonics, but will also receive valuable instruction in the Chinese tonic herbal system. It is routine practice to include a sheet or booklet within the box that each tonic comes in. These information sheets describe the actions and indications of the herbal product and list the ingredients. Many of these sheets are quite detailed providing a great deal of interesting and valuable information. Many, it will be observed, use very poor English, but the ideas are usually gotten across. Collecting these packing sheets and booklets will eventually yield an interesting collection of reference materials.

A few Chinese products no longer provide these sheets because they have been banned by the United States government for one reason or another, usually because of making claims unsubstantiated in the United States according to the Federal Drug Administration. However, even American companies such as East Earth Herbs, which produces many excellent Chinese herbal tonic products, print information sheets, though they are of course very careful to follow FDA regulations when it comes to making medicinal claims. In the late 1970's the United States government actually banned the importation of any herbal products containing *ginseng* into the United States, asserting that *ginseng* falls into the category of a "food additive" and being unapproved by the FDA, though very widely used, it could not be used without FDA testing and approval. However, *ginseng* was already being widely distributed and government efforts to stop the importation of such *ginseng* products proved unpopular and virtually ineffective, and the effort was soon abandoned.

Most of the tonic preparations manufactured for mass consumption use fine herbs, and are produced by people who have a sincere belief that their products are excellent. Another important quality of these commercial tonics is price. It often costs much less to use commercially prepared products than to make one's own tonics, even when using the identical herbs. For example, the cost of preparing a *ginseng* extract such as "Panax Ginseng Extractum" would be far greater if we were to buy the *ginseng* roots whole in a Chinese herb shop and make our own. Therefore, the commercial tonics are actually quite a bargain. However, sometimes we can buy higher grade *ginseng* and make a tonic of still higher quality, though we must pay for the improved quality.

In general though, the most common reasons for using commercial tonics are reliability and convenience. It is just so easy to take a few pills or put an extract in a cup of hot water. And because we can purchase the identical product any time, we can feel secure that we can follow a regimen for an extended period of time if so desired.

Let us now look at some of the commercial tonics available in America.

8.1 Extracts

There are many good extracts available and some great ones. Virtually all of the most important major tonic herbs are commercially available as extracts, though they may be blended with other tonic herbs.

Shou Wu Chih: Shou Wu Chih is one of the most popular commercial tonic preparations. This truly excellent product has as its primary constituents *Ho Shou Wu, Tang Kuei*, and *Rehmannia*. It is both an energy tonic and a blood tonic. It is specifically tonic to the Kidney and Liver systems, as is its King herb, *Ho Shou Wu*. Taken for a period of time, this herbal will build blood and vitality visibly. Sleep will become deep and sound, and the sex life will change significantly for the better. Continued use is said to maintain youthfulness and prolong life. A couple of tablespoons in hot water make a rich tea, to be consumed at bedtime and before breakfast.

Panax Ginseng Extractum: Panax Ginseng Extractum is made from *Kirin ginseng*. This popular mainland Chinese product is highly concentrated and of good quality. Though *Kirin* is the lowest grade of Chinese *ginseng*, it is still effective when taken regularly. This extract is mild and inexpensive. It takes many *ginseng* roots to make one bottle of this extract, so it is actually a good bargain. Several drops the extract a day in tea will provide the results expected from *ginseng*.

Ginseng-Antler Extract: This combination of two very potent tonics has been used in China for two thousand years. This formula exerts the many tonic actions of both of these herbs. It is said to strengthen physical power, regenerate energy, nourish the blood, promote the secretion of saliva, and serve as a roborant and nutrient tonic. It is further said to balance the emotional responses, inhibit over-excitation of the nervous system, nourish the brain, tranquilize the nerves, improve mental power, enhance the sythesizing of proteins and RNA, build blood, regulate carbohydrate metabolism, increase physical resistance, and accelerate healing. These are all effects of *ginseng* and *antler* extract demonstrated in the laboratory. This fine tonic includes *Ginseng* (33%), *Antler* (2%), Honey (50%), and distilled water (15%). Instructions are provided in the package.

Pantocrin: Pantocrin is the extract of *Deer Antler*. This is a premium product, and is one of the great bargains of Chinese tonic herbalism. It is manufactured and bottled in the Peoples Republic of China. This precious extract has many fine qualities that make it one of the best tonics money can buy. Pantocrin is a sweet, pleasant tasting liquid which comes with a dropper. Ten drops under the tongue are taken daily or more often, as needed, to increase physical vigor and mental acuity. Pantocrin has been proven to be beneficial to metabolism, to the heart, central nervous system and brain, to the reproductive system, and as a general tonic after childbirth. Pantocrin has central nervous system stimulating qualities and the Chinese use it as an energy tonic. It is widely used by men as a sexual tonic to improve potency. This product is well worth exploring.

Ginseng Polygona Root Extract: This combination of two of China's greatest longevity herbs is not widely distributed in America, but is available from some

sources and is well worth any trouble gone to obtain it. Li Ch'ing Yuen, who lived to be 252 years old, used this formula as his tonic for the last 100 years of his life. Both herbs are excellent energy tonics, though together they not only provide energy but have a slight sedative action which results in sound sleep. *Ginseng* affects the Spleen and Lung systems while *Ho Shou Wu* (referred to as *Polygona* in the name of this product) is a Kidney and Liver tonic. This tonic has blood tonic effects, strengthens the sinews and bones, enriches the marrow, sperm and ova, brightens the countenance, maintains the natural rich color of the hair, and if taken for a long time, is said to prolong life. A few drops of the superior tonic is taken in tea, several times a day.

Tang Kuei Gin (pronouced *jeen*): Tang Kuei Gin is produced by several different companies. It contains *Tang Kuei* as its prevalent ingredient (69%), along with small portions of *Astragulus, Paeonia, Rehmannia, Licorice, Codonopsitis, Poria,* and *Lingusticum.* Tang Kuei Gin is considered to be a superlative women's tonic. It is said to be nourishing to the blood, and regulating to the menstrual cycle. It increases physical strength, and helps build flesh. Tang Kuei Gin is also used by many men as an excellent blood tonic. This extract is taken in hot water.

Dragon Brew: A very fine herb company called East Earth Herbs produces one of the best lines of tonic products available. East Earth Herbs is an American company which deals strictly in Chinese tonics. The author has watched this company closely since its inception in the early 1970's and has come to the conclusion that it would be almost impossible to be more dedicated, to have more integrity, or to have more knowledge than East Earth Herbs.

Unlike most Chinese herb companies, East Earth Herbs uses only *premium grade* herbs in their products. For example, where other Chinese herb companies universally use *Kirin Ginseng* in any product that uses *ginseng*, East Earth Herbs uses *Shiu Chu Ginseng*, which is of a much higher quality. In one case (see "Sages' Ginseng"), they even use wild Chinese *ginseng* and semi-wild *Yi-Sun Ginseng*. The same is true of all the herbs used in East Earth Herbs' products: all are of very high grade. Remarkably, their products are not that much more expensive than their Chinese counterparts which use the less expensive commercial grade herbs. "Commercial grade" Chinese herbs are of high quality, but "premium grade" is the best you can get. East Earth Herbs' products are available in most health food stores and by mail order, but are not found in Chinese shops.

East Earth Herbs produces one liquid tonic concentrate. It is called "Dragon Brew." "Dragon Brew" is a complex and powerful tonic concentrate. It is a well-balanced herbal, using twenty-nine tonic herbs in just the right proportions to tonify and balance all of the systemic functions and to regulate the five elemental energies. Half of these herbs provide primarily Yang energy. Some of these herbs are: *Ma Huang (Ephedra sinensis) Codonopsis, Licorice root, Ginger, Atractylus, Astragalus, Eucommia bark, Ho Shou Wu, Tang Kuei,* and *Aconite.* The herbs used to tonify the Yin energies include: *Lycii berries, Orange Peel, Bupleurum root, Scutellaria root, Peony root, Schizandra berries, Poria cocos,* and *Royal Jelly.*

What makes this tonic truly unique, and impressive, is in the addition of one further ingredient. To the extract of the twenty-nine superior herbs is added a ferment, which transforms the herbs slightly so that they are more easily assimilated and utilized by the body. The culture used in "Dragon Brew" is very ancient and comes from north central Asia, where it has long been valued for its ability to stimulate intestinal action and for its ability to improve the production and circulation of *Ch'i* and blood. It builds a full force of intestinal flora in the intestines, which also produce a variety of B vitamins. The culture is a strain of one bacteria and three different yeasts.

"Dragon Brew" is definitely an energy tonic. As a matter of fact, studies made by East Earth Herbs have shown that drinking "Dragon Brew" results in three distinct energy peaks, as well as an overall balanced high level of energy lasting over a long period of time. The first energy peak comes immediately after drinking it. A second energy peak comes 20 to 30 minutes later when the *Ma Huang* takes effect. *Ma Huang* contains ephedrine, a powerful central nervous system stimulant (see in-depth discussion of *Ma Huang* in Chapter 5). Six hours later, the total effects of the twenty-nine tonic herbs results in a third noticeable energy peak as they affect the organs and the energy system. East Earth Herbs says that one's energy becomes permanently enhanced if one does not waste the energy, but instead learns to store it through meditative practices such as Zen meditation, Tai Ch'i Chuan, or the Taoist Internal Exercises (*Nei Gung*). Receiving an acupressure treatment of the higher forms, such as *Jin Shin Do* or *Tsubo Therapy*, also enhances the accumulation, circulation and storage of these energies.

It is the author's experience that it is best to start off slowly with "Dragon Brew." Use only a half dose the first couple of days and build up to a full dose over the next few days. If you experience gas from "Dragon Brew," it is because your stomach and intestines are weak. Do not be a martyr to health; instead, gradually and comfortably increase the dosage until the full dose is readily assimilated. Be aware of the energy peaks, but be careful not to abuse the energy. Instead, try to relax and allow the energy to accumulate deep in your being.

Ginseng Bee Secretion: One of the finer commercial products, "Ginseng Bee Secretion," has already made its mark on the Western market. It is available at many health food stores as well as at Chinese herb shops and markets. The thick, sweet syrup has as its ingredients: *Ginseng* (12%), *Royal Jelly* (2%), *Deer Antler* (5%), *Tang Kuei* (3%), *Astragalus* (7%), *Cordyceps* (4%), *Licorice root* (5%), and *Polygonum multiflorum* (2%). It is important to note that two versions of this product are available on the Western market: one which uses honey and one which uses sugar to create the sweet syrup. By all means, look for the variety that uses the honey base. Most health food stores carry the honey-base variety.

"Ginseng Bee Secretion" comes in a lovely bottle with a large unique "eye-dropper." The dropper's large rubber bulb has an embossed *ginseng* root on it. The dropper is used to extract approximately 15 to 20 ml. of the syrup from the bottle. This is added to tea, or may be squirted straight into the mouth. It is very sweet and pleasant tasting. It is a perfect tonic product with which to get started with Chinese tonic herbalism, because it uses the super-stars of Chinese tonic herbalism, is easy to use, and tastes good. Also, children love it because it tastes like liquid candy (they like to have it squirted straight into their little mouths). If you have a problem with sugar, this product may not be right for you; but if you do not, it is well worth the $7 for a bottle. After openning, keep "Ginseng Bee Secretion" refrigerated.

To introduce your friends to the Chinese tonic herbs, squeeze some of this tonic syrup into a regular cup of tea. They'll enjoy it.

8.2 Oral Liquids

The Chinese market a series of products known as the "oral liquids." These have proven to be an extremely popular form of Chinese tonic preparation in recent years. These liquids are bottled in small (10 c.c.) ampules and generally come in boxes of ten such vials. In most cases the glass vials containing the sterile extract must be sliced at the neck with a glass-cutting stone that is provided in the package. At the narrowest part of the neck, the stone is used to *gently* scratch a circle around the bottle. A plastic safety-cap is provided, which is fitted over the head of the ampule after the scratch has been made. With a quick snap, the head is snapped off. The nectar within is now ready to be drunk through a small straw which is provided in the package (ten such straws are provided).

These oral liquids are very popular because they generally use very famous tonic herbs and because they are very palatable—some are even delicious. It seems that people like them because of the unique and exotic packaging as well. Because of the excellence and purity of these products, which retail at very reasonable prices (between $4 and $12 a box), these are perfect for many consumers. Old-time herb-users keep a supply of their favorite oral liquids on hand at all times. The oral liquids are frequently available at health food stores and are always available in Chinese markets. Chinese shops generally carry a wider variety of these oral liquids than do health food stores.

One word of warning: always use the plastic safety-cap when breaking off the head so that you do not cut yourself. We are trying to build blood, not lose it!

Peking Royal Jelly Oral Liquid: This is one of the most popular inexpensive tonic preparations on the market. It is considered a "supertonic" by the Chinese. Each of the 10 c.c. vials of "Peking Royal Jelly" contains 250 mg. of *Royal Jelly* (bottled fresh), together with 60 mg. of *Codonopsitis* and 40 mg. of *Lycium* extracts.

This excellent formula is believed to provide physical and mental energy, make the body strong, strengthen the Lungs, Spleen and Liver and to lengthen life. It is excellent as a tonic after heavy stress, or while recovering from an illness or childbirth. Please re-read the discussions on *Royal Jelly*, *Codonopsitis* and *Lycium* in Chapter 4 to fully realize the value of this elixir.

This is another easy-to-use, effective, and tasty product with which you might start your adventure into Chinese tonic herbalism. Buy a box and consume one or two vials daily. It is the manufacturer's recommendation that the user take the herb twice daily for optimum effect—once early in the morning and again at bedtime. The nectar is delicious and easy to consume (and fun, too!). The author believes in following directions, but most people who are familiar with the Chinese tonics use the oral liquids somewhat differently than the manufacturer's suggested way. Most people take "Peking Royal Jelly," or any of the oral liquids, for that matter, anytime they please. All of the oral liquids are excellent for a burst of energy, so many people consume an ampule or two of their favorite oral liquid in the afternoon or early evening for a lift. As a matter of fact, the author just drank two bottles of his favorite oral liquid, "Pantocrin Oral Liquid" (see below for description of this product) for a late afternoon burst of mental energy.

Children love "Peking Royal Jelly Oral Liquid" and it is considered to be very good for children by the Chinese. But, because of the danger of cutting oneself on the glass, an adult should always open the ampule for them. Throw away the empty ampules immediately because they are sharp and, once opened, brittle. Discard the used straw as well. Keep your box of oral liquids out of the reach of children because they are so much fun to use that the kids may try to do it on their own just for play.

If you use "Peking Royal Jelly Oral Liquid" for a few days, you will start to feel more energy and experience a sharpening of the mind. Once you have been using tonics for a short while, you will feel the effects of this and the other oral liquids virtually immediately.

Pantocrin Oral Liquid: "Pantocrin Oral Liquid" is essentially the same product as the "Pantocrin" extract described in the previous section. However, it is diluted and prepared for direct consumption. This is one of the author's very favorite tonics. This great tonic has almost immediate effects, stimulating and invigorating the central nervous system in a mild, smooth, pleasant and profound way. The author always keeps a box of "Pantocrin Oral Liquid" on the shelf.

There is something quite extraordinary about the flavor of Pantocrin, too, which adds to one's attraction to this great tonic. This crystal clear, mildly sweet tasting oral liquid is one of the best products available at any price and should be high up on the list of herbal products to buy and try.

Red Panax Ginseng Extractum: Like "Pantocrin Oral Liquid," which is simply the pure, unadulterated extract of just one herb, *Deer Antler*, "Red Panax Ginseng Extractum" is the pure extract of just one herb, *Kirin Ginseng*. This is the oral liquid for people who just want a straight dose of *ginseng*. It is a diluted version of the Kirin "Panax Ginseng Extractum" concentrate described in the previous section. As an oral liquid, it is a simple and pleasant way to get one's daily dose of the "King of Herbs." The taste is distinctly that of *ginseng*. If *ginseng* appeals to you, read again the discussion of *ginseng* in Chapter 4 to realize the value of this great tonic herb.

Renshenfengwangjiang: It may appear difficult to pronounce, but this is still one of the most popular oral liquids, even among Americans. Actually, it is not as difficult to pronounce as it may seem at first glance. "Ren shen" is a Chinese pronunciation of *ginseng*; "feng wang" is *Royal Jelly*; and "jiang" means oral liquid. Ren-shen/feng-wang/jiang! Practice it a few times. Learn how to pronounce it—you'll impress your friends.

This preparation is very popular because it combines China's two most famous herbal tonics in a wonderful balance of Yin and Yang. "*Ginseng* and *Royal Jelly* Oral Liquid" makes a perfect simple tonic suitable for both men and women, young and old. All extracts that contain any substantial quantity of *ginseng* are dominated by its flavor. "Renshenfengwangjiang" is not as delicious as "Peking Royal Jelly Oral Liquid" or "Pantocrin Oral Liquid," but it is still quite palatable, or even good tasting to one who is used to *ginseng*. All commercial Chinese tonics (except for those produced by GMS Products and East Earth Herbs) use *Kirin Ginseng*, which is mild and can be taken daily to build energy and to expand one's adaptability. The *Royal Jelly* used in this product is bottled fresh and therefore loses none of its nutritional qualities.

Royal Jelly Oral Liquid: Though this oral liquid bears a title which seems to indicate a pure *Royal Jelly* extract, it is in fact a formulation which also contains a pair of subsidiary tonics. Each ampule of this herbal essence contains not only 250 mg. of freshly bottled *Royal Jelly*, but also contains 50 mg. of *Schizandra* extract and 25 mg. of *Kirin Ginseng* extract. *Schizandra*, as described in Chapter 4, is a major tonic herb with many substantial attributes, including the ability to beautify and strengthen the skin, strengthen the Lungs and Kidney, and increase sexual capacity in both men and women. *Schizandra* was used as a tonic by China's imperial households for centuries because of these effects.

This nectar tastes very good and is generally similar in its properties to "Peking Royal Jelly Oral Liquid" described above. Though it can be taken by men and women, young or old, it is generally favored by women.

Astragali-Codonopsitis Extract: This oral liquid is not as readily found in America as the oral liquid products described above. It is probably not as easily marketable because *Astragalus* and *Codonopsitis* are not well-known in the West, whereas *ginseng* and *Royal Jelly* have become well-established products in the health food industry and are recognized by individuals who are familiar with herbs. Although *Astragalus* and *Codonopsitis* are not as well-known as *ginseng* and *Royal Jelly*, they are certainly of equal quality and value. Both are first-class herbs. *Astragalus*, as mentioned in the thorough discussion of this herb in

Chapter 4, is often considered to be a better tonic for young, active people than *ginseng*. Like *ginseng*, it is a superb energy tonic; but *Astragalus* provides more immediate energy to the outer body, especially to the muscles. *Astragalus* is considered the perfect herb for the athlete or for the person that must work hard physically. It also improves blood circulation, and builds the immune system.

Codonopsitis is very similar to *ginseng* in its effects, it is said that any formula calling for *ginseng* can use *Codonopsitis* in its place. The high commercial grade of *Codonopsitis* used in this product is certainly as excellent a tonic as the *Kirin* (good commercial grade) *Ginseng* used in the other oral liquids. *Codonopsitis* is said to build flesh and to strengthen the muscles.

Each 10 c.c. ampule of "*Astragali-Codonopsitis Extract*" contains 4 grams of pure *Astragalus* extact and 4 grams of pure essence of *Codonopsitis*. This is actually quite potent, and therefore its taste is somewhat strong, though easily consumed. This is perhaps the most potent of the oral liquids, along with "Pantocrin," and therefore costs somewhat more than the other oral liquids which use more famous herbs, but less of them.

It is said that this product "is good for increasing vigor, nourishing blood, strengthening the Stomach and Spleen, and affords the good effects of calming the nerves, improving health and is conducive to longevity, if taken regularly." This is the best of the oral liquids for those who are into athletics or who must work hard physically because it tonifies and invigorates the musculature and improves surface circulation. Take a vial or two before working out or before work in addition to a morning dose. It is also excellent for those with low resistance to infection.

8.3 Pills and Tablets

Many fine Chinese herbal products are sold in the form of pills or tablets. These usually use honey as a binder. The pills generally have a thin sugar or honey-glazed coating, whereas the tablets have no coating. The list of such products actually numbers in the hundreds, and a visit to a Chinese herb shop, especially to one that features commercially prepared products, could be overwhelming to the beginner in Chinese tonic herbalism; unless, of course, you know what you are looking for.

In this section, we will explore the tablet and pill-formed tonics. There is not the space to discuss all of the products available so we will take a close look at the most famous and important ones. As time passes and you gain experience, explore the herb shop shelves for possible alternatives, if you like. Many of the products available in Chinese herb shops include special herbs other than the ones discussed in this book. These are often local specialties or rare products. The pills that we will be discussing here use primarily the major and minor tonic herbs described in Chapters 4 and 5.

Shou Wu Pian: "Shou Wu Pian" (pian means "pill") are simply pills made of 100% *Ho Shou Wu (Polygonum multiflorum)*. The herb is ground into powder, formed into pills, which are sugar-coated for easy consumption, and bottled. As described in detail in Chapter 4, *Ho Shou Wu* is one of China's most respected energy tonics. It has a great reputation as a rejuvenation herb and for expanding one's life-span. It is considered to be an excellent tonic to the Liver and Kidney functions. Taken regularly, "Shou Wu Pian" is said to increase vigor, preserve youthfulness, strengthen the sexual function, and lengthen life.

Halonyuan (Black Dragon Tonic Pill): "Halonyuan" is one of the most prized tonics in the Chinese pharmacopia. These pills are made by combining *ginseng*, *Deer Antler*, and a number of other high-grade tonics. It is believed that Halonyuan can promote health, generate vitality, and make a person look and feel younger. One to three pills are to be taken twice daily with warm water or soup. It is said that a person taking Halonyuan can expect to feel calm and stronger after just two or three days. After using Halonyuan for two or three weeks, dramatic changes might occur: the mind becomes conscious and quick, the memory becomes sharp, the skin develops luster, the Kidneys become strong (also implying improved sexual functioning), sleep becomes deep and satisfying, and the body becomes strong.

Halonyuan is of equal benefit to men and women. This famous supertonic is used by tens of thousands of people. The formula is an ancient one, famous as a Kidney tonic of the highest order.

Cerebral Tonic Pills: These popular pills use fourteen herbs to achieve the desired result of strengthening the mind. *Tang Kuei, Schizandra, Lycii berries*, and the seeds of the *Red Jujube Date* are the dominant tonic herbs in the formula.

"Cerebral Tonic Pills" are used as a mental and general tonic to aid, in particular, the function of the Kidney. It is said in the Chinese health arts that the power of the mind is dependent upon the energy of the Kidney function. Therefore, any good Kidney tonic is also a "cerebral tonic." However, these pills contain a rare product: the fossilized bone of the Mastodon, which the Chinese call "*Dragon Bone*." This rare substance has been proven to be a superb, though mild, natural tranquilizer. Therefore the Cerebral Tonic Pills have a general sedative action while tonifying those functions that will result in a stronger memory and clearness and quickness of thought. The pills also have a positive side-effect of being a fine blood tonic. They are especially beneficial to people who have been under heavy mental and/or emotional stress and who wish to overcome their mental fatigue.

Shih Chuan Ta Pu Tonic Pills: These pills contain *Tang Kuei, Licorice root, Atractylus, Codonopsitis, Astragalus, Rehmannia, Cinnamon, Poria, Paeonia* and *Ligusticum*, all of which are described in Chapters 4 and 5. With such a complete range of tonic herbs, this herbal cannot help but do wonders. It is considered to be tonic to all of the functions of body and mind. This fine herbal tonic preparation is said to build energy and blood, to regulate the five elemental energies, to regulate the appetite, to add strength to the muscles and joints, to develop a strong mind, to balance the emotions, and if taken regularly, to lengthen life. This is a fine general tonic suitable for both men and women.

Tabellae Tang-Kuei: These pills are composed of 100% *Tang Kuei*, except for a thin sugar-coating to help them go down easier. They are used primarily by women as a general tonic. *Tang Kuei*, as described in detail in Chapter 4, is an excellent blood tonic and has wonderful effects upon the female reproductive system.

It is worth mentioning, at this point, that Western health food stores now carry many brands of 100% *Tang Kuei* pills, tablets, and capsules. It is difficult to assess which is of the highest quality. It is the author's opinion that if you want to be assured of getting the most out of your herbs, you should purchase a high quality whole *Tang Kuei* root from a reputable source and take this on a daily basis (preparation is described in Chapter 4). However, for the lazy, "Tabellae Tang-Kuei" or other such commercially prepared *Tang Kuei* pills are sufficient.

Angelica Tablets: Angelica is *Tang Kuei*. "Angelica Tablets" are sugar-coated pills used primarily as a woman's tonic. They contain 70% *Tang Kuei*, and 10% each of *Atractylus, Red Jujube Dates* and *Ligusticum*. This is an excellent woman's tonic, being tonic and regulating to the female reproductive functions, and is a superb blood tonic. The three herbs that are used here to supplement *Tang Kuei* vastly enhance the actions of *Tang Kuei* and make this a product superior to plain *Tang Kuei* pills unless the *Tang Kuei* is known to be of a high grade. To be effective, 3–5 tablets must be consumed three times daily with warm water, tea or soup.

Ginseng Antler Pill: This herbal pill consists of not only *ginseng* and *Deer Antler*, but also a long list of other superior tonics, including: *Codonopsitis, Lycii berries, Poria, Rehmannia, Atractylus, Schizandra, Licorice,* and *Dioscoria*. This is a popular and, indeed, a fine general tonic. Two to four pills are taken three times a day with warm liquid.

Tienchi Ginseng Tablet: See Chapter 5 for a detailed discussion of *Tienchi Ginseng*. These tablets are 100% raw *Tienchi*. *Tienchi* has long been used to rejuvenate and strengthen the organs, tissues and functions of the Circulatory system. *Tienchi* has been proven to reduce hypertension, and to benefit the heart.

Dragon Eggs: As mentioned earlier in this chapter while discussing "Dragon Brew," a company known as East Earth Herbs produces a superb line of products, most of which come in tablet form. These tablets they call "Dragon Eggs." Again, East Earth Herbs stands out because they use only the highest grade herbs and because the integrity of the people at East Earth Herbs is unsurpassed in the field.

The people at East Earth Herbs are very knowledgeable. They, like the author of this text, have focussed all of their attention, as far as herbs are concerned, upon the superior class of Chinese tonics. They were among the first Americans to travel to Post-revolutionary China and to this day have the best contact for high quality herbs that the author is aware of (along with GMS Products). Over the years, they have produced many fine herbals. For some years they marketed a series of "five elements teas." However, it appears that these products were too

esoteric to be widely marketable at the time in America and have apparently been discontinued. In the last several years, East Earth Herbs has produced the "Dragon Eggs" line of products which have met with a great deal of consumer acceptance and approval. These "Dragon Eggs" are absolutely sensational, as the following discussion will bear out.

We will look here at a representative sample of the "Dragon Eggs" tonic herbals. East Earth Herbs puts out a fine pamphlet called the *Energy Guide*, which provides insight into the nature and actions of all of the "Dragons Eggs" and contains much information about all the Chinese tonic herbs. Please refer to the Bibiography at the end of this book.

Four Ginseng Dragon Eggs: This is an extremely potent energy tonic, virtually unsurpassed by any other commercial product, except perhaps for some of the other "Dragon Eggs" and GMS products. It uses as its base four varieties of *ginseng: Shiu Chu, Kirin, Prince Ginseng* and *Siberian Ginseng.* The four varieties of *ginseng* are supported by twenty-six other tonic herbs. Only East Earth Herbs uses *Shiu Chu Ginseng* in their products. Remember that *Shiu Chu* is the highest grade of cultivated Chinese *ginseng* available and is much more potent than *Kirin Ginseng,* which is the basic commercial grade of *ginseng* used by virtually all other manufacturers of Chinese herbals. Not that *Kirin Ginseng* is a bad product; on the contrary, it is quite good. But it does not compare with *Shiu Chu Ginseng.*

The twenty-six tonic herbs used with the four varieties of *ginseng* in this formula, according to East Earth Herbs, "help to circulate and support the *ginseng* energy, and provide Yin cooling energies for balancing. They keep the Liver from retaining the Yang *ginseng* energy and becoming too fiery. They add Yin to the Heart meridian and they circulate energy in a balanced manner through the five phase energy cycle." *Kirin Ginseng* is a mild variety of *ginseng* and is generally felt to be safe to use alone. But the higher grades of *ginseng* can sometimes be too Yang for some people and may result in an excessive build-up of Yang energy, called "false fire," in the viscera and in the upper parts of the body unless they are balanced out in the formula with cooling herbs. This is precisely what East Earth Herbs has done in this formula. It is formulated so as to enhance the free circulation of the energies provided by the four *ginsengs,* as well as the other tonic herbs, throughout the body. These "Dragon Eggs" may be used by men or women. They will result in a definite yangizing of one's condition. If you feel that you are becoming too Yang from these herbs (aggressive, assertive, highly active and extroverted, sexually active), you may wish to cut down on the dose and/or to use a balancing herbal such as the "Peaceful Dragon Eggs," which have a Yin tonic effect (they are distinctly dispersive and sedative). Women who take "Four Ginsengs" may wish to use "Women's Longevity Dragon Eggs" or "Tang Kuei Dragon Eggs." For complete details as to how the "Dragon Eggs" might be combined, see East Earth Herbs' *Energy Guide.*

Women's Longevity Dragon Eggs: This formula is designed for use by women as a tonic, focusing on female energies and functions. This formulation was developed to be nutritive to the blood; to improve blood, fluid, and energy circulation; and to improve those organic functions associated with the female fertility cycle. As is true of all the "Dragon Eggs," the formula is sophisticated and uses quite a few herbs to achieve its goals. It uses *Astragalus, Tang Kuei, Atractylus*, and a *Poria Cocos* to tonify the Spleen function, which is in charge of making blood, and of fluid circulation. *Rehmannia, Ho Shou Wu, Atractylus, Poria cocos*, and small red (*Azuki*) beans are used to tonify the Kidney function, which controls the female hormonal balance. *Peony root, Ligusticum, Peony bark, Lycii berries*, and *Orange Peel* are used to tonify and cleanse the Liver, which is in charge of the storage of blood, of the genitalia, of the sex drive and of the degree of muscular tension. *Tang Kuei, Tangerine Peel, Red Jujube seed* and *Cinnamon* are used to tonify the Heart function, which is in charge of central blood circulation, the emotions and is the center of the feelings of Love.

Women who use this formulation will experience a noticeable change within a few days. Extended use will result in a whole new experience of life, balanced emotionally and physiologically.

Sages' Ginseng: With this astounding product, East Earth Herbs has definitely taken a gigantic step in Chinese commercial herbalism. "Sages' Ginseng" contains genuine *wild* Chinese *ginseng*. Wild Chinese *Tung Pei Ginseng* is virtually unavailable on the American market, even in Chinese herb shops, except by special order. Genuine wild roots sell for $3,000 to $10,000 per ounce when available in China. East Earth Herbs has one of the few connections for this herb in China and is absolutely the only herbal manufacturer that uses it in an herbal preparation.

As East Earth Herbs literature notes: "Wild Chinese *ginseng's* effect is very profound on one's spiritual nature. It is deeply penetrating and broadly tonifies the body's basic energy (*Ch'i*). The life giving energy from wild Chinese *ginseng* is beyond any other herb, drug or food on this planet."

One milligram of wild Chinese *ginseng* is contained in each tablet of "Sages' Ginseng." To this is added semi-wild *Yi-Sun Ginseng* (also rare and expensive), *Tienchi*, American wild *ginseng, Lung Chih mushroom* (one of China's "mushrooms of longevity"), *Poria cocos* (one of China's premiere Kidney tonics), *Lycii berries* (a powerful life-prolonging herb), and *Schizandra berries* (rememeber that the *Lycii-Schizandra* combination was used by the emperors of China and their wives as their main tonic for longevity, sexual vigor and beauty).

The basic effects of the "Sages' Ginseng" formula are an energizing of the Heart/Mind function and the building of large amounts of *Ch'i* to the entire system, much of which is stored and is used as adaptogenic energy. The overall effect of "Sages' Ginseng" is reasonably close to taking pure wild Chinese *ginseng*. However, it seems to the author that this product may even be better in the long run than would be pure wild *ginseng* because of the other superb herbs used in the masterful formula.

Not enough can be said about the potential of this herbal for changing the lives of those who consume it. It is worth noting that *Yi-Sun Ginseng* alone would be generally considered remarkable in any commercial product, and is not, to the author's knowledge, used in any other product. *Yi-Sun Ginseng* is also rare, though available, and costs about $1,000 an ounce on the American market. These are the beautiful and spectacular roots on display under glass at some Chinese herb shops.

East Earth Herbs also produces other "Dragon Egg" products: *"Express"* tablets are a powerful energizer. *"Express"* is potent both as an immediate energizer and as an extremely well-balanced general tonic. *"Tang Kuei"* tablets are a formula similar to "Women's Longevity"; *"Shiu Chu Ginseng"* tablets emphasize the virtues of *Shiu Chu Ginseng*, the top-of-the-line commercial-grade Chinese *ginseng*; and **"Dragon Diet"** tablets, a formulation similar to that of the *"Express"* tablet, harmonizes the body's functions, improves energy, regulates metabolism, and has a carefully balanced stimulating effect. Please read the literature provided by East Earth Herbs for detailed descriptions of these products.

"Peaceful" tablets are a Heart/Mind tonic that has the profound ability to break up energy blockages, and which has a strong tranquilizing effect. As the *Energy Guide* states, "A problem with tonifying energy in the internal organs is that you can add only so much energy to the organs and then the energy gets stuck and cause problems. *"Peaceful"* tablets are a remedy for this situation. Anytime energy gets stuck, we are also talking about emotional energy. *"Peaceful"* tablets force the *Ch'i* to move in the heart. This clears out the channels in the heart center letting the energy circulate very freely. The result of this action is a very peaceful state of mind. Use only when you notice your energy becoming excessive, in static emotional states, or when you need solutions to a mental problem that would be helped by more smoothly flowing energy." It is *fundamental* to Chinese herbalism that balance always be both the means and goal of any formulation. Herbs need to be balanced in the formula so that no harsh effects result. As discussed in Chapter 4 in the section on *Ginseng*, and again in the section on Compounding the Chinese Tonic Herbs in Chapter 7, "hot" herbs must be combined with "cool" or "neutral" herbs so that the final product is "neutral" or just "warm" in overall energy. This is why it is traditional, when preparing *ginseng*, to add enough *Red Jujube Dates* to yield a "warm" tonic brew. The *dates* have a "neutral" energy and are a Yin tonic. The function of the *dates* is to assure the free circulation of the abundant energy generated by the *ginseng*. All formulae follow this principle, though often in a more complete way. This is why *"Peaceful"* tablets are worth keeping around. If any tonic causes "false fire" symptoms (anxiety, neck and shoulder tension, a headache, and/or feelings of frustration, irritability or anger), a couple of *"Peaceful"* tablets should be able to disperse the blockages and relieve the "false fire" symptoms. The "Cerebral Tonic Pills," mentioned previously, as well as a simple brew made of six or seven *Red Jujube Dates*, would serve the same purpose. At any rate, do not accept discomfort from the tonics. The tonics should be balanced in the first place, but if they are not, know how to rectify the situation. Balance is the secret of life.

And finally, the most powerful commercially prepared tonic available. "**Ching**

Tablets" are a formulation based on a tenth century imperial formula. "Ching" means "primal energy," and that is exactly what this formula provides.

It was used primarily as a men's tonic, especially as a sexual tonic, but also as a brain tonic and longevity herbal. It is not an aphrodisiac in the usual sense of a stimulant. It takes a little time for the pills to take effect (several days is common), and it is said that it will take 100 days for the *full* effects to take place (though obvious results occurs almost immediately). A tenth century classic in the Chinese bedroom arts states in connection with this formula: "Be careful! Do not use this formula if you are womanless."

The "**Ching Tablets**" currently available (See Sources in Appendix) are fairly expensive, but are an overwhelming favorite among those who can afford *the best*. The formula contains six powerful yang herbs and six potential yin herbs. The yin herbs nourish the organs and tissues and provide vast resources of potential energy. The yang herbs provide the spark needed to ignite our potential energy. All twelve ingredients in this formula are of plant origin except sea horse, a powerful yang herb renowned in China as an aphrodisiac and Kidney tonic. Ginseng, Deer Antler, and *Astragalus* are among the better known herbs. The "**Ching Tablets**" produced by GMS Products (beware of cheap imitators) use the very highest quality herbs available. For example, the ginseng used is North Korean Heaven Grade 10! No other commercial product uses such a high grade in significant quantity (**Sages' Ginseng Dragon Eggs** included). North Korea Heaven Grade 10 Red Ginseng is universally recognized as the best ginseng in the world available on a commercial (albeit very rare) basis, and costs over $1,000 per pound. The Antler used is the soft core of spotted deer from Kirin China, and is again the best available in the world, costing about $800 per pound. The *Astragalus* is likewise the highest grade grown in China, from Shaxi Province, costing about $100 per pound. In the same way, each of the other nine herbs are selected on the basis of quality only. The price of the final product ($100 for one months supply) reflects the high costs tremendous care used in creating these tablets, but so do the results. The author has heard some *remarkable* stories of rejuvenation from men who have used "**Ching Tablets**" and has himself found them to be what they are historically said to be. Ching Tablets can be obtained through the Four Seasons Herb Co. and through other sources.

In this chapter we have explored a sample of the commercial products available to the Western herbalist. Other products are also available, many being of excellent quality. Unfortunately, the author has not had the time in his lifetime, nor the capacity, to try every available product. The above-described products, however, are the generally-recognized "cream of the crop" and would serve as a perfect foundation for starting one's adventure with the Chinese tonic herbs.

Most people who use the Chinese tonics seriously enjoy purchasing, preparing, and consuming the herbs bought in bulk from the herbalist's shelf. In this way, it is possible to select the highest quality herbs available (or affordable) and to prepare the formula exactly to one's personal specifications. But even old-time herbalists keep stocks of their favorite commercial products on hand for times when they do not feel like cooking, or for when they are traveling.

Looking at my own herb shelf tonight, as I approach the end of this book, I have on my shelf the following items: a jar each of "Sages' Ginseng, Express, and Peaceful Dragon Eggs," a jar of "Ching Tablets," a couple of boxes of "Pantocrin Oral Liquid," and a box of "Astragali-Codonopsitis Oral Liquid." In my refrigerator, I have a bottle of "Shou Wu Chih," a bottle of "Ginseng Date Juice" and a bottle of "Ginseng Bee Secretion." I often have other products, but tonight's selection is indeed representative of my normal collection.

I remember that the first real Chinese herbal tonic that I ever used was "Shou Wu Chih." I used it religiously for several weeks, at the advise of someone that I admired and respected very much. This herbal tonic absolutely and profoundly changed my life. I continued using it daily for several years, in addition to other tonics that I came to learn about. I still drink several cups of "Shou Wu Chih" a week, and am sure to take some tonic every day.

Generally, once I open a bottle or jar of a tonic preparation, I follow the instructions and continue consuming it until the bottle is empty. However, this is not a rule, especially with products like the oral liquids, which can be taken when needed for energy. Generally, though, consistency has its virtues and benefits, especially with herbals like "Shou Wu Chih," "Womens Longevity," or "Ching Tablets," which have an accumulative effect.

In Conclusion

In using the Chinese tonic herbs, remember always, above all else, *DO NO HARM*. Use all tonics with wisdom and respect. If in doubt, get expert advise. If ill, see a doctor. There is no folly like arrogance. Remember that the herbs described in this book are *tonics*, not medicines, and are not used to treat disease, On the other hand, follow your instincts and tap into the great source of knowledge and understanding: TAO. By following a balanced, natural, harmonious path, *you will succeed.* How do you find Tao? Again the words of China's greatest teacher, Lao Tze:

> "Many words cannot fathom it,
> But look, it is in your heart!"

With the new-found energy that you obtain by using the Chinese tonic herbs, do good by your fellow man, and strive to improve what can be improved in the world. In giving, we receive; and the more we give, the more we will receive. This is the Law of Tao, and is one of the great secrets of life. Those who apply this principle to their lives become the masters of their own destinies, and will find wisdom, health and happiness. Indeed, in the Taoist sense, they will become "immortal."

 *Appendixes*

Sources of Herbs, Herbal Products and Suppliers

It is possible to obtain the herbs discussed in this text from a wide variety of sources. Many of the commercially prepared products are available in health food stores. Those who live in cities where there is a Chinese, Korean, or Japanese community will have many sources to choose from. Those who do not live in such localities can easily obtain the herbs and products by mail-order.

In fact, it is a bit unfair to mention but a few "sources" when there are literally thousands of herb shops, health food stores and other suppliers of the Chinese tonic herbs in America. Do some exploring in your own town to see what might be available. If nothing is, or if you want something in particular, simply shop by mail.

Mail Order

Many Chinese and Korean herbs shops will sell by mail as long as you do *not* inquire about medicinal cures. There is one company that concentrates exclusively on Chinese tonic herbs by mail-order.

Four Seasons Herb Co.
17 Buccaneer Street,
Marina Del Rey, CA 90292

This company sells Chinese tonic herbs, herb products and supplies by mail only. It sells all the major and minor tonic herbs described in this text plus another fifty or so tonics not mentioned here. Four Seasons generally maintains a full selection of the various grades of each of the herbs. Besides selling the herbs in bulk (1 oz. minimum), many pre-mixed formulas are also available. Many, if not most, of the formulas described in this text are currently pre-packaged by Four Seasons. All you have to do is order them and take them as directed.

Four Seasons Herb Co. also sells quite a selection of herbal formulas that are of a highly sophisticated nature and are not described in this basic text because they contain rare herbs or the formulas are simply too complex.

Many are of Taoist origin and some use very rare herbs. The "Ching Tablets" discussed in Chapter 8 is an example of a sublimely potent formula which uses some common tonic herbs (though of *un*commonly high quality) and some rare herbs. "Ching Tablets" and other similar products are almost always available through Four Seasons Herb Co. You should send for their free catalogue. And watch for their specials. Four Season's prices are *very* reasonable, apparently due to low overhead (no store-front and no media advertising). Customers who buy from them regularly receive special notices, informing them of the availability of limited quantities of certain excellent products which occasionally become available. They also offer discounts on quantity purchases.

Books, Pyrex pots, ginseng cookers and other supplies are also available from Four Seasons. They offer a money-back guarantee and ship out the same day they receive an order. And don't be surprised to find free goodies included in your package. Once, the author (who admittedly had done much business with these people) received a Shin Chu 15 Ginseng root as a gift along with his order of herbs. It was the largest Shin Chu root this herbalist had ever seen, and it turned out to be one of the best he ever took—and it was a gift (it wasn't a sales gimmick, because when the author tried to purchase more, he was informed that there were none for sale. This had been a special purchase of just one catty [15 roots], brought back personally from the Peoples Republic of China and the roots had simply been sent to good customers as a gift). Occasionally you will get a free sample of a new product or some literature, all of which the author has found useful and informative.

By all means, send for Four Seasons Herb Co's catalogue and price list as soon as you're ready to get into the herbs. Just remember, do not request medical help from Four Seasons; they cannot serve this role. For medical help, see a medical specialist. However, if you have questions about the origins, quality, or preparation of an herb or compound, Four Seasons will respond.

Health Food Stores

There are some fine Chinese tonic preparations that are not generally sold in Chinese or Korean herb shops. These products are manufactured by Western companies. These are found in health food and natural food stores. As excellent example of this type of store is the famous "Erewhon Natural Foods" store located in Los Angeles. They carry a small but truly excellent selection of Chinese tonic products such as Dragon Eggs, Dragon Brew, and many other great extracts, tinctures, capsules, etc. The finer health food and natural food stores throughout this country generally carry these fine products. Some health food stores carry herbs in bulk.

Herbal Categories

Herbs According to Tonic Types

Yang	Energy	Yin	Blood
Schizandra	Ginseng	Schizandra	Tang Kuei
Cinnamon	Licorice	Raw Rehmannia	Lycium
Deer Antler	Ho Shou Wu	Codonopsis	Steamed Rehmannia
Ginger	Astragalus	Dendrobium	Tienchi (Steamed)
	Codonopsis	Red Dates	Paeonia
	Atractylus	Asparagus	Cordyceps
	Red Dates	Tienchi	Alisma
	Royal Jelly	Royal Jelly	
	Deer Antler	Eucommia	
	Magnolia flower	Scute	
	Bupleurum	Paeonia	
	Cyperus	Citrus peel	
	Cordyceps	Acorus	
	Citrus peel	Poria	
	Acorus		
	Alisma		
	Ephedra		

Herbs According to Flavor

Salty	Sour	Bitter	Sweet	Pungent
Schizandra	Schizandra	Ginseng	Ginseng	Tang Kuei
Dendrobium	Cornus	Ho Shou Wu	Tang Kuei	Schizandra
Deer Antler	Peony	Schizandra	Licorice	Cinnamon
	Citrus peel	Rehmannia	Ho Shou Wu	Ginger
	Magnolia	Atractylus	Schizandra	Cyperus
		Asparagus	Lycium	Acorus
		Tienchi	Astragalus	Ephedra
		Royal Jelly	Rehmannia	
		Eucommia	Codonopsis	
		Magnolia flower	Atractylus	
		Scute	Dendrobium	
		Peony	Red Dates	
		Citrus peel	Cinnamon	
		Bupleurum	Asparagus	
		Magnolia	Eucommia	
		Cyperus	Deer Antler	
		Cordyceps	Ephedra	
		Alisma	Poria	

Herbs According to Atmospheric Energy

Cold	Cool	Neutral	Warm	Hot
Raw Rehmannia	Dendrobium	Licorice	Ginseng	Cinnamon
Asparagus	Asparagus	Lycium	Tang Kuei	Korean Ginseng
Bupleurum	Peony	Codonopsis	Ho Shou Wu	
	Citrus peel	Red Dates	Schizandra	
	Acorus	Tienchi	Astragalus	
	Scute	Royal Jelly	Steamed Rehmannia	
	Cyperus	Eucommia	Atractylus	
		Alisma	Deer Antler	
		Poria	Magnolia flower	
			Cornus	
			Ginger	
			Ephedra	
			Cordyceps	
			Acorus	

5 Elements of Herbs and their combinations

Wood	Fire	Earth	Metal	Water
Peonia	Tang Kuei	Ginseng	Poria	Ho Shou Wu
Moutan	Astragalus	Licorice	Schizandra	Red beans
Ho Shou Wu	Tangerine peel	Dates	White fungus	Licorice
Lycium	Jujube	Codonopsis	Ginseng	Rehmannia
Orange Peel	Rehmannia	Atractylus	Cordyceps	Atractylus
Ligusticum	Cinnamon	Pinellia	Pueria	Poria
Cyperus	Prince ginseng	Ginger	Codonopsis	Cornus
Magnolia	Lycium	Orange Peel	Magnolia	Schizandra
Bupleurum	Asparagus		Licorice	Asparagus
				Black beans

OPTIONAL BREWS

Wood	Fire	Earth	Metal	Water
Peonia	Tang Kuei	Ginseng	Poria	Ho Shou Wu
Moutan	Lychium	Dates	Pueria	Rehmannia
Magnolia	Asparagus	Atractylus	Magnolia	Poria
Bupleurum	Tangerine		Licorice	Asparagus
Orange Peel				Cornus
Lycium	Astragalus	Atractylus	Schizandra	Ho Shou Wu
Cyperus	Jujube	Licorice	Poria	Red beans
Ligusticum	Cinnamon	Pinellia	White fungus	Asparagus
Orange Peel	Tangerine	Ginger	Cordyceps	Schizandra
				Licorice
Ho Shou Wu	Prince Ginseng	Codonopsis	Ginseng	Rehmannia
Peony	Rehmannia	Atractylus	Codonopsis	Ho Shou Wu
Bupleurum	Asparagus	Dates	Schizandra	Black beans
Orange Peel	Cinnamon	Orange peel	Pueria	Asparagus
	Tangerine		Magnolia	Licorice
			Licorice	Schizandra

Chinese Tonic Herbs Chart

Scientific Name	Chinese name	Common name	Chinese character	Part used	Tonic action	Taste	Atmospheric energy	Grades available	Primary meridians	Notes
Panax Ginseng C. A. Mey	Renshen	Ginseng	人參	root	Energy tonic	Sweet and Slightly bitter	warm	*Korean Red* Heaven Earth Man size 10–60 (lower is bigger) *Korean White* Heaven Earth 15–60 *Chinese* Wild Tung Pei Yi Sun Shiu Chu (15–60) Kirin	Lung, Spleen and to a lesser degree all meridians	The best Korean ginseng comes from the office of the monopoly. However, instant ginseng products are generally weak.
Radix Angelica sinensis	Tang Kuei	Tang Kuei	當歸	root	Blood tonic	sweet-pungent	warm	High Low	Heart, Liver, Spleen, Kidney	the larger and sweeter, the higher the quality
Glycyrrhiza uralensis	Kan Tsao	Licorice root	甘草	root	Energy tonic	Very sweet	neutral	High Low	Spleen, Stomach, Kidney, Lung, and to some degree all meridians	sweeter roots with deeper yellow color are best
Polygonum multiflorum	Ho Shou Wu	Ho Shou Wu	向首烏	tuber	Energy tonic	bitter-sweet	warm	Good Regular	Liver and Kidney	dark pieces are best
Schizandra chinensis	Wu Wei Tza or O Mi Ja	Schizandra	五味子	berries	yin and yang Tonic	sour-salty, with sweet, pungent and bitter overtones	warm	Good Regular	Lung, Kidney and Liver	dark, full berries are best

Scientific Name	Chinese name	Common name	Chinese character	Part used	Tonic action	Taste	Atmospheric energy	Grades available	Primary meridians	Notes
Lycium chinensis	Kou Chi Tza	Lycium	枸杞子	berries	Blood tonic	sweet	neutral	High Good Regular Poor	Liver, Kidney, and Lung	Large, sweet, deep red berries are best. Dry, brown, bitter, small, or died berries are worst and weakest.
Astragalus membranaceus	Huang Ch'i	Astragalus	黃耆	root	Energy tonic	Sweet	Warm	High Good Regular	Spleen, Lung, Triple Warmer	Large, yellow, well shaped roots are best
Rehmannia glutinosa	Ti Huang	Rehmannia	地黃	rhizome	Steamed: Blood Tonic / Raw: Yin Tonic	bitter-sweet / bitter-sweet	warm / cold	all good / all good	Heart, Kidney, Liver / Kidney, Heart, Small Intestine	
Codonopsis lanceolata	Tang Shen	Codonopsis	黨參	root	Energy and yin tonic	sweet	neutral	High Good	Lung, Spleen	larger, straight roots are best
Atractylus orata or lancea	Pai Shu	Atractylus	白朮	rhizome	Energy tonic	sweet-bitter	slightly warm	all good	spleen and Stomach	
Dendrobium hancockii	Shih Hu or Suk Gok	Orchid	石斛	stems, leaves, and pods	Yin tonic	sweet and lightly salty	cool	High Good	Kidney, Lung, Stomach	well preserved, golden herb is best
Zizyphus jujube	Suan-tsao-jen	Red Dates	大棗	fruit	Yin and Energy tonic	sweet	neutral	Small Large	Stomach, but also all 12 meridians	small dates are better
Cinnamomum cassia	Kuei Pi	Cinnamon	肉桂	bark	Yang tonic	sweet-pungent pungent	hot	High Good	Kidney and Circulation	large, sweet, strong-tasting bark is best

Latin Name	Name	Common	Chinese	Part	Tonic	Taste	Temperature	Quality	Organs	Best
Asparagus lucidus	Tien Men Tong or Chung Dong	Asparagus Root	天門冬	root	Yin tonic	sweet-bitter	cold to cool	High Good	Kidney, Lung, Heart	Large, sweet, clean, soft pieces are best
Radix Pseudoginseng	San-chi or Tienchi	Tienchi	三屯 or 田屯	root	Blood and Yin tonic	bitter	neutral	all good	Heart, Kidney	larger are better
Royal Jelly	Feng Wang	Royal Jelly	蜂王	bee secretion	Yin and Energy tonic	bitter	neutral	all good	Triple Warmer, Kidney	fresh pure secretion is best
Eucommia ulmoides	Tu Chung	Eucommia	杜仲	bark	Yin tonic	bitter-sweet	neutral	all good	Heart, Kidney	
Cornu Cervi parvum	Lu-Jung	Deer Antler	鹿茸	antler	Yang and Energy tonic	sweet-salty	warm	High Good	Kidney, Liver, Heart, Brain	all antler is excellent
Magnolia officionalis	Hou P'o	Magnolia Flower	辛夷	flower	Energy tonic	sour-bitter	warm	all good	Triple Warmer, Lungs, Spleen	
Cornus officionalis	Shan Chu-Yu	Cornus	山茱萸	fruit	Yin tonic	sour	warm	all good	Kidney and Liver	
Bupleurum chinensis	Chai-hu	Bupleurum	柴胡	root	Energy tonic	bitter	cold	all good	Liver, Stomach, Small Intestine	
Scutellaria macrantha	Pan-chih Lien or Huang Chir	Scute	黃芩	root	Yin tonic	bitter	cool	all good	Heart, Lung, Kidney	
Paeonia albiflora	Shao Yao or Pai Shao	Peony root	芍藥 or 白芍	root	Blood and yin tonic	bitter-sour	cool	High Good	Liver, Spleen, Stomach, Small Intestine	Large, straight pinkish slices of the root are best
Cyperus rotundus	Hsiang-fu	Cyperus	香附	tubercles	Energy tonic	slightly bitter, pungent	Cool	all good	Kidney, Lung, Spleen	

Scientific Name	Chinese name	Common name	Chinese character	Part used	Tonic action	Taste	Atmospheric energy	Grades available	Primary meridians	Notes
Cordyceps sinensis	Tang Chung Hsia Tsao	Cordyceps	冬虫夏草	fungus	Energy and Blood tonic	sweet	warm	all good	Lung, Kidney	
Citrus aurantium	Chen-pi	Citrus peel	陳皮	fruit rind	Yin and Energy tonic	bitter-sour	cool	High Good	Stomach, Kidney, Liver, Triple Warmer	the older the better
Acorus calamus	Shih-chang-Pu	Acorus	石菖蒲	rhizome	Energy and Yin tonic	pungent	warm		Spleen, Stomach, Kidney	
Zingiber officionale	Kan-chiang	Dried ginger	乾姜	rhizome	Yang tonic	pungest	warm	Stomach, Spleen		
Alisma plantago	Tse-hsieh	Alisma	澤瀉	tuber	Energy and Blood tonic	bitter	neutral	all good	Kidney	
Ephedra sinensis	Ma'Huang	Ma Huang or Ephedra	麻黃	stem	Energy tonic	sweet-pungent	warm	all good	Lung, Kidney	do not use too much
Poria cocos	Fu-ling	Poria or Hoelen	茯苓	fungus	Yin tonic	sweet	neutral	all good	Kidney, Lungs, Spleen	
Dioscoria batatas		Dioscoria	山藥	tuber	Yin tonic	sweet	neutral	all good	Stomach, Spleen, Lung Kidney	

 *Bibliography*

The following are the source materials used in the preaparation of this book. It omits, of course, the oral transmission of information to the author by various authorities on the subject. All the listings here presented would be well worth reading by anyone interested in Oriental health care and in Chinese tonic herbalism in particular.

Taoist Literature

Blofeld, John. *Taoism: The Road to Immortality*. Boulder: Shambala Publications.
———. *Gateway to Wisdom*. Boulder: Shambala Publications, 1980. John Blofeld is one of the great modern writers on Chinese philosophy. He has had a great impact upon the author. He is a superb writer and has written a number of other great books, such as *The Secret and the Sublime*, the stories of his adventures as a wanderer in pre-revolutionary China—truly fantastic reading.
Chang Chung-yuan. *Creativity and Taoism*. New York: The Julian Press, 1963. An easy to read and enlightening exposition by a great modern scholar on the fundamental principles of Taoism.
Chu Hsi. The Great Extreme (or First Cause of Existence). *Shrine of Wisdom* 10 (Spring): pp. 79–88, 1929. The first of a series of articles in successive issues translating the writings of one of China's greatest philosophers. Here he discusses Yin and Yang and Tao.
———. Heaven and Earth. *The Shrine of Wisdom* 10 (Summer): pp. 103–11, 1929. This treatise by Chu Hsi deals with man's relationship with Nature and the Cosmos.
———. *Yin and Yang—The Five Elements and the Seasons* 1929. This classic document of Taoism describes the nature of cyclicity and man's place in the natural scheme of things.
Huai Nan Tsze. The History of Great Light. *The Shrine of Wisdom* 18 (Spring): pp. 281–90, 1937. Another classic of Taoism written in 206 B.C. delving into the fundamentals of Taoist philosophy.
Ko-Hsuan. The Classic of Purity. *The Shrine of Wisdom* 11 (Winter): pp. 314–19, 1930. A short but powerful piece of ancient literature that some scholars attribute to Lao Tze.
Merton, Thomas (translator). *The Way of Chuang Tzu*. New York: New Directions Books, 1969. A great translation of China's most witty Taoist philosopher, Chuang Tzu, who was Lao Tze's disciple. This selection of artfully translated short, easy to read, fun short stories and poems make sense out of Taoism, a philosophy that often seems too mystical to be comprehensible.

Western Physiology

Becker, Robert O. Electrophysiological Correlates of Acupuncture Points and Meridians. *Electroenergetic Systems* (pp. 105–12). 1976. A monumental research study by esteemed

Western researchers, validating the Chinese energy system scientifically and proposing a modern theoretical basis for the system.

Li, C. P. *Chinese Herbal Medicine*. Washington D. C.: Dept. of Health, Education, and Welfare Publication No. (NIH) 75–732, 1974. This excellent booklet comprehensively details the scientific research that had been done up to that time on numerous Chinese herbs, many of which are in the tonic class, validating scientifically many traditional claims and even discovering new actions of these old drugs.

Luce, Gay Gaer. *Biological Rhythms In Human and Animal Physiology*. New York: Dover Publications, 1971. This is an excellent source of information on the new study of biological rhythms.

Schlossberg L. and Zuidema, G. D. *Human Functional Anatomy*, 2nd ed. Baltimore: John Hopkins Univ. Press, 1980. This is a great anatomy book, comprehensible by laymen but of professional quality and detail. The plates are wonderful and the writing is short and to the point.

Selye, Hans. *The Stress of Life*, rev. ed. New York: McGraw-Hill, 1978. A great book by one of modern medicine's greatest and most respected researchers and thinkers, this classic deals with the physiology of stress and adaptation.

Strand, Fleur L. *Physiology: A Regulatory Systems Approach*. New York: McMillan, 1978. By far the best physiology book on the market today, this thoroughly up-to-date physiology text stresses the functional unity of the human body, mind, and environment. Thoroughly modern, scientific, and (unadmittedly) holistic.

Eastern Healthcare and Chinese Herbalism

Berk, William. *Chinese Healing Arts*. Culver City, California: Peace Press, 1979. This book on Taoist Yoga describes many yogic exercises and also deals with Taoist tonic herbalism.

Chu, David. *Tienchi Ginseng—The Miracle Root for the Preservation of Health*. Los Angeles: Chinese Research Center, 1979. This fine book details the history, usage and scientific knowledge of Tienchi Ginseng, one of China's great tonic herbs.

Da Liu. *Taoist Health Exercise Book*. New York: Links Books, 1974. A great little book on Taoist health practices.

———. *The Tao of Health and Longevity*. New York: Schocken Books, 1978. Another fine book by this living Taoist master dealing with Taoist health practices.

East Earth Herbs. *Energy Guide*. Reedsport, Oregon: East Earth Herbs, 1983. An excellent discourse on Chinese tonic herbalism, especially as it pertains to their fine product line.

Fulder, Stephan. *The Tao of Medicine—Ginseng, Oriental Remedies and the Pharmacology of Harmony*. New York: Destiny Books, 1980. This excellent treatise on a topic similar to that of this book focuses on Ginseng as an example of an adaptogenic agent. It presents an in-depth discussion of the Chinese medicine of harmony and how it can be encorporated into modern medicine and lifestyle.

Harriman, Sarah. *The Book of Ginseng*. New York: Pyramid Books, 1975. Excellent book on Ginseng with many tonic recipes.

Heffern, Richard. *The Complete Book of Ginseng*. Milbrae, California: Celestial Arts, 1976. A good thorough discussion of Ginseng.

Hsu Hong-Yen. *Bulletin of the Oriental Healing Arts Institute of U.S.A.* Hawaiian Gardens, California. This journal deals exclusively with Chinese herbalism and is of superb quality.

Hyatt, Richard. *Chinese Herbal Medicine*. New York: Schocken Books, 1978. A good book on Chinese medicine herbalism.

Kang, Young S. *Oriental Medicine in Modern Practice*. New York: Carlton Press, 1972. A great book on Oriental medicine.

Khan, Hazrat Inayat. Health. *The Sufi Vessage, Molume IV*. (pp. 15–95) London: Barrie and Jenkins, 1972. In the author's opinion, this is the highest and most profound discourse on healing ever written in the English language. Hazrat Inayat Khan was not a Taoist, he was a Sufi; but there is little difference. Read this discourse and your perspective on health and healing will be uplifted forever more. There are 80 pages of discussion by a truly enlightened being blessed with the ability to express his thoughts and feelings both eloquently and beautifully. You'll enjoy this, and any other book by this great universal master.

Kimmens, Andrew C. (editor). *Tales of Ginseng*. New York: William Morrow, 1975. One of the author's favorite books. This book of traditional Oriental tales, stories and myths about Ginseng is truly wonderful, magical reading. Some are excellent children's stories.

Li Shih Chen (translated by Smith, F. P. and Stuart, G. A.). *Chinese Medicinal Herbs*. San Francisco: Georgetown Press, 1973. A poor but useful translation of Li Shih Chen's tremendous classic on Chinese herbalism, the *Kang Mu Pen Tsao*.

Lu, Henry. *Chinese Herbal Therapy*, a correspondence course. Vancouver: North American College of Chinese Herbalism, 1976. A superb, though lengthy course in Chinese herbalism.

———. *Chinese Health Foods*. Vancouver: Academy of Oriental Heritage, 1977. One of the many books by Dr. Lu, this one gives the traditional qualities of Chinese foods.

———. *Use and Abuse of Ginseng*. Vancouver: Academy of Oriental Heritage, 1977. A very useful book by one of the greatest scholars on Oriental medicine in the West. Dr. Lu publishes many excellent books and correspondence courses on the various Chinese healing arts.

Mann, Felix. *The Meridians of Acupuncture*. London: William Heinemann Medical Books, 1964. The most detailed book in the English language on the subject of the organ-meridians by the very highly respected british scholar.

Revolutionary Health Committee. *A Barefoot Doctor's Manual*. Mayne Isle and Seattle; Cloudburst Press, 1977. Now a classic, this book provides basic information on current Chinese healthcare as practiced in the fields of China, with much herbal information.

Teeguarden, Iona. *Acupressure Way of Health—Jin Shin Do*. Tokyo: Japan Publications, 1977. The art of Jin Shin Do Acupressure is the perfect compliment to Chinese tonic herbalism. This is a comprehensive, well-illustrated introductory description of this great art. For information on Jin Shin Do classes and literature, contact the Jin Shin Do Foundation, P.O. Box 1800, Idyllwild, CA 92349

Veith, Ilza. *The Yellow Emperor's Classic of Internal Medicine*. Berkeley: University of California Press, 1972. This is *the* classic of Chinese medicine, but very little about herbs in the segments here translated. However, philosophically, this book is quite revealing.

Veninga, Louise. *The Ginseng Book*. Felton, California: Ruka Publications, 1974. One of the best books on Ginseng. Ms. Veninga has much insight and has written a charming book worth owning.

Wallnofer, Henrich and Von Rottauscher, Anna. *Chinese Folk Medicine*. New York:

Crown Books, 1972. One of the great classics on the Chinese healing arts in English. It is interesting, accurate, easy reading and deals with all the Chinese healing arts, including a fine section on the major Chinese herbs.

Ware, James R. (translator). *Alchemy, Medicine and Religion*. New York: Dover, 1980. This book deals with very esoteric Taoist practices.

Ziglar, Walter. *The Ginseng Report*. Huntington Beach, California: 1979. Worthwhile reading on Ginseng and related herbs.

 *Index*